T0330115

Financing Nonprofits and Other Social Enterprises

To Selma and Polly, Noah and Asher, and Lydia, Isaiah and Micah, grandchildren who make my world a better place

Financing Nonprofits and Other Social Enterprises

A Benefits Approach

Dennis R. Young

Executive in Residence, Cleveland State University and Professor Emeritus, Georgia State University, USA

 Edward Elgar
PUBLISHING

Cheltenham, UK • Northampton, MA, USA

Published by
Edward Elgar Publishing Limited
The Lypiatts
15 Lansdown Road
Cheltenham
Glos GL50 2JA
UK

Edward Elgar Publishing, Inc.
William Pratt House
9 Dewey Court
Northampton
Massachusetts 01060
USA

A catalogue record for this book
is available from the British Library

Library of Congress Control Number: 2016959933

This book is available electronically in the **Elgar**online
Business subject collection
DOI 10.4337/9781783478293

ISBN 978 1 78347 827 9 (cased)
ISBN 978 1 78347 829 3 (eBook)

Typeset by Servis Filmsetting Ltd, Stockport, Cheshire
Printed and bound in Great Britain by TJ International Ltd, Padstow

Contents

About the author

Dennis R. Young is Executive in Residence in the Maxine Goodman Levin College of Urban Affairs at Cleveland State University and Professor Emeritus at Georgia State University. Previously he was Professor of Public Management and Policy in the Andrew Young School of Policy Studies where he directed GSU's Nonprofit Studies Program and held the Bernard B. and Eugenia A. Ramsey Chair in Private Enterprise. From 1988 to 1996 he was Director of the Mandel Center for Nonprofit Organizations and Mandel Professor of Nonprofit Management at Case Western Reserve University. His research interests include nonprofit economics and finance, social enterprise and entrepreneurship, and management and governance of nonprofit organizations. He is the founding editor of the journal *Nonprofit Management and Leadership* and founding and current editor of *Nonprofit Policy Forum*, and past president of the Association for Research on Nonprofit Organizations and Voluntary Action (ARNOVA). His books include *A Casebook of Management for Nonprofit Organizations, Economics for Nonprofit Managers* (with Richard Steinberg), *Corporate Philanthropy at the Crossroads* (with Dwight Burlingame), *Effective Economic Decision Making for Nonprofit Organizations, Wise Decision-Making in Uncertain Times, Financing Nonprofits, Handbook of Research on Nonprofit Economics and Management* (with Bruce A. Seaman), *Civil Society, the Third Sector and Social Enterprise: Governance and Democracy* (with Philippe Eynaud and Jean-Louis Laville), and *The Social Enterprise Zoo* (with Elizabeth A.M. Searing and Cassady V. Brewer). In 2013, his 1983 book *If Not for Profit for What? A Behavioral Theory of the Nonprofit Sector based on Entrepreneurship* was digitally reissued with new commentaries from contemporary scholars by the Georgia State University Library (http://scholarworks.gsu.edu/facbooks2013/1/). Professor Young received ARNOVA's 2004 Award for Distinguished Achievement and Leadership in Nonprofit and Voluntary Action Research, and the Award for Innovation in Nonprofit Research from the Israeli Center for Third Sector Research at Ben Gurion University in 2005. In 2010 he was awarded an honorary doctorate from the University of Liège in Belgium for his work on social enterprise and entrepreneurship. He served on the governing board of the National Council of Nonprofits from 2008 to 2014 and the Advisory Board of the Foundation Center/Atlanta from 2005 to 2015.

Foreword

As a young entrepreneur with a passion to serve some 40 years ago, I thought a "call" to serve, a passion to feed the hungry, and a strong work ethic would ensure success. And while it was essential to continue to clarify the call and rely on my passion and hard work, I found out quickly that was only the beginning of what I needed to know. Not everyone saw the "value" of what I offered or exactly what or how to invest in my new idea. It became clear from the beginning that I was not able to articulate the value proposition in a way that motivated investment or strategic partnerships. It also became clear that I was not organizationally or administratively ready for what I was asking for.

I began the Atlanta Community Food Bank in the basement of a downtown church, and over 36 years grew the organization into one of the largest, most effective social purpose organizations in Georgia. There was much to learn along the way. If only I had a guide to better understand the benefits theory that is articulated so well in this book.

In this book, Dennis Young has laid out a very clear and comprehensive way to understand the value of benefits theory in financing social purpose organizations. Without sustained income and strong support from all sectors of the community even the best organization will not grow or sustain itself over time. This book offers a clear and comprehensive explanation to guide students, managers, and leaders toward finding the best mix of income sources for their organizations and stimulates additional research on financing of nonprofits and other forms of social enterprise.

Today I find that students and managers, as well as those contemplating working in different sectors, could certainly benefit from a better understanding of benefits theory. There is a tremendous new interest in entrepreneurship and looking at the nonprofit social sector to address many of society's ills. This will require many creative approaches that often have not been tried before. From my perspective this is a very positive development. People from all walks of life feel empowered to address many of the social ills and social needs of our communities. And many of our traditional social purpose organizations need to grow and embrace change to survive. But no matter how many new ideas emerge or how many young entrepreneurs try their hand at developing and marketing their ideas, there are some basic values that will always remain true. Dr. Young addresses these essential approaches with clarity and some great case studies.

Organizations may differ in their ability to cultivate certain income sources that may correspond to the services and benefits they produce. Understanding the theory, assets and skills needed to implement the appropriate sources of support can prevent managers from investing in the wrong approach at the wrong time, and can inform them on how to develop the skills to be successful. Benefits theory stipulates that social purpose organizations are most effectively financed by income sources that correspond to the types of public and private benefits they generate through their services, taking account of the transactions costs associated with engaging those income sources. I can remember learning this painful lesson well.

When it looked like everyone was getting into the direct mail business we jumped right in. I learned quickly that I did not have the skills or back office support to be accountable to or nurture those donors. And when everyone was encouraging us to create special events such as the Hunger Walk or Golf Tournament we learned quickly that we needed strategic partners and sponsors to grow and sustain our events. We also needed much more "people power" than we ever imagined. When State and Federal officials came to us to partner with them in after school and summer feeding programs we learned that we needed additional administrative resources to account for and sustain the contract. There was a whole new language to learn and partners to nurture and support. We needed to hold our ground and manage expectations, not taking on more than we could manage well.

And when it was pointed out that we were in a perfect position to create "earned income" by providing a management service to the food industry little did we know how much they would be requiring extra assurance that we were meeting all federal and state regulations. Who knew that we would need to bring on attorneys to review contracts and ensure our agreements met our stated mission or extra tax accountants to ensure we paid unrelated business tax?

We lived and thankfully learned. We embraced change and new ideas, engaged new partners, and involved thousands of volunteers from every sector. But I wish I had better understood benefits theory from the beginning. By learning the hard way we left money on the table and people unfed. I recommend anyone considering starting or growing their organizations to read and learn from this book. I encourage students to take this book seriously if they want to work in the sector or to progress in their careers.

Dr. Young has made a substantial contribution to knowledge and to management practice in a field that increasingly demands transparency and excellence.

Bill Bolling

Chairman, Food Well Alliance

Senior Consultant, Georgia Food Bank Association

ABOUT BILL BOLLING

Bill Bolling is a teacher, mentor, convener, facilitator, entrepreneur, and successful CEO. He founded the Atlanta Community Food Bank in 1979 and served as its executive director for 36 years before stepping down in June 2015. Under Bill's leadership, the Food Bank distributed more than half a billion pounds of food and grocery products through a network of nonprofit partner organizations that feed the hungry. As a charter member of Feeding America, the national network of food banks, Bill was instrumental in the start-up of food banks across Georgia and across the country. Bill recently created Food Well Alliance, a nonprofit organization that connects and supports urban farms, community gardens, farmers markets, school gardens, and other members of Atlanta's local food movement. He currently serves as Chairman of Food Well Alliance and as senior consultant for the Georgia Food Bank Association. Bill is a frequent speaker on topics related to sustainable food, hunger, poverty, regionalism, affordable housing and public policy reform. His skills in bridging various economic sectors have made him a leader in strengthening the community to serve those most in need. Prior to his association with the Food Bank, he served as director of community ministries for St. Luke's Episcopal Church in Atlanta.

Preface

The first presentation of "benefits theory" in the literature did not even coin the phrase. In *Financing Nonprofits: Putting Theory into Practice* which I edited for publication in 2007, I wrote the concluding chapter entitled "Toward a Normative Theory of Nonprofit Finance" which outlined the rudiments of the theory. That book was the joint effort of eighteen distinguished scholars who came together to examine the various different parts of the proverbial elephant of nonprofit finance – fees, gifts, government funding, investment income, volunteering, and so on – and also consider how these components came together into nonprofit income "portfolios." The book still serves as an important resource in the nonprofit management field and I continue to use and recommend it, if only for the star-studded cast I want my students to be exposed to and the solid thinking that went into each of the chapters.

In addition, that book set in motion two important developments. First, the field now had a resource book that could be used to teach nonprofit income development in a more comprehensive way, embracing not only charitable fund-raising but all of the other important streams of nonprofit income as well. Ever since the book's publication I have taught annually my nonprofit finance course from this perspective. In the first few years, the Andrew Young School of Georgia State University allowed me the luxury of jointly developing and teaching the course with my good friend and colleague John O'Kane, then an adjunct instructor and principal in the Coxe Curry consulting firm. Eventually austerity caught up with us and I went solo with the course, but I continued to teach benefits theory with John in the Executive Leadership Program for Nonprofit Organizations (ELPNO), a short course that we had established in Atlanta for nonprofit executives in the Southeast. John and I continue to teach our mini-version of benefits theory in the ELPNO program to the present day. Meanwhile, the baton has been taken up elsewhere in the university world, including at institutions such as American University and University of Wisconsin/ Milwaukee where my former doctoral students Lewis Faulk and Grace Schultz are now members of the faculty, and indeed at Georgia State where the course continues to be taught since my retirement from that institution. I have not tracked the dissemination of benefits theory into nonprofit management curricula beyond that, but it seems now to have become part of the common lingo for faculty in this field and enjoys a place in David Renz's *Jossey-Bass Handbook of Nonprofit Leadership and Management* (Renz, 2016).

A second key development helps explain why benefits theory has been taken up in the educational realm and indeed how it got its name. When I wrote the chapter for the 2007 book I described the nascent theory as a "normative theory," meaning that this is how we "should" think about nonprofit finance. However, it soon became apparent that benefits theory had some explanatory power and could also serve as a framework for research on extant patterns of nonprofit income. That is, the logic of the theory was intuitive and thus it wasn't surprising that nonprofit leaders seemed to gravitate to its expectations even if they did not do so consciously. This set into motion what has become a modest but increasingly robust stream of empirical research, kicked off by three papers that I co-authored with Amanda Wilsker, Rob Fischer and Mary Grinsfelder (see Chapters 3 and 11), which confirmed a strong relationship between the public/private nature of the benefits produced by a nonprofit and the mix of income sources by which it is funded. Since that initial research, papers by various scholars hinging on benefits theory have regularly appeared in scholarly field journals and nonprofit research conferences. As a result, benefits theory is now part of the knowledge base, hence repertoire for faculty who teach about nonprofit finance. This development has been both gratifying and perplexing: Gratifying because the theory apparently makes good sense as a way of approaching nonprofit finance in a holistic way. Perplexing because if nonprofits already behave this way, then why do we need to teach it as a normative approach?

The answer to the latter question is not too difficult to tease out, however. There is ample evidence that nonprofits struggle with their finances and that many of them fail (see Chapter 1). And clearly, some of this failure is attributable to an inability to effectively mobilize and manage resources. Moreover, while most nonprofit organizations may sense the right combinations of financial sources to support themselves, they do not obviously optimize those mixes. That is, they may not take full advantage of the financial opportunities implicit in their missions – opportunities that would follow from explicit analysis from a benefits perspective; and they may not be making the right trade-offs between some sources and others.

How to address these concerns? There was as yet no educational resource up to the task. While the 2007 book and the subsequent stream of research supporting benefits theory constituted an expanded knowledge base for the field, this knowledge required piecing together into a coherent whole. That, in short, is the purpose of this book, which is intended to help students in school and those in practice gain a fuller grasp of the theory and how to apply it, in addition to guiding researchers who wish to extend the frontiers of knowledge on this subject.

One other important development plays into the formulation of this book and its title and terminology. Both in the U.S. and around the world, we no longer think exclusively of traditional nonprofit organizations when we consider how private organizations can contribute to the public good. In particular the roles of social enterprise and social entrepreneurship are ascendant and they are now manifested through a variety of organizational forms including cooperatives, socially-oriented businesses, and public/private partnership arrangements. Indeed, the sectoral map has become so complex, and the variety of forms so diverse, that it now makes sense to use the more generic term "social purpose organization" (SPO). Several colleagues and I have recently published another book that documents this variety and its implications (Young, Searing and Brewer, 2016). While SPO is not yet the widely used generic term, I adopt it in this book so that benefits theory thinking can be appropriately expanded beyond traditional nonprofits. It remains to be determined if the theory is a powerful way of explaining or guiding the finance of cooperatives, social businesses and the like. I believe it is. Thus, this book extends the application of benefits theory beyond the boundaries of nonprofits per se, and into the more general realm of social enterprises. Indeed, I argue that benefits theory is generic to social mission-driven organizations and that legal forms can be adjusted and adapted to best serve this mission by exploiting a wide variety of income opportunities.

Given this broad scope of application, I believe that this book will be helpful at three levels. First, it should be useful in the classroom, at the graduate and advanced undergraduate levels to teach finance of nonprofits and social enterprises. Second, I hope that leaders and managers of social purpose organizations, board members as well as executives and staff, will read and learn from the book. I have consciously written it in accessible language without too much technical complexity to make it helpful for practice. Third, I hope the book will assist scholars in their own quests to extend knowledge in this field. Doctoral students should find the book useful for identifying research issues and questions of their own. Experienced researchers will be familiar with much of the underlying literature but perhaps will be guided by the frontiers I have sketched here and will find ways to deepen and extend the knowledge base. We still need to know a lot about the nuances and applications of benefits theory, especially in terms of the numerous variants within general income classes such as earned, gift or government funding; the various conventional and new instruments of capital finance; the ways in which finance decisions are made within alternative forms of social enterprise; and the management of complex income portfolios.

While social purpose organization finance is still a nascent field of knowledge, I was almost overwhelmed by the task of writing the book. As I delved further into each facet of the subject, I realized that volumes could be written on the topics of virtually every chapter here. In my mind, the task grew encyclopedic. But I had a deadline, and a specific intent to produce a manageable volume, for me and for the reader. However, I hope this book will grow in future editions, perhaps taken up by some of my younger colleagues and former students, so that each aspect of the subject can receive the fuller examination that it deserves.

That said, for those wishing to build a graduate course around this book, I would recommend several supplemental sources for students who wish to dig deeper in various ways. The aforementioned 2007 volume is still relevant and informative. Our new book on social enterprises contains a chapter by Elizabeth Searing and me on benefits theory applied to social enterprises, but as importantly, it explores the various organizational and economic issues surrounding social enterprise, including the diverse legal forms it now assumes, and its various national and industry contexts (Young, Searing and Brewer, 2016). And for a comprehensive picture of the social economy of the United States, I highly recommend the text by Laurie Mook, John Whitman, Jack Quarter and Ann Armstrong (2015). On the issues of capital financing of social ventures and social innovation, I suggest the impressive volume edited by Alex Nicolls, Rob Paton and Jed Emerson (2015). As general resources on economic thinking applied to social purpose organizations and on general management issues, I recommend, respectively, the long awaited second edition of Young and Steinberg's *Economics for Nonprofit Managers and Social Entrepreneurs*, forthcoming with two additional authors, Rosemarie Emanuele and Walter Simmons and now extended to social enterprise (2018); and the 4th edition of Dave Renz's *Handbook* (2016). And I would be seriously remiss if I failed to recommend Woods Bowman's (2011) book on nonprofit financial management, especially because I had the privilege of hosting Woods at Georgia State in the course of his writing that book, in which he generously included a section on benefits theory.

As a related and poignant aside, I wish to note that I feel a personal loss of several close colleagues and friends who were leading thinkers in the field of nonprofit finance and who were part of the 2007 volume. Woods Bowman was one. Howard Tuckman and Estelle James are the others. I am indebted to all three for their friendship and their contributions to my thinking. Their legacies live on in the literature of nonprofit finance and in the minds and hearts of their peers and students.

Volumes like this are rarely the product of a single isolated individual. In this case I had plenty of help along the way. First, the reader will note that there are numerous case studies, vignettes and examples included throughout the book. For this I would like to thank my doctoral student Jung-In Soh for her multiple, substantial efforts on this aspect of the book. In addition, many individuals in the various organizations discussed here provided their help and guidance and substantial information. These include Kevin Spear, Ann Holt-Wiolland, Lee Fisher, Russ Klimczuk, Daniel Lehman, William Weisberg, John Anoliefo, Justina Kwesiga, Latchmee Bhual, Greghan Fischer, Danielle Paskowski, Brian Kenyon, and Jenny Northern. In addition, several colleagues including Jack Quarter, Andrea Bassi, Laurie Mook, Lewis Faulk, Elizabeth Searing, and Jesse Lecy led me toward interesting and appropriate cases.

I also benefitted from many guests in Atlanta who spoke in my classes on nonprofit finance over the years. These include Joe Arnold, David King, Valarie Wilson, Clay Rolader, Bobbi Cleveland, John Floyd, Patricia Showell, Suzanna Stribling, Catherine Mickle and Janice Wolfe. I learned something new every time they spoke.

Importantly, I am indebted to several colleagues who took the time to read all or parts of an earlier draft of this book and provided me with excellent ideas for changes, additions and alterations. These include Jack Quarter, Lewis Faulk, Jung-In Soh, Thad Calabrese, Elizabeth Searing, David King, John O'Kane, Grace Schultz, and Scott Taitel. Bill Bolling also read the draft manuscript and generously wrote the Foreword.

Finally, all authors know that completing a book can make you grouchy and irritable at times. I thank my lovely wife Linda Serra for putting up with me and supporting me throughout the process.

Dennis R. Young
September 2016

REFERENCES

Woods Bowman, 2011. *Finance Fundamentals for Nonprofits*, Hoboken, NJ: John Wiley & Sons.

Laurie Mook, John R. Whitman, Jack Quarter and Ann Armstrong, 2015. *Understanding the Social Economy of the United States*, Toronto: University of Toronto Press.

Alex Nicolls, Rob Paton and Jed Emerson, 2015. *Social Finance*, Oxford: Oxford University Press.

David O. Renz (ed.), 2016. *The Jossey-Bass Handbook of Nonprofit Leadership and Management, Fourth Edition*, Hoboken, NJ: John Wiley & Sons.

Dennis R. Young (ed.), 2007. *Financing Nonprofits: Putting Theory Into Practice*, Lanham, MD; AltaMira Press.

Dennis R. Young, Elizabeth A.M. Searing and Cassady V. Brewer (eds), 2016. *The Social Enterprise Zoo*, Cheltenham, UK and Northampton, MA, U.S.A: Edward Elgar Publishing.

Dennis R. Young, Richard Steinberg, Rosemarie Emanuele and Walter O. Simmons, 2018. *Economics for Nonprofit Managers and Social Entrepreneurs*, Cheltenham, UK and Northampton, MA, U.S.A: Edward Elgar Publishing.

1. Introduction

If you're ever in Stockholm, Sweden you should visit the Vasa Museum (Vasamuseet in Swedish). It is one of Stockholm's most popular tourist attractions and one of the most popular museums in Europe. The museum was built for the sole purpose of displaying the reconstructed warship *Vasa* and educating the public about Swedish life in the 1600s and the circumstances surrounding the sinking of the *Vasa* (Vasa Museum, 2016). That story serves nicely as a metaphor for understanding the finances of social purpose organizations.

The *Vasa* was a wooden warship, built during the 30 Years War of 1618–1648 after Sweden lost a dozen ships and needed new vessels to support King Gustav II Adolph's military campaign in the Baltic. The *Vasa* was the largest ship in the history of the Swedish fleet, with an extra cannon deck that the king himself had ordered during its construction. On August 10, 1628 the *Vasa* left her mooring at the royal palace for the first time, with 130 crewman and wives on board (for the celebration). It sailed some 1300 meters out toward the sea before a gust of wind caused it to heel over to its port (left) side. Water poured through the open cannon ports and the ship sank in the 32 meters deep channel of Stockholm harbor; 53 lives were lost. Hearings were held following the disaster but no precise cause was found and no one was held accountable. It was not until 1961 that the *Vasa* was successfully salvaged. The salinity of the water and the shelter of the harbor had preserved its remains to a remarkable extent (Fairley, 2016). The ship was reconstructed over time and the Vasa Museum built around it, adjacent to the harbor (Vasa Museum, 2016).

A variety of factors seem to have contributed to the sinking of the *Vasa* (Fairley, 2016) including an escalation of size and armament requirements, lack of knowledge about how to build such a large and innovative (two-gun deck) ship or calculate its stability and performance characteristics, and management and planning problems including failures of communication and accountability. In retrospect, however, the physics of the *Vasa* just didn't add up. In essence, the *Vasa* took on an ambitious new mission as the largest and mostly heavily cannoned warship to date, without the proper foundations. The *Vasa* was top-heavy with an extra cannon deck but not enough ballast to maintain its stability. Nor, given its design, could it have added enough ballast without compromising its mission. In particular, adding the required ballast would have pulled its lower cannon deck below the waterline.

SHIPWRECKS AND COURSE CORRECTIONS

What does the *Vasa* story have to say about the finances of social purpose organizations? For one thing, the great success of the Vasa Museum is a tribute to its inspired conception and economic support structure. Its mission was very clear and compelling from the start, allowing it to sustain itself on fee revenue, with a small margin of grants funding and sponsorships from public and private sources (Persson, 2016; Swedish National Maritime Museums, 2016). (The museum is overseen by the Swedish National Maritimes Museums, along with two other museums but stands largely on its own financially.) That coordination of mission with sources of financial sustenance is a central theme of this book. For another, the *Vasa's* sinking parallels the dangers of trying to achieve a mission without the requisite financial foundations in place. Far too many important social purpose organizations have floundered in recent years and many have indeed sunk while others have had to trim their sails or change course. Here are just a few examples:

In July 2016 the Arizona Theatre Company announced that it would close its doors if it could not raise an additional $2 million to finance the 2016–2017 season. An appeal to donors was sufficiently successful to keep the doors open (Hijazi, 2016; Arizona Theatre Company 2016).

Architects for Humanity was founded in 1999 and grew to $12 million in revenues by 2012. AFH became recognized, receiving the TED prize and providing leadership in the open architecture movement. But it had serious funding challenges, relying almost completely on donations and experiencing budget overruns and declining donations in recent years. In 2015 it filed for bankruptcy (Lecy and Searing, 2016).

You Gotta Believe is a homeless prevention program for youth in foster care in New York City and Long Island. Until 2015 it received 40 percent of its annual $700,000 budget under contract with NYC's Administration for Children's Services (ACS). In 2015 ACS enacted severe cuts, reducing YGB's government support to 10 percent of its budget. The shortfall threatened YGB's viability. However, an online petition by a well-known radio host and a playwright on change.org resulted in an annual fundraising event called

Voices for the Voiceless that secured $500,000 for YGB in its first year. YGB also implemented a new fee for service model for some of its programs. YGB staff and board are now optimistic about the future, under its new finance strategy (Schaffer, 2016).

The National D-Day Memorial in Bedford, Virginia, opened in 2001 in the town that suffered the most casualties per capita in the D-Day invasion. The private foundation that supports the memorial has struggled financially since its inception, with donations, admission fees and endowment returns failing to keep pace with debt from construction and operating costs. The Memorial seeks to be taken over by the National Park Service (Dunn, 2014).

In 2013 Cooper Union, the esteemed private college established by industrialist Peter Cooper in 1859 to provide quality education in science and the arts for talented students regardless of economic circumstances, faced a traumatic financial crisis that led it to impose tuition fees for undergraduates, breaking a century-old tradition (Kaminer, 2013).

After liquidating its depleted endowment in 2009 to cover costs, the New York City Opera filed for bankruptcy in 2013 and closed its doors after 70 years of operation. The Opera faced mounting debt after years of deficit operations, borrowing from endowment and failure to raise new funds or collect on pledges (Stewart, 2013).

In 2012, Hull House, the venerated settlement house/social services organization established by Jane Addams in 1889, closed its doors as a result of bankruptcy stemming from chronic deficits and failures to control costs and establish sustainable revenue streams (Cohen, 2012).

In 2009 the Shriners Hospitals, after having lost substantial value in its endowment and facing chronic deficits, considered closing six of its hospitals. In 2011 the organization modified its 89-year-old policy to provide free specialized care to children by deciding to collect insurance payments (Osby, 2013).

WCLV was established in 1962 by two co-owners as a commercial radio station licensed to broadcast classical music in northeast Ohio. As classical commercial radio stations disappeared from radio spectra across the country under competitive pressures, WCLV continued to focus on its stated mission to keep classical music on the radio. As the owners grew older, they searched for a way to maintain this mission in perpetuity. In 2001 they worked with the Cleveland Foundation and the local (nonprofit) public radio and television organization in Cleveland, called Ideastream, to establish the WCLV Foundation, a new 501(c)(3) public charity to which they donated WCLV. Later, the foundation was closed and WCLV was transferred to Ideastream as one of its in-house programs (Lewis, 2012).

In 1998 Joan Kroc gave $90 million to the Salvation Army to build a comprehensive, luxurious community center in San Diego. Based on this model, Ms. Kroc left $1.8 billion in her estate in 2003 for the SA to build thirty more such centers around the country. The bequest paid for construction costs and an endowment to cover operating costs. However, the value of the gift was arguably insufficient and its value was substantially depleted by the recession of 2008–2009, requiring major additional local fundraising efforts in the cities where the new centers were to be located. Two centers were cancelled but by 2014, 25 were operating and total of 28 were scheduled for completion (Strom, 2009).

In 2008, the Milwaukee Shakespeare theater company went out of business after the Argosy Foundation, the principal funder of its $1.3 million operating budget, declined to renew its sustaining grant. Argosy, a family foundation, faced a cash shortage as a consequence of the national financial crisis and recession (Milwaukee Journal Sentinel, 2008).

In 2007 New York State eliminated its funding for zoos, botanical gardens and aquariums; this along with reduction in support by New York City and lagging earned revenues as a result of recession caused severe financial distress for the New York Botanical Garden in the Bronx. The NYBG cut its operating budget by 12 percent, laid-off staff, canceled several programs and delayed construction of its new parking garage. With a well-diversified income portfolio, NYBG was able to weather the storm, restored its programming and regained its financial footing by 2010 (Pogrebin, 2009).

Ben & Jerry's was established as an ice cream store in 1978 by Ben Cohen and Jerry Greenfield with the intent of pursuing a "double bottom line" of profits and social benefits generated through socially responsible workforce, environmental and agricultural practices. The company was established as a for-profit corporation with a board of shareholders including the entrepreneur–owners. In 2000 the company was bought by Unilever, a multinational consumer goods corporation. Controversy followed as to whether Ben & Jerry's had abandoned its social goals, whether it was required by corporate law and market forces to sell out, and whether the social purpose activities and practices it had pioneered would continue under the new ownership (Page and Katz, 2012).

It should come as no surprise that many contemporary nonprofit and other private social purpose organizations (SPOs) face serious financial challenges and conflicting economic pressures. Many of the foregoing cases are large organizations, prominent enough to draw media attention. Yet it is well-known that small and young organizations are especially vulnerable. Social scientists call this the "liability of newness," a condition of particular concern in the social sector, given the recent growth of social entrepreneurship, new forms of social business and the continued proliferation of nonprofit organizations (Lecy and Searing, 2016).

Social purpose organizations, small and large and mid-sized – social service agencies, schools, health care organizations, arts institutions, policy advocacy associations, environmental groups, socially-oriented businesses and cooperative enterprises – are asked to perform a delicate balancing act: achieving a social mission while sustaining themselves economically. Devoted to their social missions, they have limited leeway in pursuing financial success at the expense of mission; required to break even or face financial ruin, they are also chastened to pursue their missions with suitable restraint and risk tolerance. The tensions that result from this situation can manifest themselves in a variety of ways, sometimes exploding in spectacular fashion as some of the above cases demonstrate. Indeed, even some of the most esteemed organizations, such as Hull House, Shriners Hospitals and Cooper Union have been severely distressed financially in recent years. Some such as Hull House and the New York City Opera have succumbed to the pressures. Others, such as the New York Botanical Garden, WCLV and the Salvation Army have demonstrated their resilience under fiscal stress. Indeed one may argue that the tension between mission and financial sustainability experienced by social purpose organizations can also be a source of strength. Unlike conventional businesses, SPOs are normally not solely dependent on market sales. Managed smartly, they can take advantage of other sources of finance from parties that support their social missions. That indeed, is the prime message of this book, and the basis of effective financing strategy for social purpose organizations.

Of course, the causes of financial distress are not simply financial. Economic circumstances change over time – both in terms of cost factors and changes in demands for services, leadership and governance failures abound, and missions become obsolete. Organizations ranging from Drexel University (Paul, 2008) to the New-York Historical Society (Guthrie, 1996) to the New York City Opera (Levy, 2015) to Hull House (Cohen, 2012) are replete with management, governance and strategic failures and even corruption. Every SPO has its own story to tell. Nonetheless, generating sufficiently robust sources of income to support the chosen mission is always critical, and poor choices of income strategy constitute a common factor associated with an SPO's inability to make ends meet or to grow. Moreover, as emphasized in this book, the opportunities for income development vary from organization to organization. Given competent management and governance as prerequisites this book offers a guiding framework with a set of principles and income strategies that can be adapted to a broad spectrum of SPO circumstances. It is helpful, however, to begin with a working definition of a social purpose organization and some historical perspective on the financial context within which SPOs now operate.

SOCIAL PURPOSE ORGANIZATIONS

SPO is not (yet) a commonly used term. More usual designations include nonprofit organizations and social enterprises but these terms are too restrictive for the purpose here. As conceived in this book, *SPOs are private organizations (separate from government and operating in a market economy) which include a social or public purpose as an integral and explicit part of their missions.* This certainly embraces traditional nonprofit organizations and the various manifestations of what is now termed social enterprise. However, neither of the latter terms fully reflects the notion of SPO. For example, nonprofits that lack an earned income component are often excluded from consideration as social enterprises, while the term "social enterprise" is not always used in a way that encompasses forms such as sustainable businesses, public/private partnerships, socially-focused cooperatives or charitable nonprofits. While some scholars argue for an expansive definition of social enterprise (Young, Searing and Brewer, 2016) the term SPO is less fraught and more explicitly accommodating of a variety of organizational forms and international variations. The need for such more inclusive terminology stems from the historical evolution of market economies as understood by scholars and policymakers.

Fifty years ago, the economy of the United States, as well as those of other industrial democracies, was viewed simplistically as having two essential parts – business and government. Textbooks in economics and public finance ignored the presence of charities, associations, cooperatives and other mutual and public service organizations, and little consideration was given to businesses that pursued anything other than profits. Citizens, of course, realized that there was more to it than this, but they did not associate their churches, hospitals, schools, museums, orchestras, community centers, advocacy groups, social service organizations, or even grant-making foundations, with any cohesive "third sector" commensurate with business or government. Rather, such organizations were thought of as charities, associations or community groups having little to do with one another, and supported primarily by charitable giving and volunteering. That conception began to change in the 1960s and 1970s in the U.S. when the federal government's Great Society programs poured massive funding into nonprofit organizations for the delivery of social, health, education, arts and cultural and environmental services; when foundations came under attack for their social activism in civil rights and education; and when scholars began to take notice by formulating new theories of the nonprofit sector.

Still, the notion of the third sector consisting essentially of charities supported primarily by donations and volunteering persists, in the U.S. and elsewhere. Even in large contemporary established nonprofit organizations, development officers focus primarily on charitable giving from individuals and grants from foundations and corporations, giving short shrift to the broader picture of nonprofit finance as considered in this book. Similarly, in higher education, where a plethora of graduate and undergraduate programs in nonprofit management and social enterprise has blossomed over the past thirty years across hundreds of universities in the U.S. and abroad, the teaching of resource development primarily focuses on traditional (charitable) fund-raising for nonprofit organizations. Only recently have the concepts of "social entrepreneurship" and broader-based "social investing" infiltrated these curricula in a serious way.

CHANGES IN THE SOCIAL SECTOR

The reality of the third sector – what the management guru Peter Drucker liked to call the "social sector" – is much more complex than it was even thirty years ago – in at least two important ways. First, charitable giving, while it has grown in absolute terms, is now relatively a much smaller part of the overall finances of nonprofit or other social purpose organizations. Good numbers on this are hard to find because most estimates (in the U.S. at least) derive from tax data that have limited detail and fail to cover smaller organizations or churches. Still, the available numbers are striking. As recently as 1980 private donations constituted 34 percent of the revenue of philanthropic organizations, the rest deriving from fee income, government grants, and investments (Rudney, 1987). Even that statistic shows that many nonprofits were never just simple charities. However, by 2010 that number had declined to somewhere between 10 percent and 13 percent (Salamon, 2012; Roeger et al., 2012). Fee income from private sources alone currently constitutes half of nonprofits' operating income, with fees and contracts from government accounting for another 24 percent.

This is not to argue that the charitable component of social purpose finance is no longer important. Indeed, the charitable share of nonprofit revenue is much higher in certain segments of the sector such as churches and the arts. Moreover, when a value is put on volunteering, the share of income from charitable support increases by roughly half (McKeever, 2015). Rather the point is that the primary focus on charitable fund-raising for nonprofit finance is misplaced and needs to be broadened to include other more abundant sources including fees for service and government support.

The second way in which social sector finance is more complex today than it was thirty or fifty years ago is that the sector itself has changed in important ways. In particular, scholars have highlighted the "blurring" of the sectors (Billis, 2010), wherein nonprofits are now much more engaged with business than they used to be, running their own commercial ventures for profit, as well as partnering with for-profit business in numerous variations of joint ventures and sponsorship and ownership arrangements (Cordes et al., 2009). Moreover, nonprofits themselves, while still dominant as a legal form, are no longer considered the only kind of private social purpose organization in the U.S. Indeed, the broader concept of "social enterprise," once narrowly conceived in the U.S. as commercial activity carried out by nonprofits in service of their social missions, has become a much more inclusive idea – encompassing a variety of legal forms and arrangements (Young, Searing and Brewer, 2016). These include new for-profit entities such as low profit, limited liability companies (L3Cs), various types of "benefit" or social purpose corporations, so-called B Corps – for-profit companies certified by the nonprofit B Lab as meeting specified standards of social and environmental responsibility, as well as social purpose cooperatives and various types of public/private partnerships which often involve combinations of nonprofit, for-profit and government organizations. Although these for-profit and low profit alternatives currently represent only a small fraction of social purpose activity in the U.S., there are a growing segment of the social sector (Brewer, 2013) that cannot be ignored and indeed show considerable promise for addressing some of the chronic and intractable social problems of the present day, such as poverty, literacy and environmental degradation. Moreover, nonprofits per se, while growing in prominence in other parts of the world, are not necessarily as dominant elsewhere as they are in the U.S. The cooperative form, for example, has been adapted to social purposes such as work integration for marginalized populations in Europe and is an important structure for social enterprise in other regions as well. So-called "social cooperatives" are conceived as occupying the intersection of nonprofit organizations and member-serving cooperatives (Defourny and Nyssens, 2012). In some countries such as Italy and Sweden the government provides substantial funding for social cooperatives (Kerlin, 2012). In the United Kingdom, the Community Interest Company (CIC), a newly devised hybrid nonprofit/ for-profit form has made substantial inroads as a vehicle for social enterprise over the last decade (Regulator, 2010).

While this book concentrates largely on the financing of public benefit nonprofit organizations per se (designated as 501(c)(3) charitable organizations by the IRS in the United States), the blossoming of social enterprise and the blurring of the sectors favors use of the term social purpose organization (SPO) as the generic default. Clearly the financing of these various types of organizations encounters different sets of constraints, legal requirements and resource opportunities. However, they also share a challenge common to all entities with a social purpose that must sustain themselves financially in the market economy – how to support the provision of goods and services or ventures with social purpose, in a market context and a democratic society, where the market is geared to consumers shopping for private goods and investors seeking to gain from the profits of businesses in which they buy and sell shares or debt; and where government is drawn to the preferences of a majority while protecting minority interests. In this context, all SPOs must negotiate the margins of the marketplace where public benefits are symbiotic with profitmaking, where the niches of government programming may coincide with their particular social goals, and where the diverse philanthropic impulses that motivate generous individuals and charitable institutions can be rallied for support of their particular missions.

Taking this broad, generic approach to the finance of SPOs makes certain things immediately apparent. First, the marketplace, government and philanthropy are all imperfect mechanisms for pursuing social benefits through private organizations. The marketplace does not easily accommodate goods and services that cannot be sold for a profit, no matter how socially beneficial. Some connection between social purpose and private gain must be made in order for market revenues to support social ventures. Government does not automatically respond to socially beneficial projects either; who receives and who pays for those benefits matter and coalitions must be successfully assembled to enlist taxpayer support. And philanthropy can be a haystack of potential donors requiring careful sifting to match and engage donors of diverse preferences with ventures having particular social goals. Given the wide variety of missions addressed by SPOs, and the diverse potential mechanisms for their support, there is no simple financial formula that will suit all SPOs, or even all SPOs within broad categories such as social service or the performing arts. For example, consultants who may recommend a simplistic "one-thirds strategy" for nonprofits – one third fees, one third government, one third gifts – are just flying by the seat of their pants.

FASHIONS IN FINANCIAL STRATEGY AND BENEFITS THEORY

Nonetheless, different financial strategies tend to come into fashion over time. In the heyday of the Great Society programs of the late 1960s and early 1970s, government financing of nonprofits in the U.S. expanded significantly in many different fields, including the arts, and securing government grants and contracts seemed the smart thing to do. Later, with the success of American Express's sponsorship of the restoration of the Statue of Liberty and corporate support of the 1984 Olympic Games in Los Angeles, *cause-related marketing* became the rage and many nonprofits were encouraged to pursue this strategy. Following the examples of endowment managers at Yale, Harvard, Stanford and other large nonprofits in the booming 1990s, *building an endowment* became the strategy of choice for many nonprofits. More recently, *social enterprise* has entered the lexicon of SPO finance. Based on the relatively diminishing role of philanthropy and the proliferation of nonprofits and other SPOs since the 1990s, it was now thought that every nonprofit should *commercialize* its products and find ways to price and sell its mission-related services and engage in additional ventures that could turn a profit. Of course all of these strategies have a place in the arsenal of SPO financing options, but *none constitutes a panacea*. Paradoxically, however, neither is *diversification of income sources* necessarily a preferred strategy for every SPO or nonprofit organization. The issue of diversification is a complex one that will be discussed in Chapter 11. Suffice it to say here that an underlying theory is required to determine just how much an individual SPO's income should be diversified and what its particular mix of income sources should be. That is the overriding goal of this book – to offer the "benefits theory" of SPO finance as a framework for choice of the sources and mixes of financial support for any given SPO.

There are two common aspects of SPOs on which the benefits theory is built: First, that all SPOs have social missions to which they are dedicated; accordingly, benefits theory is anchored in the pursuit of mission. This is important although it takes different forms for different types of SPOs. Nonprofit organizations are perhaps the most straightforward case. Nonprofits are established for the explicit purpose of achieving a social (charitable) mission and all of its resources must ultimately be dedicated to that purpose. Other types of SPOs such as social purpose businesses, public/private partnerships and cooperatives often incorporate an element of (usually limited) profit distribution to those in control (members, owners or shareholders) and are concerned with private gain to some degree in addition to their social missions. This book is concerned primarily with the financing of the public aspects of the missions of SPOs in a manner that assures the organization's economic viability. This does not restrict the analysis of SPOs that include a component of private benefit, but the latter is of interest only as it applies to helping support the SPO's social mission.

The second common feature of SPOs on which the benefits theory is based is that almost all sources of support for SPOs are *transactional* in nature. Passive investment income which does not entail direct exchange of services or benefits, is arguably an exception although the sources of capital for such investments indeed often require transactions with donors or other sources (see Chapters 8 and 10). In this dimension benefits theory recognizes that all SPOs operate in the marketplace, broadly defined, and each must make ends meet in the most effective way. The transactional character is of course most obvious for SPOs that take the form of for-profit businesses that transact with their customers and investors. In the same spirit, cooperatives are engaged in transactions with their members, and in many cases the consumers of their products. Traditional nonprofit organizations are more subtle in this respect, but this is where the benefits theory makes its biggest contribution. Nonprofits do depend largely on fee income which generally derives from private market transactions. In addition, government support can take the form of grants or contracts, but in either case the funding agency expects something in return for its financial support. Gift income is even more nuanced, but understanding the interests and reciprocal expectations of donors, institutional funders and volunteers is critical to the securing of such resources as well. Overall, the "benefits" that SPOs offer, reflecting the preferences of their various resource providers (and the constituencies whom those providers seek to serve), are thus key to what they can negotiate for resources in return.

ORGANIZATION OF THE BOOK

The remainder of this book is organized as follows. The next chapter examines in greater detail the economic, political and social context in which nonprofits and other SPOs have operated in recent years – the patterns and trends that SPOs must understand and negotiate in making their decisions about sources of support. This context is dynamic and diverse, featuring various cross-currents stemming from changes in public policy, vicissitudes in the economy, changes in technology, fashions in management strategy, international differences, and new social problems and challenges, which in turn have affected the relative availability and perceived efficacy of different sources of economic support. However, unlike businesses and government organizations which tend to blow with the economic and political winds in pursuit of profits or votes, social purpose organizations presumably use their individualized missions as their compasses. As a result, SPOs tend to be resilient in the face of cross-currents and formulaic panaceas, and relatively steadfast in their financial underpinnings over time. This echoes a cornerstone of the benefits theory of SPO finance – that SPOs' income portfolios are anchored in mission and adaptive in adjusting to circumstances in a dynamic environment that both threatens their stability and offers them new opportunities.

The third chapter explicitly presents the benefits theory framework of SPO finance. The main idea is that mission determines what kinds of goods and services an SPO provides and whom it serves and benefits. This in turn drives the possibilities for finance. Some evidence from research shows that this is indeed how SPOs tend to operate, if only intuitively. Recognizing and codifying this rationale allows SPOs to exploit it more effectively.

The fourth chapter examines the nature of benefits, beneficiaries and income contributors and their connections with mission and services. Here the language of public and private goods as developed by economists is employed and adapted to distinguish the outputs of SPOs in various fields of service. The recognition that SPOs vary by mission, services and benefits helps explain why the income portfolios of SPOs are so (justifiably) varied and why a homogenous approach to SPO finance is naïve and inappropriate.

Chapters 5 through 9 explore the financing of SPOs reliant on alternative sources of income, respectively fee or earned income, gifts and grants, governmental funding, returns from investments, or diversified among these sources. Each of these chapters describes how the nature of the services connects with the particular type of income secured, and the various strategies that may be employed for that purpose – for example alternative pricing strategies in the case of earned income, or different approaches to fund-raising in the case of gifts and grants. Each chapter offers case studies of SPOs that support themselves primarily through the source of income under scrutiny. In Chapter 9 a similar analysis is presented for SPOs with highly diversified income portfolios, indicating how that pattern conforms to the mixed character of their missions, services and beneficiaries.

Chapters 5 through 9 focus principally on operating income. In Chapter 10 attention turns to capital funding because SPOs with different cost structures and legal forms have substantially different capital requirements and alternatives for funding them. Here the benefits theory is applied to the raising of capital funds for endowments, buildings and other assets, so as to connect sources of capital with long-term benefits and beneficiaries.

Chapter 11 further develops the concept of an SPO's "income portfolio," in the context of risk management, financial solvency and growth. Here it is noted that SPOs must manage a variety of interconnected portfolios including portfolios of programs, assets, investments and income sources. Classical portfolio theory from the financial management field is considered as a perspective for understanding SPO income portfolios. In particular, we consider the virtues and challenges of "diversification" of income as a way of buffering an organization from financial perturbations and storms. Certain aspects of income portfolios, however, limit or complicate the application of classical theory, including the possibility of unanticipated shocks in the economic environment. Still, portfolio theory requires estimates of return on investment in alternative income sources which benefits theory can help supply. Two conclusions follow from this analysis. First, that diversification must be supplemented by other means of risk management, such as the maintenance of reserve funds. Second, that benefits theory serves as an overarching framework for shaping SPO income portfolios, and providing the information for a robust risk management and income development strategy.

Finally, Chapter 12 offers some practical advice and tools for SPO resource development. This includes the notion implied throughout the book, that SPOs require broader staff capacities, focused not just on charitable fund-raising but on the wider set of possible (and likely) sources of income support. With this in mind, some general principles of SPO income development strategy are summarized and templates and tools offered to facilitate the thinking of SPO leaders and development personnel of the 21st century. The reader is invited to apply and adapt these templates and tools to cases offered throughout the book and to his or her own organizations.

REFERENCES

Arizona Theatre Company, 2016. www.arizonatheatre.org/.

David Billis (ed.), 2010. *Hybrid Organizations and the Third Sector*, Basingstoke: Palgrave Macmillan.

Cassady Brewer, 2013. Social Enterprise Entity Comparison Chart, working draft, George State University College of Law, October.

Rick Cohen, 2012. "Death of the Hull House: A Nonprofit Coroner's Inquest", *Nonprofit Quarterly*, August.

Joseph J. Cordes, Zina Poletz and C. Eugene Steurele, 2009. "Examples of

Nonprofit-For-Profit Hybrid Business Models", Appendix 3.1 in Joseph J. Cordes and C. Eugene Steurele (eds), *Nonprofits & Business*, Washington, DC: Urban Institute Press, pp. 69–82.

Jacques Defourny and Marthe Nyssens, 2012. "Conceptions of Social Enterprise in Europe: A Comparative Perspective with the United States", Chapter 3 in Benjamin Gidron and Yeheskel Hasenfeld (eds), *Social Enterprises: An Organizational Perspective*, Basingstoke: Palgrave Macmillan, pp. 71–90.

Donna Dunn, 2014. "What Will Become of the National D-Day Memorial?", *Lynchburg Living*, retrieved on December 9, 2016 from www.lynchburgliving.com, June.

Richard E. Fairley (2016), "Why the Vasa Sank: 10 Lessons Learned", draft, retrieved on December 9, 2016 from http://faculty.up.edu/lulay/failure/vasacasestudy.pdf.

Kevin M. Guthrie, 1996. *The New-York Historical Society*, San Francisco, CA: Jossey-Bass Publishers.

Jennifer Hijazi, 2016. "Arizona Theatre Company Feels the Love – But Needs a Lot More", *Tucson Weekly*, retrieved on December 9, 2016 from www.tucsonweekly.com/TheRange/archives/2016/07/11/arizona-theatre-company-feels-the-lovebut-needs-a-lot-more.

Ariel Kaminer, 2013. "College Ends Free Tuition, and an Era", *New York Times*, April 23.

Janelle A. Kerlin, 2012. "Defining Social Enterprise across Different Contexts: A Conceptual Framework Based on Institutional Factors", Chapter 4 in Benjamin Gidron and Yeheskel Hasenfeld (eds), *Social Enterprises: An Organizational Perspective*, Basingstoke: Palgrave Macmillan, pp. 91–117.

Jesse Lecy and Elizabeth A.M. Searing, 2016. "Changes Over the Life Cycle of Social Enterprise Animals", Chapter 6 in Dennis R. Young, Elizabeth A.M. Searing and Cassady V. Brewer (eds), 2016. *The Social Enterprise Zoo: A Guide to Perplexed Scholars, Entrepreneurs, Philanthropists, Leaders, Investors and Policymakers*, Cheltenham, UK and Northampton, MA, USA: Edward Elgar Publishing, pp. 113–140.

Reynold Levy, 2015. *They Told Me Not to Take That Job*, New York: PublicAffairs Books.

Zachary Lewis, 2012. "Cleveland's WCLV FM/104.9 planning to switch to non-commercial format", *The Plain Dealer*, September 26.

Brice McKeever, 2015. *The Nonprofit Sector in Brief*, Washington, DC: The Urban Institute, October.

Milwaukee Journal Sentinel, 2008. "Milwaukee Shakespeare to Close After Argosy Cuts Funding", retrieved on December 9, 2016 from www.jsonline.com/entertainment/arts/33456084.html.

Liv Osby, 2013. "Shriners Hospital expanding services after weathering financial crisis", *GreenvilleOnline.com*, July 17.

Anthony Page and Robert A. Katz, 2012. "The Truth about Ben and Jerry's", *Stanford Social Innovation Review*, Fall, retrieved on December 9, 2016 from www.ssireview.org/articles/entry/the_truth_about_ben-and-jerrys.

David A. Paul, 2008. *When the Pot Boils: The Decline and Turnaround of Drexel University*, Albany, NY: State University of New York Press.

Maria D. Persson, 2016. Vasa Museum; personal correspondence.

Robin Pogrebin, 2009. "In New York, Proposed Budget Shuts Out Zoos, Aquariums and Gardens", *New York Times*, January 21.

Regulator of Community Interest Companies, 2010. *Community Interest Companies Information Pack*, London: Department for Business Innovation and Skills.

Gabriel Rudney, 1987. "The Scope and Dimensions of Nonprofit Activity", Chapter 4 in Walter W. Powell (ed.), *The Nonprofit Sector: A Research Handbook*, New Haven: Yale University Press, pp. 55–64.

Katie L. Roeger, Amy S. Blackwood and Sarah L. Pettijohn, 2012. *The Nonprofit Almanac 2012*, Washington, DC: The Urban Institute Press.

Lester M. Salamon, 2012. *America's Nonprofit Sector: A Primer*, Third Edition, New York: The Foundation Center.

Jim Schaffer, 2016. "Funding Crisis as Opportunity: Nonprofit Enterprise Transformation", *The Chronicle of Social Change*, July 27, retrieved on December 9, 2016 from https://nonprofitquarterly.org/2016/08/02/funding-crisis-nonprofit-opportunity-enterprise-transformation/?utm_source=Daily+Newswire&utm_ca mpaign=a54827a7a1-Daily_Digest_23628_2_2016&utm_medium=email&utm_ term=0_94063a1d17-a54827a7a1-12331785.

James B. Stewart, 2013. "A Ransacked Endowment at New York City Opera", *The New York Times, Business Day*, October 11.

Stephanie Strom, 2009. "Plan for Dozens of Salvation Army Centers Falters", *New York Times*, June 14.

Swedish National Maritime Museums, 2016. www.maritima.se/sv/Om-oss/ Arsredovisning/.

Vasa Museum, 2016. www.vasamuseet.se.

Dennis R. Young (ed.), 2007. *Financing Nonprofits: Putting Theory into Practice*, Lanham, MD: AltaMira Press.

Dennis R. Young, Elizabeth A.M. Searing and Cassady V. Brewer (eds), 2016. *The Social Enterprise Zoo: A Guide to Perplexed Scholars, Entrepreneurs, Philanthropists, Leaders, Investors and Policymakers*, Cheltenham, UK and Northampton, MA, USA: Edward Elgar Publishing.

2.   Cross-currents in SPO finance

> But the principal failing occurred in the sailing
> And the Bellman, perplexed and distressed,
> Said he *had* hoped, at least, when the wind blew due East
> That the ship would *not* travel due West!
> Lewis Carroll, 'The Bellman's Speech' (Oxford Dictionary of Quotations, 1979)

Think of a social purpose organization as a ship at sea (hopefully not the *Vasa!*). The compass has two dimensions: North-South and East-West. North is the direction of positive social impact – achievement of the organization's social mission. East is the direction of financial reward or surplus. All social purpose organizations want to head North but not necessarily true North. Traditional nonprofit organizations whose bottom line is social impact want to travel as close to true North as possible, allowing for sufficient margin of financial surplus to ensure their organizational integrity, growth and vitality. Cooperatives and other limited-profit distribution SPOs, such as the U.K.'s community interest companies (CIC's) want to tack slightly more to the East to satisfy their chosen balance of mission impact and net remuneration to investors or members. Social businesses constrained less by strict limits on profit-taking (for example, L3Cs as discussed later) would tack even further to the East, and avowedly socially responsible or sustainable businesses (for example, B corporations) even more so to the East. Purely profit-maximizing businesses wanting to be socially responsible would of course head a bit north of due East.

All this seems clear enough, but as any sailor as well as Lewis Carroll's Bellman, knows, the sea is a tricky environment, with few safe harbors, where the winds change and the weather is stormy as often as not. Moreover, the seas are not homogeneous, with different patterns of current flow in different regions – calmer seas in some places, rougher and more volatile in others – and in any case, different from one place to the next. In the environment of social purpose organizations, various winds have blown in and out over the past several decades, and different policies and conventions govern conditions in different parts of the world.

For nonprofits in the U.S., for example, evidence from research suggests that although the number of organizations has increased markedly in recent years, these organizations are facing increasing levels of demand for their services (Harrison and Thornton, 2014). Thus, to the degree that funding has not kept pace with latent demand factors such as population growth, they must compete more aggressively for resources. Meanwhile, the role of philanthropy has changed as the sector outgrows its original philanthropic base, and as the desires and practices of donors themselves have evolved. The role of government too is changing, as public services once generously funded by the welfare state have been privatized and incentivized for results, and funding of social welfare services, even privately delivered, has become more limited. Markets, always a major source of economic sustenance for SPOs, loom increasingly large, manifested in multiple ways that suggest that SPOs must adopt more business-oriented strategies. Thus, over time, SPOs have been variously importuned to engage in earned income ventures, partner with corporations in cause-marketing arrangements, develop sophisticated performance metrics to attract philanthropic "investors," business partners and government funding, and become sophisticated investors of their endowment funds. Furthermore, SPOs have been encouraged to become more skilled resource managers, for example by adopting efficient operating practices and diversifying their sources of support to more safely execute their risky voyages.

Some of these cross-currents have already been glimpsed in Chapter 1. This chapter reviews them in greater detail and completeness in order to set the stage for deeper analysis of SPO financial strategy. These cross-currents include the changing roles and character of philanthropy and government support, the enlarged role of markets, and broad international patterns including differences between those parts of the world (for example, the U.S. and U.K.) that use the nonprofit sector as their main frame of reference for the social sector, and other parts (for example, continental Europe and Quebec) that think in terms of the broader "social economy."

To push the maritime metaphor just a bit further, the theory developed in the next chapter can be appreciated as a sextant or compass to help SPOs plot their chosen directions, tack appropriately and avoid being pulled too far off course by the strong winds of change that buffet the social sector. Most SPOs are already oriented toward such steadfastness because of their generally tenacious mission orientation, but they often require greater guidance to maintain their viability and direction and adapt where necessary. The benefits theory developed in this book is based on the belief that organizational mission (however it may balance social impact and market success) serves as the navigational north star from which appropriate financial strategy may be developed.

THE CHANGING ROLE OF PHILANTHROPY

In the United States, gifts and grants have always been central to the
identity and support of social purpose organizations, the primary form
of which has been the charitable not-for-profit corporation classified as
501(c)(3) under the U.S. tax code. The 501(c)(3) designation allows donors
to take a charitable deduction from their taxable income or corporate
profits, thus providing an important incentive for charitable giving. As
noted in Chapter 1, however, even in the U.S. charitable giving is not
the dominant source of income support for nonprofit organizations,
even most 501(c)(3)public charities, and it has become less prominent
in the income portfolios of nonprofits in recent decades. In other parts
of the world, however, private philanthropy has not been as significant
historically (Salamon, 2012a) though it is growing, inspired by the classical
American model of deductible contributions and the formation of private
grant-making foundations.

Chapter 6 offers a more complete picture of philanthropy as a source
of SPO finance. For now, suffice it to say that philanthropy remains
a critical source of income for many nonprofits and other SPOs and
will continue to be so. But it is also important to understand why
philanthropy in its classical forms has diminished in its relative importance to SPOs and why it may continue to decline. A lesson developed
in Chapter 6 is that philanthropy may well have an important place in
the income portfolio of any given SPO but that place must be strategically chosen relative to the predilections and priorities of individual and
institutional donors.

In the U.S., philanthropy certainly continues to grow in absolute terms.
Based on data from the *Giving USA Foundation*, Roeger et al. (2012)
estimated that total private giving rose from approximately $118 billion in
1970 to $291 billion in 2010 in inflation-adjusted terms (2010 dollars), a
three-fold increase. On a per capita basis, for individual giving, the growth
is smaller but still impressive – increasing by approximately 50 percent
over the same period. What is really notable, however, is the stability of
charitable giving as a percentage of national income. Over the 1970 to
2010 period, this figure remained within a narrow range bracketing 2
percent of national income, never rising above 2.1 percent or falling below
1.5 percent over the entire forty year period. In all but seven of these
years, the figure held to the range of 1.7 percent to 2 percent. Even with
national campaigns such as the *Give 5* project promoted by Independent
Sector in the 1980s, and imitated by various charitable groups since then,
the figure has never budged much. Still, it is worth noting that even at the
modest 2 percent level, private philanthropy as proportion of national

income (or its reflection in GDP) the U.S. figure well exceeds that of other developed countries (Salamon, 2012a).

This stability of charitable giving as a proportion of income is important in the context of growth of the social sector. Specifically, the sector (even limited narrowly to charitable nonprofits) has grown faster than the economy as a whole over recent decades, and certainly faster than the 2 percent of national income commonly allocated to charitable giving. Essentially, the social sector tracks the growth of the service economy, which has long increased at a faster rate than the economy as a whole in developed countries such as the U.S. Various statistics tell this tale (Roeger et al., 2012). Nonprofit employment in the U.S. has risen steadily from 8.8 percent of the non-farm workforce in 1998 to 10.6 percent in 2010. The number of reporting charities rose at an average annual rate of 3.9 percent over the 2000–2010 period. And total expenses of these charities rose at an average annual rate of 6.9 percent over the same period. During the same period, real GDP in the U.S. (and hence 2 percent thereof) increased at an annual rate of only 1.6 percent over the 2001–2011 period, similar to that of the U.K. and exceeding that of most European countries and Japan (*Economist*, 2014).

In summary, while private philanthropy will remain an important strategic component of SPO finance, it represents a diminishing proportion in quantitative terms, and a relatively small part of the finances of SPOs overall. The role of philanthropy varies widely in importance by field of activity, however, and is still the dominant source for many SPOs. Moreover, innovations in fund-raising facilitated by the revolution in communications technology, such as crowd-funding, may yet have the potential to stem the relative slide in philanthropic support (Lehner, 2015). Thus, navigating the narrow channel of opportunity for securing charitable funding will remain important for the captains of many SPOs for the indefinite future.

That said, the changing character of philanthropy is having a pervasive and subtle influence on the management and financing of social purpose organizations. In particular, so-called "venture philanthropy" has helped transform much of institutional philanthropy from old-style relatively "hands off" grant-making (more like gift giving) to a regime featuring more intensive involvement of funders in the strategy, governance and development of proposed ventures, more emphasis on seeking out talented social entrepreneurs with good business plans, greater use of performance metrics, as well as implementation of "pay for success models" that explicitly connect performance with payment (John and Emerson, 2015). In addition, some foundations are making increasing use of so-called "program-related investments" (PRIs) that allow them to leverage the corpus of their endowments (in addition to their investment returns) to support organizations that address social needs, through loans and other instruments that provide a financial as well as social return to the funder, thus permitting a recycling of allocated funds (Searing and Young, 2016; Motter, 2013). While PRIs have been around for a long time, foundations have been slow to embrace them until recently. However, leading foundations including the Packard, Gates, Knight and MacArthur foundations now promote this approach.

BUSINESS INVESTING AND CORPORATE PHILANTHROPY

The venture philanthropy movement arose from a generation of business leaders who made their fortunes in high tech and related areas in the late 20th and early 21st centuries, and sought to apply their problem-focused, results-oriented, entrepreneurial methods to their philanthropy and investing, in a movement that came to be called "philanthrocapitalism" (Bishop and Green, 2015). This movement went beyond traditional philanthropy, influencing the broader realm of business investment and corporate giving. In particular, socially-oriented investors began to seek out financial investments that could demonstrate significant social impacts as well as financial returns in efforts to address broad scale social problems. Concurrently, business corporations began rethinking their corporate social responsibility (CSR) strategies, seeking to become more socially responsible and environmentally sustainable, and moving their attention to initiatives that could be both financially rewarding and socially beneficial – the idea of creating "shared value" (Smith and Kramer, 2014). These developments in turn helped widen the spectrum of social purpose organizations to include partnerships and hybrid arrangements participating in socially focused initiatives, and involving business corporations, social enterprises, cooperatives, microfinance institutions and community development finance institutions (Oleksiak, Nicholls and Emerson, 2015).

MARKET STRATEGIES TO SUSTAIN THE STABILITY AND GROWTH OF SPOs

The uncertainty in government funding and the relative decline of philanthropy have led SPOs to explore a variety of market-oriented strategies to maintain their vitality and continue to grow. Here several such strategies are reviewed, with further analysis of some of them reserved for later chapters. These have become part of the repertoire of contemporary SPOs, and new ones continue to emerge. Ongoing strategies include cause marketing and partnerships with business, developing of new commercial enterprises, increasing fees and pricing formerly free services, building endowments and pursuing sophisticated investment strategies, and diversifying funding sources. Newer strategies include performance-based instruments such as social impact bonds and other financial arrangements tied to outcomes, crowd-funding and other Internet-based approaches, and new legal forms designed to facilitate the pursuit of social purpose in a market context by attracting new sources of support. In some ways, the latter strategies are simply a matter of "keeping up with the Joneses" as technologies change over time for all economic actors. More broadly they represent a turn to the market by SPOs for financial support. However, while these various strategies reflect both fresh opportunities and new dangers, they do not fundamentally alter the nature of SPO finance. SPOs still need to figure out the best "value proposition" for their current and prospective beneficiaries and supporters.

Commercial Ventures and Social Enterprise

Earned income has always been an important segment of the support of social purpose ventures, dating back well into the 18th century in the United States (McCarthy, 2003). In the 1820s, for example, sales accounted for half of the revenue of the American Bible Society. Girl Scout cookie sales are, of course, legendary and still a mainstay of Girl Scout finances; and New York University is famous for having owned the Mueller Spaghetti Company – setting off a sequence of events leading to the codification of the Unrelated Business Income Tax on charitable nonprofits in 1950. In the 1980s the Rockefeller Brothers Fund commissioned a study that documented widespread engagement of nonprofit organizations in commercial activity (Crimmins and Keil, 1983). The strategy of pursuing commercial revenues as a means to subsidize mission-focused nonprofit activity was first formalized in theory by Estelle James (1983) and later studied extensively by a team of colleagues led by Burton Weisbrod (1998). Recently, overall reliance on market-derived sources of income appears to be accelerating in response to developments in philanthropy and government support. Salamon (2012a) notes, for example, that 58 percent of the growth of the revenue of U.S. nonprofit organizations between 1997 and 2007 derived from fee income, thus nudging upwards the sector's overall reliance on this source of support. It is fair to say, however, that in recent years the increased reliance on earned income is just one facet of the stronger commercial orientation of the social sector. Additional dimensions include the adoption of business practices by SPOs, the engagement of commercial businesses with SPOs, and the manifestation of new forms of social business.

Adoption of Business Practices

The growing reliance on earned income has brought with it increased attention to market-based decision-making by SPOs. This is perhaps best illustrated by the issue of pricing of services. Pricing is often where the rubber meets the road in balancing social purpose against financial success. Even the American Bible Society had to decide when to sell its bibles and when to give them away. In the modern era, nonprofit hospitals balance charity care with financial return, and private colleges and universities design financial aid schemes to accommodate deserving students of modest means, even risking anti-trust action in one instance by allegedly colluding to ensure that tuition did not determine student choices (Eckel and Steinberg, 1993). As pressures to increase earned income have grown, some SPOs with historic missions to provide their services free of charge, such as Cooper Union (see Chapter 8) and Shriners Hospitals have faced excruciating decisions to implement pricing schedules. Of course there is a long tradition of SPOs offering "sliding scales" or various discounts to needy or worthy groups of consumers. While economists would call this "price discrimination," the rationales for such practices are really quite different for SPOs than for profit-oriented businesses. However, as a result of their deeper involvement in markets, SPOs have had to become much more sophisticated in their pricing policies and designs. (This subject is addressed in Chapter 5.)

Another area of business practice that SPOs have had to embrace is performance measurement. Here SPOs operate at a considerable disadvantage relative to business. For SPOs, profits are not a sole measure of success, though they serve as a partial indicator for social businesses that combine profitmaking and social objectives, or as a helpful measure of sustainability for those SPOs with non-distribution or limited distribution of profits constraints (such as traditional nonprofit organizations and many cooperatives). Moreover, SPOs are engaged in social ventures, ranging from youth development, to environmental conservation, to poverty alleviation, to public health and education, whose impacts are not so easily measured. Nonetheless, few new social ventures succeed in attracting funding without a formal business plan that includes measures of impact and effectiveness.

In part, the pressure for SPOs to adopt performance measures that reflect both financial sustainability and social mission impact has come from the necessity to compete successfully with for-profit businesses in some markets such as education, health care or the arts. Perhaps ironically, pressure has also come from philanthropic and governmental funders of SPOs who now demand greater accountability for receipt of their increasingly scarce resources. In addition, much of the new philanthropic wealth now driving institutional philanthropy derives from the high tech boom of the 1990s, whose entrepreneurs now seek to apply standards similar to those that helped them become successful in the private sector (Morino, 2011).

A particularly interesting confluence of business investment and performance measurement for the achievement of social goals is the "social impact bond," a device that has been used in the U.S., U.K. and elsewhere to attract investors to the achievement of social goals through contingent government funding of projects carried out through SPOs. Under this arrangement, investors recover their investments plus a financial return paid only if the goals are achieved. For example, in 2014, the Goldman Sachs Social Impact Fund and other partners invested $9 million to expand services provided by Roca, a nonprofit organization in Massachusetts, to achieve stipulated outcomes for high risk youth. Repayment of the loan by the state was directly tied to the achievement of future decreases in incarceration and increases in employment among participants in the Roca program (Goldman Sachs, 2014). (Social impact bonds and other performance-related financial instruments are examined further in Chapter 10.)

Building Endowments

For-profit businesses do not build endowments; they generally prefer to reinvest so as to grow their businesses and/or reward owners or share-holders with dividends and higher stock prices. Businesses do sometimes accumulate large cash reserves which they may use to buy back shares or take over other firms if such strategies promise greater returns than alternative investments. However, these reserves are not endowments wherein the capital is preserved in order to generate streams of investment income over an indefinite or specific period of time. SPOs, on the other hand, can often make good use of endowments. As discussed in Chapter 8, investment revenues can serve several purposes in balancing SPO income portfolios including offsetting high fixed costs, and managing risk. Building endowments has at various times been encouraged by business sector thinking and practice. In particular, many SPOs have been influenced by the financial industry with the promise of extraordinary returns on investments. This is especially true in higher education in the U.S. where the endowment performance of exemplar institutions such as Yale and

Harvard have served as bell-weathers. Though recently discredited for the financial debacle of 2007–2009, the investment management and securities industries have surely influenced the behavior of many SPOs, especially large ones, some of which have taken inordinate risks or become victims of unscrupulous investment managers such as Bernie Madoff. Though tales of endowment mismanagement are not especially rare, the New York City Opera being a tragic recent example (Levy, 2015), and although the Great Recession was punishing to well-endowed institutions, these experiences have likely reinforced the need for sophisticated (prudent) business thinking about endowments by SPOs. Meanwhile the recovery of the economy and parallel rise of the stock market continue to attract interest in endowments as a source of reliable income for appropriately positioned organizations.

As with performance measurement, the connections of endowment strategy with philanthropy are palpable and perhaps ironic as well. Generally speaking, endowments are funded through philanthropy, especially by major individual donors who can put their names on programs, buildings, scholarships, professorial or curatorial chairs, in exchange for their large permanent gifts of financial assets. It is possible, of course, to build endowments through other means, such as retained earnings. (Though this is less common, it is another way that SPOs can model themselves on traditional business for the accumulation of capital. See Chapter 10.) Moreover, the funding of endowments through philanthropy can be problematic if the gifts obligate SPOs to cover unanticipated costs or threaten to divert them from their missions. For example, the recent case of Joan Kroc's bequest to the Salvation Army to build a series of community centers entailed both of these tensions (Hrywna, 2012).

In summary, the contemporary environment of fiscal stress helps account for SPOs' continuing interest in endowment development. As discussed in Chapter 8, endowments are not for everyone, nor are they likely to account for the bulk of operating income for the vast majority of SPOs. But they remain a viable option for some SPOs that seek to stabilize and grow their operations over the long term. While the role of income from philanthropy has declined in relative terms in recent decades, the longevity of many venerated institutions – Harvard, the Cleveland Museum of Art, and Shriner's Hospitals among them – can be attributed in large measure to the cultivation and proper stewardship of their endowments over time.

Diversification of Income Sources

Analogous to managing large diversified investment portfolios, the notion of diversifying sources of operating income has infiltrated the thinking of SPO managers more strongly in recent years. As discussed further in Chapters 9 and 11, the basic idea is simple: prudence requires not putting all your eggs in one basket. This is a concept drawn from various parts of the business sector, including financial management of securities portfolios and industrial strategies of mergers, acquisitions and divestments. For SPOs, there is a small but growing literature on diversification of income sources that demonstrates limits and trade-offs to applying a strategy of diversification. In particular, research on nonprofit organizations shows, tentatively at least, that diversification can help stabilize a nonprofit's finances but at a possible cost of slower growth, not a surprise if you accept the comparison with financial portfolios that balance risk-taking and financial return (see Chikoto and Neely, 2014). In fact, the issue is more complex than this and across-the-board prescriptions of income diversification for all SPOs is misplaced. Indeed, the intent of this book is to provide a more fundamental rationale for appropriately diversifying an SPO's income sources in a manner corresponding with its particular mission. Nonetheless, the call to diversify is an often compelling message in the contemporary economic environment of SPOs, if only to supplement current but stagnant or declining sources of income with new ones.

Partnering with Business

Market-based strategies for helping to finance SPOs are by no means limited to internal financial and management practices. Some entail deeper involvements with for-profit businesses themselves. For example, nonprofits often decide to pursue their commercial income strategies through for-profit subsidiaries. Indeed, nonprofit/for-profit hybrid or conglomerate arrangements have become increasingly common and complex (Cordes et al., 2009; Tuckman 2009). The decision to separately incorporate commercial activity hinges on both tax considerations including requirements for maintaining a nonprofit's tax exempt status (Brody, 2009) and strategic management issues including risks associated with mission drift and clash of mission-focused and profit-oriented staff cultures. In any case, the engagement of for-profit business forms for pursuit of earned income is a widespread and often viable nonprofit practice.

More generally, there is a long history of corporate support of the social sector, dating back at least to the philanthropies of industrial giants such as John D. Rockefeller, Andrew Carnegie and Henry Ford. Such pioneers (some would say self-redeeming robber barons) gave from their personal fortunes and established private foundations to carry on their good works in perpetuity. Later, corporate philanthropy became institutionalized through internal giving programs and foundations established within the framework of corporations themselves. Interesting tensions have manifested themselves around the practice of philanthropic giving by businesses. While small private business owners can support causes in their communities as they see fit, public corporations have stockholders, some of whom believe that corporations have no right to dispense charity at the expense of dividends or shareholder value. However, another school of thought is that corporate philanthropy is a strategic exercise aimed to build good relations and environmental conditions supportive of maximum long-term profits (Burlingame and Young, 1996). While the latter strategic argument has won general favor today, the tensions still persist and affect SPOs in at least two ways.

First, it has become clear that corporate support is a two-way street. Companies are generally looking for benefits they can accrue in exchange for their gifts. The development of so-called "cause-marketing" is a good illustration. The original American Express credit card initiative supporting the Statue of Liberty Foundation helped restore that national monument by providing a percentage of sales revenue to the foundation. It also helped to boost sales made with American Express credit cards. The practice of corporations' sponsoring or otherwise assisting charitable organizations is now widespread with thousands companies and SPOs engaged. For SPOs, such arrangements require careful strategic consideration as well. SPOs entrust their reputations to their corporate sponsors and they must seek good value for taking that risk, and ensure that their reputational capital is not devalued as a result of their relationships with their corporate partners.

Second, the stockholder tensions associated with traditional corporate philanthropy have spawned a new movement to create social businesses with legal formats that protect social investing as well as profit-seeking, as discussed next.

New Business Forms of SPO

In the U.S. especially, the connection between pursuit of social purpose and engagement in profitmaking business has now expanded to include the creation of new legal forms designed in part to overcome some of the resource limitations of traditional nonprofit organizations (Young, Salamon and Grinsfelder, 2012). In particular, traditional nonprofit organizations are constrained in their ability to raise capital funds (see Chapter 10) because they cannot sell equity. The new forms of social business have the potential to attract investors who may share an SPO's social goals and also seek a financial return. The new social business forms may also be an avenue for grant-making foundations to invest their funds in a manner that contributes both to the financial returns on their investments and the social missions they seek to promote. In particular, so-called Low Profit Limited Liability Companies (L3Cs) were devised with the thought that these foundations would expand their use of so-called Program-Related Investments (PRIs; see below), although this practice has not been endorsed by the Internal Revenue Service; the continued interest in L3Cs thus remains in doubt.

Several other forms of social business have been legislated in various U.S. states, including Benefit Corporations, Flexible Purpose Corporations, and Benefit LLCs (limited liability companies) (Brewer, 2016). These various forms are designed to protect managers from legal challenges of investors who claim that social initiatives are undertaken at the expense of financial returns to shareholders, as well as to ensure that company resources are indeed devoted in part to the achievement of social objectives. None of these alternatives offer tax exemption benefits to investors or owners but they are designed to signal management's intent to address social as well as financial goals. Further, these forms may also entice consumers interested in patronizing businesses that are socially or environmentally responsible. Another manifestation of social business that is growing in popularity is the Certified B Corps, which is not a legal form but rather a certification process that allows for-profit companies to brand themselves as socially and environmentally responsible. The certification is provided by the nonprofit B Lab which applies a set of social impact, management and environmental standards before allowing a company to use its "good housekeeping seal of approval."

One question that arises, especially for L3Cs, LLCs and B Lab certified companies, is whether they are all truly social purpose organizations, as there is little in their make-up that ensures giving priority or continued devotion to social goals over time. Unlike conventional nonprofits, or other innovations such as Community Interest Companies in the U.K, or Social Purpose Cooperatives in Europe, these new social business forms do not include an "asset lock" that ensures that resources of the company must remain committed to social mission, nor do they severely limit profit-distribution to owners. Issues of trust may arise where investors or consumers suspect some of these entities to be for-profit wolves in SPO sheep's clothing. Moreover, the ability of conventional business corporations or LLCs to become certified as socially focused businesses raises the question of boundaries between SPOs and conventional business (Young and Lecy, 2013). Clearly a Newman's Own type company which allocates all of its profits to charity deserves such recognition but does a company like Coca Cola which engages in a vigorous program of corporate social responsibility while pursuing commercial interests that may have negative health and environmental consequences? This book does not attempt to parse this question, but rather it addresses the resource strategies of organizations, in whatever form, that do give priority to their social missions. Those strategies will, of course, be affected by legal form. It is unlikely, for example, that SPOs in for-profit form can attract philanthropic resources as easily as nonprofit charitable organizations, just as charitable nonprofits are less likely to attract investors who are primarily profit-minded.

GOVERNMENT SUPPORT AND THE HOLLOWING OF THE PUBLIC SECTOR

In the United States, the social sector, comprised primarily of charitable nonprofits, grew rapidly in the late 1960s and 1970s largely as a result of massive government funding associated with President Lyndon Johnson's Great Society programs. Essentially, social welfare spending increased not so much by expanding government itself but by contracting with private, mostly nonprofit organizations, through a regime that Lester Salamon labelled "third party government" (Salamon, 1987). Thus, government funding became a substantially more important component of the financing of the social sector than it had previously been. New organizations were created which depended largely on government funding and existing social service, health care and other SPOs expanded and shifted their reliance toward government support of current and new programming. Since then, however, the situation has become more ambiguous. With some exceptions, for example, during the Clinton administration in the 1990s and in response to the great recession of 2008–2009, governmental funding of social programming has slowed as a result of austere government policies at the federal and state levels. In particular, while government social welfare spending grew at an average annual (inflation adjusted) rate of 6.8 percent between 1965 and 1980, the corresponding figures for 1980–1990 and 1990–2009 are 1.9 percent and 3.2 percent, respectively (Salamon, 2012a).

These trends have had mixed effects on the support of SPOs by government. On the one hand, during recent periods of slowing government funding, the resources available for supporting services in fields where SPOs are active have been constricted. On the other hand, a smaller proportion of those services are now provided directly by government, expanding the opportunities for SPOs to garner government support via grants and contracts for privately delivered public services. In particular, during the episodic periods of growth, SPOs have had the opportunity to expand as government continued to curtail direct governmental service delivery.

As Salamon (2012a) documents, changes in government social welfare spending in the U.S. have varied substantially by field of service. From 1990 through 2009, for example, total governmental social spending increased at an average annual rate of 3.2 percent overall, but much of this was concentrated in the health sector which experienced a 4.7 percent annual increase compared to only 2.2 percent in welfare and social services and 2.3 percent in education.

The nature of government funding of SPOs has also changed over recent decades, moving away from relatively unrestricted grants and more toward contracts for specific services and payments for services rendered to individuals through reimbursement from Medicaid and other government insurance-type programs. In effect, there has been a "marketization" of government support of social welfare services (Salamon, 2012b), blurring the lines between private fee income derived from the marketplace and governmental support via third-party reimbursement. A related development is a growing "pay for success" orientation embodied in innovative approaches to government funding, such as social impact bonds and PBR (payment by results) contracts (Mulgan, 2015; Nicholls and Tomkinson, 2015).

Overall, governmental sources remain a large proportion of SPO revenues in the U.S. (estimated at roughly 38 percent of revenues of reporting public charities in 2007; see Salamon, 2012a), second only to private fee income (at 52 percent) overall. Indeed this is quite close to the 35 percent figure reported by Rudney (1987) for the year 1980. Thus, private fees and governmental funding have largely taken up the slack for the relative slippage of philanthropy as a pillar of support for SPO financing in the U.S. The future remains less certain, however, despite the seeming resilience of government funding of SPOs.

INTERNATIONAL DIFFERENCES AND THE SOCIAL ECONOMY

The forgoing discussion has been framed mostly around the U.S. context. While many of the generic finance issues are similar across the globe, it is useful here to recognize the wide variety of contexts in which social purpose organizations operate from one place to another. It is not within the scope of this book to do justice to this subject. However, it is worth examining an alternative paradigm for understanding the third sector in many places – the idea of the "social economy." While this concept has recently been applied very insightfully to the U.S. (see Mook et al., 2015), it is a frame of reference most closely associated with continental Europe,

Quebec, Latin America and other parts of the world where worker and consumer cooperatives, mutual, self-help and community organizations, sports associations and other solidarity-driven organizations play a larger role in the economy. In essence, the social economy encompasses more than strictly nonprofit organizations exclusively devoted to social mission (as the nonprofit sector is defined in the U.S. with its non-distribution of profit constraint) but also organizations that pursue a mix of public and private goals (and limited profit distribution) through member-governed structures and partnerships with government and business.

Still, it is interesting to compare the context of the "third sector" in different countries. The Johns Hopkins Comparative Nonprofit Sector Project has done just that, using a generic definition of "nonprofit organizations" that seeks to accommodate the nuances in what may be interpreted as a social purpose third sector organization. For example, although these criteria include the non-distribution of profits constraint, this is interpreted to allow some forms of cooperatives, mutual associations and credit clubs (Casey, 2016). As reviewed by Casey (2016) a representative selection of 16 countries reveals a wide range of reliance on different sources of income. For example, reliance of nonprofit organizations on fee income ranges from less than 30 percent in Israel to more than 90 percent in the Philippines, with mirror image reliance on government support ranging from almost 70 percent to less than 10 percent in these two countries. Alternatively, reliance on philanthropy runs from roughly 40 percent in Pakistan to less than 10 percent in the Philippines, Mexico, Australia and Finland. At the same time, the missions and activities undertaken in the nonprofit sector also vary widely across countries, from a dominant service delivery orientation in Peru, Israel, Pakistan, the U.S. and other countries, to a dominant "expressive" social or advocacy orientation in Sweden, Slovakia, Hungary and Finland. The latter is one reason for the widely different ways in which social purpose organizations finance themselves in different countries, a factor consistent with the thrust of benefits theory as developed in this book.

In those parts of the world that embrace the social economy paradigm, the prominence of cooperatives is particularly notable. According to the International Co-operative Alliance (ICA; 2016), cooperatives employ 250 million people worldwide and constitute 12 percent of total employment in G20 countries (19 major industrialized countries plus the European Union). This alliance includes membership across 96 countries (Michie, 2015). The United Nations declared 2012 as the year of the cooperative, one of its objectives being "increasing public awareness about cooperatives and their contributions to socio-economic development and the achievement of the Millennium Development Goals" (Michie, 2015, p. 141).

In the U.S., the cooperative sector is relatively small and under-studied, though still quite important. A recent study by the University of Wisconsin Center for Co-op Studies (Deller et al., 2009) has illuminated the size and character of U.S. cooperatives. According to this study, there are roughly 30,000 cooperatives in the U.S. divided among four principal types by purpose: worker cooperatives, producer cooperatives, purchasing cooperatives and consumer cooperatives. The latter is by far the largest group, constituting over 90 percent of the organizations, 98 percent of the members, more than 60 percent of the assets and more than half the revenues. Cooperatives in the U.S. participate primarily in four sectors of the economy – commercial sales and marketing, social and public services, financial services and utilities, with the bulk of revenues concentrated in the first and third of these categories, but the largest number of cooperatives (more than a third) in the second category – social and public services. The latter category signals the importance of cooperatives among social purpose organizations. Social and public service cooperatives in the U.S. provide health care, child care, housing, transportation, and education services of various kinds, offering a mix of benefits to their members and to the general public. However, one cannot conclude that social purpose cooperatives are confined to the latter group. Indeed, the subsector of Commercial Sales and Marketing includes cooperatives devoted to marketing of bio-fuels, grocery cooperatives and arts and crafts, many of which address a mix of public and member serving goals. Grocery cooperatives, for example, "have pioneered nutritional labeling, open dating, unit pricing, bulk sales, informative advertising, consumer education, and innovative institutional structures. . .[and]. . .have also consistently been in the forefront of consumer protection through selective merchandising and boycotts, political lobbying, and ongoing consumer education. . .[and]. . .their pioneering introduction of natural and organic foods" (Deller et al., 2009, p. 20). Similarly, cooperatives in Financial Services include credit unions and mutual insurance companies, and cooperatives in the Utilities field provide electric and telephone services in rural areas, all of which involve a mix of services to members and general public benefits. Credit unions, for example, "were associations born of a social mission to provide credit or loans to people who could not access them from other financial institutions and to provide them at affordable interest rates" (Mook et al., 2015, p. 815).

The legal form for cooperatives in the U.S. differs by state of incorporation. According to Deller et al., 2009, p. 5):

[U]nder some state statutes, cooperatives are considered a type of nonprofit corporation, since a cooperative's primary orientation is to benefit members, providing goods or services at cost. Thus an organization incorporated under a cooperative statute may be considered a cooperative business in one state, but may be considered a nonprofit corporation in another. Cooperative entities may also be incorporated under other statutes not specific to cooperatives such as corporation, limited liability company (LLCs), or nonprofit laws.

In the U.S. there is no specific legal form for "social" cooperatives.

As noted, cooperatives are more prominent outside the U.S. and in some cases so-called "social cooperatives" have been given a specific legal designation. In Italy, for instance, social cooperatives are regulated by National Law 381 and operate in two fields of service – care services and work integration services. Altogether, there are more than 11,000 social cooperatives in Italy compared to some 54,000 traditional cooperatives. The social cooperatives are incorporated as nonprofits and receive most of their funding from government whereas other cooperatives are organized as private enterprises and are funded mostly by market sales. The latter operate in a variety of fields including agriculture, construction or for the interests of consumers, workers and fishermen (Bassi et al., 2016).

Mook et al. (2015) characterize cooperatives as "social economy businesses" in the U.S. and the ICA notes on its website that "As member-owned, member-run and member-serving businesses, coopera- tives empower people to collectively realize their economic aspirations, while strengthening their social and human capital and developing their communities" (ICA, 2016).

Despite their relative obscurity in the U.S., cooperatives clearly fall within the universe of social purpose organizations whose financing can be usefully examined with an eye toward achieving desired mixes of public and private goals. In general, experience with cooperatives internationally suggests that social purpose organizations come in various forms and that legal designations can be misleading.

THE RELATIVE STABILITY OF SPO FINANCE AND ITS IMPLICATIONS

Despite the turbulence of the economic environment, SPOs are resilient in finding ways to support themselves and maintain their mission-focus (Salamon, 2012b). As argued in this book, being driven by a mission implies a certain logical base of income support. Thus, despite the finan- cial storms, SPOs should be both relatively stable in their chosen mixes of income support and creative in the ways they maintain or improve those mixes. The first decade of the 21st century was especially turbulent for the social sector, as the economy endured an early recession followed by economic boom in mid-decade and financial collapse in 2008–2009. It is interesting and informative, therefore, to examine how some key segments of that sector navigated these financial seas and whether they tended to stay the course or adjust their sails to the prevailing winds. Toward this end, a sample of nonprofit organizations in two broad fields of service – arts and culture and social services – in three different U.S. cities – Atlanta, Cleveland and New York (Manhattan) was examined (Young and Soh, 2013). For the period 2002–2010 nonprofits in these categories were classified according their dominant sources of income, defining dominance as dependence on a particular source of income for more than half of operating income in a given year, using data from 990 income tax forms provided by the National Center for Charitable Statistics. The four dominance categories are fees, private contributions, government grants and income from investments. A fifth category encompasses nonprofits for which none of these sources represents half or more of operating income in a given year. The results are displayed in Tables 2.1 and 2.2.

Two patterns stand out in the Table 2.1 and 2.2 matrices. First, the majority (57 percent) of organizations remained in the same financially dominant (or non-dominant) category in 2010 as they were in 2002. And as Table 2.2 shows, more than 70 percent of the latter organizations never changed their funding dominance status at all during the entire decade. Second, those organizations that did switch categories exhibited a roughly random pattern of transitions from one state to another, with no obvious trend in a particular direction. That is, for example, roughly as many nonprofits transitioned from a contributions-dominant state to a fee-dominant state as moved in the reverse direction, and so on.

Note that there are important limitations to this data. First, this is a relatively small sample, especially when it is sliced up into components. Second, form 990 data conflate some categories of income (such as private fees and government contracts) and are not as precise or as carefully scrutinized as audited financial statements, hence subject to error. Finally, transitions from a source-dominant category to the diversified non-dominant category can entail relatively small changes from just over to just under the 50 percent mark for dominance classification. However, there is no reason to suspect that these errors bias the results in any particular direction. Still, the analysis can only be suggestive.

The observed relative stability of nonprofit income mixes over time, especially during a turbulent period such as the first decade of the 21st century, is consistent with the notion that something more basic than the winds of environmental economic change is responsible for the choices that SPOs make for sustaining themselves over time. Presumably, that basic factor is SPOs' anchoring in their particular social missions. Hence benefits theory.

Table 2.1 2002 and 2010 funding dominance for Atlanta, Cleveland, and Manhattan social service and arts organizations

2002 Funding Dominance	2010 Funding Dominance					2002 Total
	Government	Private Contributions	Fees	Investment	Nondominant	
Government	14	3	4	0	0	21
Private Contributions	4	32	6	2	13	57
Fees	3	6	27	0	7	43
Investment	1	1	0	0	2	4
Nondominant	2	7	3	0	13	25
2010 Total	24	49	40	2	35	n=150

Represents nonprofit organizations with stable funding dominance categories in 2002 and 2010.

Table 2.2 *Interim changes in funding dominance among stable social service and arts organizations, 2002–2010*

2002 and 2010 Funding Dominance (n=86)	Interim Changes in Funding Dominance				
	Government	Private Contributions	Fees	Investment	Nondominant
Government (*n*=14)	13	–	–	–	–
Private Contributions (*n*=32)	–	23	–	–	–
Fees (*n*=26)	–	–	20	–	–
Investment (*n*=0)	–	–	–	0	–
Nondominant (*n*=14)	–	–	–	-	5

▮ Represents nonprofit organizations that never changed funding between 2002 and 2010.

CLOSING COMMENT

The environment in which social purpose organizations operate is dynamic and diverse, subject to strong cross-winds buffeting their interfaces with philanthropy, business and government, and varying considerably across national borders. While pressures to rely on earned income and to operate more like businesses appear to be ascending, it would in fact be misguided for social purpose organizations to simply blow with the wind or adapt chameleon-like to local circumstances or current fashions. For one thing, the winds can change direction over time. For another, the unique thing about SPOs is that they anchor themselves in a social mission that is likely to be stable over the long term, providing them with a beacon for adapting to transient conditions without radically changing course. While such adaptation may entail marginal shifts in their programs and their reliance on different sources of income over time, the main issue for SPOs is to determine what services, target groups, and sources of income most effectively address the mission at hand. That is the subject of the following chapters and the essence of benefits theory.

REFERENCES

Andrea Bassi, Jung-In Soh and Dennis R. Young, 2016. Draft, "Applying the Benefits Theory of Nonprofit Finance to Social Cooperatives", 12th International conference of the International Society for Third Sector Research, Ersta Sköndal University College, Stockholm, Sweden, June 28 to July 1, 2016.

Matthew Bishop and Michael Green, 2015. "Philanthrocapitalism Comes of Age", Chapter 4 in in Alex Nicholls, Rob Paton and Jed Emerson (eds), *Social Finance*, Oxford: Oxford University Press, pp. 113–129.

Cassady V. Brewer, 2016. "The Zoo and the Ongoing Evolution in Social Enterprise Legal Forms", Chapter 3 in Dennis R. Young, Elizabeth A.M. Searing and Cassady V. Brewer (eds), *The Social Enterprise Zoo: A Guide to Perplexed Scholars, Entrepreneurs, Philanthropists, Leaders, Investors and Policymakers*, Cheltenham, UK and Northampton, MA, USA: Edward Elgar Publishing, pp. 33–64.

Evelyn Brody, 2009. "Business Activities of Nonprofit Organizations", Chapter 4 in Joseph J. Cordes and C. Eugene Steuerle (eds), *Nonprofits & Business*, Washington, DC: The Urban Institute Press, pp. 83–127.

Dwight F. Burlingame and Dennis R. Young (eds), 1996. *Corporate Philanthropy at the Cross-Roads*, Bloomington, IN: Indiana University Press.

John Casey, 2016. *The Nonprofit World: Civil Society and the Rise of the Nonprofit Sector*, Boulder, CO: Kumarian Press.

Grace L. Chikoto and Daniel Gordon Neely, 2014. "Building Nonprofit Financial Capacity: The Impact of Revenue Concentration and Overhead Costs", *Nonprofit and Voluntary Sector Quarterly*, 43(3), June, pp. 570–588.

Joseph J. Cordes, Zina Poletz and C. Eugene Steuerle, 2009. "Examples of

Nonprofit-For-Profit Hybrid Business Models", Appendix 3.1 in Joseph J. Cordes and C. Eugene Steuerle (eds), *Nonprofits & Business*, Washington, DC: The Urban Institute Press, pp. 69–82.

James C. Crimmins and Mary Keil, 1983. *Enterprise in the Nonprofit Sector*, New York: Rockefeller Brothers Fund.

Steven Deller, Ann Hoyt, Brent Hueth and Reka Sundaram-Stukel, 2009. *Research on the Economic Impact of Cooperatives*, Report. Madison, WI: University of Wisconsin-Madison Center for Cooperatives.

Catherine C. Eckel and Richard Steinberg, 1993. "Competition, Performance and Public Policy Toward Nonprofits", Chapter 2 in David C. Hammack and Dennis R. Young (eds), *Nonprofit Organizations in a Market Economy*, San Francisco: Jossey-Bass Publishers, pp. 57–81.

The Economist, 2014. *Pocket World in Figures*, London: Economist Newspaper.

Goldman Sachs, 2014. "Social Impact Bonds", retrieved on December 13, 2016 from www.goldmansachs.com/our-thinking/impact-investing/massachusetts-social-impact-bond/index.html.

Teresa Harrison and Jeremy Thornton, 2014. "Too Many Nonprofits? An Empirical Approach to Estimating Trends in Nonprofit Demand Density", *Nonprofit Policy Forum*, 5(2), October, pp. 213–229.

Mark Hrywna, 2012. "Sal Army Completing Kroc Heiress' Dream For Centers", *The Nonprofit Times*, June 1. Retrieved on December 13, 2016 from www.thenonprof ittimes.com/news-articles/sal-army-completing-kroc-heiress-dream-for-centers/.

International Co-operative Alliance (ICA), 2016. "Facts and Figures", retrieved on December 13, 2016 from http://monitor.coop/en/facts-and-figures.

Estelle James, 1983. "How Nonprofits Grow: A Model", *Journal of Policy Analysis and Management*, 2 (Spring), pp. 350–365.

Rob John and Jed Emerson, 2015. "Venture Philanthropy", Chapter 7 in Alex Nicholls, Rob Paton and Jed Emerson (eds), *Social Finance*, Oxford: Oxford University Press, pp. 185–206.

Othmar M. Lehner, 2015. "Crowdfunding in Social Finance", Chapter 16 in Alex Nicholls, Rob Paton and Jed Emerson (eds), *Social Finance*, Oxford: Oxford University Press, pp. 521–542.

Reynold Levy, 2015. *They Told Me Not to Take That Job*, New York: PublicAffairs Books.

Kathleen D. McCarthy, 2003. *American Creed: Philanthropy and the Rise of Civil Society 1700–1865*, Chicago, IL: The University of Chicago Press.

Jonathan Michie, 2015. "Co-operative and Mutual Finance", Chapter 5 in Alex Nicholls, Rob Paton and Jed Emerson (eds), *Social Finance*, Oxford: Oxford University Press, pp. 133–155.

Laurie Mook, John Maiorano, and Jack Quarter, 2015. "Credit Unions: Market Niche or Market Accommodation?", *Nonprofit and Voluntary Sector Quarterly*, 44(4), pp. 814–831.

Mario Morino, 2011. *Leap of Reason: Managing to Outcomes in an Era of Scarcity*, Washington, DC: Venture Philanthropy Partners.

Nicole Motter, 2013. "Why Program-Related Investments are Not Risky Business", retrieved on December 13, 2016 from www.forbes.com/sites/ashoka/2013/02/21/why-program-related-investments-are-not-risky-business/#58ec42eb1f8e.

Geoff Mulgan, 2015. "Social Finance: Does 'Investment' Add Value?", Chapter 1 in Alex Nicholls, Rob Paton and Jed Emerson (eds), *Social Finance*, Oxford: Oxford University Press, pp. 45–63.

Alex Nicholls and Emma Tomkinson, 2015. "The Peterborough Pilot Social Impact Bond", Chapter 12 in Alex Nicholls, Rob Paton and Jed Emerson (eds), *Social Finance*, Oxford: Oxford University Press, pp. 335–380.

Anna Oleksiak, Alex Nicholls and Jed Emerson, 2015. "Impact Investing", Chapter 8 in Alex Nicholls, Rob Paton and Jed Emerson (eds), *Social Finance*, Oxford: Oxford University Press, pp. 207–249.

The Oxford Dictionary of Quotations, Third Edition, 1979. Oxford: Oxford University Press, "Lewis Carroll" p. 133, no.6.

Katie L. Roeger, Amy S. Blackwood and Sarah L. Pettijohn, 2012. *The Nonprofit Almanac 2012*, Washington, DC: The Urban Institute Press.

Gabriel Rudney, 1987. "The Scope and Dimensions of Nonprofit Activity", Chapter 4 in Walter W. Powell (ed.), *The Nonprofit Sector: A Research Handbook*, New Haven: Yale University Press, pp. 55–64.

Lester M. Salamon, 1987. "Partners in Public Service: The Scope and Theory of Government-Nonprofit Relations", Chapter 6 in Walter W. Powell (ed.), *The Nonprofit Sector: A Research Handbook*, New Haven: Yale University Press, pp. 99–117.

Lester M. Salamon, 2012a. *America's Nonprofit Sector: A Primer*, New York: The Foundation Center.

Lester M. Salamon (ed.), 2012b. *The State of Nonprofit America*, Washington, DC: Brookings Institution Press.

Elizabeth A.M. Searing and Dennis R. Young, 2016. "Feeding the Animals", Chapter 5 in Dennis R. Young, Elizabeth A.M. Searing and Cassady V. Brewer (eds), *The Social Enterprise Zoo: A Guide to Perplexed Scholars, Entrepreneurs, Philanthropists, Leaders, Investors and Policymakers*, Cheltenham, UK and Northampton, MA, USA: Edward Elgar Publishing, pp. 93–112.

Dane Smith and Mark Kramer, 2014. "Shared Value", Chapter 11 in Urs. P. Jager and Vijay Sathe (eds), *Strategy and Competitiveness in Latin American Markets: The Sustainability Frontier*, Cheltenham, UK and Northampton, MA, USA: Edward Elgar Publishers, pp. 161–181.

Howard P. Tuckman, 2009. "The Strategic and Economic Value of Hybrid Nonprofit Structures", Chapter 5 in Joseph J. Cordes and C. Eugene Steuerle (eds), *Nonprofits & Business*, Washington, DC: The Urban Institute Press, pp. 129–153.

Burton A. Weisbrod (ed.), 1998. *To Profit or Not to Profit: The Commercial Transformation of the Nonprofit Sector*, New York: Cambridge University Press.

Dennis R. Young and Jesse Lecy, 2013. "Defining the Universe of Social Enterprise: Competing Metaphors", *Voluntas*, 17(3), pp. 246–262.

Dennis R. Young and Jung-In Soh, 2013. "The Determinants and Dynamics of Nonprofit Organizations' Income Portfolios", conference paper, ARNOVA Annual Conference, November.

Dennis R. Young, Lester M. Salamon and Mary Clark Grinsfelder, 2012., "Commercialization, Social Ventures, and For-Profit Competition", Chapter 14 in Lester M. Salamon (ed.), *The State of Nonprofit America*, Washington, DC: Brookings Institution Press, pp. 521–548.

3. Benefits theory

INTRODUCTION

Benefits theory is a conceptual construct to foster understanding of how social purpose organizations are financed. As "positive theory," to the degree that its assumptions correspond to how SPOs actually behave, it is useful in describing how SPOs finance themselves in practice. Evidence from research suggests that the theory rings true to a substantial degree, explaining observed financing patterns (see below). Perhaps more importantly, benefits theory is also normative, offering guidance on how SPOs can most successfully finance themselves while pursuing their chosen missions. The essence of the theory is simply that by carrying out its particular mission, an SPO generates a specific mix of public and private benefits for its various beneficiary groups and that these beneficiaries, or their proxies, in turn support the SPO through alternative types of financing mechanisms. Elaboration of the theory involves fleshing out the different kinds of benefits and beneficiaries, and articulating how financing mechanisms appropriate to each can translate benefits into resource support.

The concept of "exchange" is fundamental to benefits theory. Indeed, the sustenance of organizations throughout the economy can be understood in terms of exchange. Participants in, or clients of, organizations provide monetary or in-kind support in exchange for goods or services rendered. This is most obvious in the business sector where consumers receive goods or services for which they make monetary payments to vendors and where investors buy stocks and bonds or other securities or capital goods (for example, real estate) in exchange for anticipated future profits or dividends.

In the public or governmental sector, finance is also transactional although the precise nature of the exchange is more varied and subtle. Governments charge fees in exchange for consumption of certain services such as water and sewer, public housing, the right to drive an automobile or enjoy a state or national park. Of course governments also impose taxes, which may be designed to finance a specific service such as public education or maintain state roads, or to support public services more broadly through a general tax fund allocated through a governmental budgeting process. In the latter case, one can understand the exchange as a social contract between the citizens of a jurisdiction and its government which embraces the mutual expectations of citizens and public officials within a constitutional framework. The exchange relationship for financing government agencies extends to financing of capital goods such as bridges, roads, parks and other infrastructure. Such projects may be financed through the sale of tax free bonds for which investors expect to receive a competitive return. Indeed, as Thomas Piketty (2014) keenly observes, governments create quite a bit of private wealth by selling their securities to investors.

So in these various ways, business and government finance can be understood as *transactional* in character. The same is true of nonprofit and social enterprise finance, although there are many dimensions to the exchanges that take place in this realm. This should not be terribly surprising since, as the last two chapters have noted, much of the financing of SPOs comes from government and business, or through the sale of goods and services in the marketplace. Generally speaking governments expect outputs and results in return for their financing of SPOs and businesses expect marketing and other benefits in exchange for their largesse as well. The nature of these expectations will be elaborated in subsequent chapters. Perhaps less apparent is the notion that charitable gifts and volunteer efforts are also usefully understood in terms of exchange. The subject of altruism has, of course, been extensively studied and is not belabored here. Suffice it to say, however, that at one level or another, exchange is fundamental. One broad distinction developed by Andreoni (1990) and others is that between pure and impure altruism. In the latter case, the giver receives some degree of direct satisfaction or "warm glow" from the act of giving, no matter what is secured or achieved with her gift. In contrast, in the case of pure altruism, the giver is concerned only with the output or the results. One consequence of pure altruism is that donors may refrain from giving if the output in question is financed some other way such as by government funding or fee income. In such circumstances, the impure altruist may continue to give, avoiding so-called "crowd-out" between giving and other sources. Empirical studies suggest that altruism is generally impure, with some but not full crowd-out resulting from increases in other sources of finance to nonprofit organizations (Steinberg, 1991).

Whether pure or impure, however, philanthropy can still be understood within a transactional framework. Pure altruists expect to see an impact of their giving in the output or achievement of the SPO that receives their gifts; impure altruists expect to feel good about their giving (perhaps through suitable recognition or appreciative gestures). Donors with both needs will want some of each. Furthermore, as discussed in Chapter 6, some donors will also be attracted by "tie-in" sales such as the receipt of special (private) goods or services (tee shirts, free parking, and so on) in which case the exchange between donor and SPO is multifaceted.

Similar observations extend to volunteering, which as noted in Chapter 1, is of the same overall order of magnitude in value as monetary giving. Again, there is a rich literature on volunteering (Leete, 2006) that suggests a wide variety of motives ranging from direct private benefits such as access to services or networking with peers, to pure altruism. Even in the latter case, the volunteer is the beneficiary of an exchange – albeit the simple knowledge that his or her efforts have made a difference.

BENEFITS THEORY

Benefits theory is based on the premise that SPOs have missions and services aimed at benefitting various groups of clients, consumers or constituents directly through their goods and services, for which they or their sponsors are willing to pay. Moreover, SPOs reward investors or major donors by providing opportunities to gain monetary or less tangible returns in exchange for capital gifts or investments. The trick to successful financing therefore is to identify those benefits and beneficiaries and then determine what kind of transactions are best suited to effecting the exchange of benefits for financial or other types of income support. It is argued here that the nature of the transaction is highly dependent on the character of the benefits, especially their public versus private nature, hence the degree to which the market or other mechanisms may be employed.

There are at least three levels of complexity to this analysis. First, SPOs are not all purely social mission-driven. Many are, by design or intent, determined to produce both private benefits for their owners or investors and mission-related benefits for their target audiences. In such cases, the market usually can be relied upon to support a substantial part of SPOs' finances. Second, SPOs often provide complex goods entailing both private benefits to individual beneficiaries as well as public goods for societal groups collectively. The particular mix of public and private benefits associated with an SPO's output can be expected to influence the mix of sources for which its financing is best suited. Third, most substantial SPOs offer more than one kind of good or service, with different offerings likely to vary in their public versus private nature. Again, this will influence the appropriate mechanisms for an SPO's financing. The relationships among the various services in an SPO's portfolio of programs are also relevant, as considered further in Chapter 11. For example, the ability to generate profits from some services may allow an SPO to subsidize the costs of other services important to its social mission.

HOW BENEFITS THEORY WORKS IN PRACTICE

Benefits theory can be understood in terms of both the demand and supply of social goods and services. From the demand perspective, the theory stipulates that there is economic demand in the form of potential willingness to pay by beneficiary groups (or their sponsors) that desire the benefits that SPOs can provide. Through exploitation of the different potential sources of income, this demand can be manifested in the various commercial, charitable and public sector "marketplaces." From the supply perspective, social entrepreneurs of various stripes can sense these opportunities for achieving social purposes and work to exploit latent demands with appropriate programming initiatives by their organizations. Given the constraints and limitations of alternative incomes sources, the available choices of organizational vehicles, and other factors such as interactions among alternative revenue sources (or example, crowd-out; see Chapter 11) and risk management issues (to be considered in Chapter 12), an adjustment process is required to ensure that resulting income portfolios are sustainable.

Graphically, this line argument can be illustrated as follows: Figure 3.1 represents the essence of benefits theory – the matching of financial

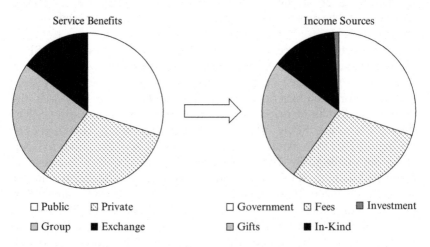

Figure 3.1   Matching benefits with income sources

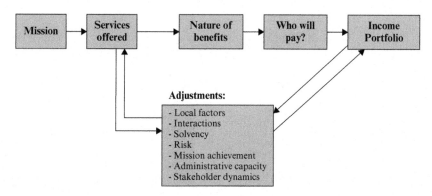

Source: Adapted from Figure 15.1 in Young (2007).

Figure 3.2   Demand-side view of benefits theory

resources with the benefits that can be supported through the various income mechanisms. Figure 3.2 then illustrates benefits theory from the demand side while Figure 3.3 does the same from the supply side.

Figure 3.1 distinguishes among four broad types of benefits – private, public, group and exchange benefits. These distinctions are elaborated in Chapter 4. Basically, private benefits redound to individuals while public benefits impact a broad segment of society as a whole. Group goods are similar to public goods except that they impact a smaller, specific group (such as alumni or art lovers) while exchange benefits involve two specific parties, such as an SPO and a corporate sponsor. The point is that the different types of benefits generally favor different sources of finance – fees, gifts, governmental support and quid pro quo exchange of payments or other resources. Benefits theory stipulates that the distribution of an SPO's benefits should be reflected in its portfolio of income sources.

Figure 3.2 presents a more robust picture of the process as seen essentially from the perspective of demand for an SPO's services. Here it is assumed that an SPO is grounded in its basic social mission which determines the kinds of services it offers. However, support for those services depends on the kinds of benefits it provides to its constituents or beneficiary groups. A first pass through the top level of the diagram would yield a distribution of income sources corresponding to its intended service offerings and consequent income strategies. The feedback loop in the lower part of the diagram recognizes that various adjustments may be required to account for a number of organizational and environmental factors, including the local climate for giving, governmental support or

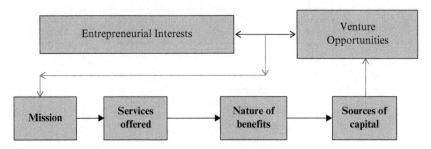

Figure 3.3   Supply-side view of benefits theory

fee revenue (for example, competition from other SPOs), impacts of one income source on another (that is, potential crowd-out), the capacity of the organization to administer multiple income sources, risks associated with a concentrated versus diversified income portfolio, stakeholder interests in maintaining particular sources and programs (such as cherished special events) and indeed whether, when all is said and done, the income yield is sufficiently robust to pay for stipulated programs. With such factors in mind, SPOs would complete the feedback loop by adjusting their service offerings to better address to these realities. Note, an outer feedback loop could be added to the diagram which would acknowledge that in severe circumstances, adjustment of the mission itself (and perhaps the legal form) can be brought into play.

Figure 3.3 pictures a supply-side characterization of the process, from the viewpoint of social entrepreneurs seeking to determine how to support their social ventures (Young, 2015). This view is especially apropos for considering capital financing where SPOs must determine where to look for investment capital to establish and build their organizations, start new programs, or maintain, expand or change the capacity or direction of existing programs. The logic is that entrepreneurial interests (on the part of start-up entrepreneurs or current organizational leaders) connect with latent opportunities in the social and economic environment to formulate a venture's mission, services and benefits which, along with institutional constraints (see Table 3.2), then influence what sources of capital can be pursued. To complete the loop, those potential sources of capital, reflecting potential benefits and beneficiaries, help define the set of possible venture opportunities. Many of the same considerations come into play here as on the demand side, including organizational capacities which shape entrepreneurial interests, and environmental conditions which influence the form and availability of sources of capital. This view, however, recognizes that the missions and programs of SPOs originate from the proactive involvement of leaders who identify latent opportunities from sources reflecting potential beneficiaries.

While the formal framing of SPO finance in terms of *benefits theory* is new (Young, 2007), the practice of finance by SPOs, particularly nonprofit organizations, suggests that most SPOs intuitively understand this way of thinking and tend to follow its precepts. The purpose of developing this framework explicitly here is to help SPOs take maximum advantage of the strategies implied by the theory. The contention is that an SPO that fully exploits benefits theory strategies is *less likely to leave money (or other forms of income) on the table*. In the present era when SPOs compete for increasingly scarce resources, this can mean the difference between success and failure.

BENEFITS THEORY IN PRACTICE

In the field of nonprofit organizations, there is clear evidence that SPOs implicitly pursue benefits theory logic. A simple examination of the financing patterns of broad nonprofit subsectors is immediately revealing. As shown in Table 3.1, for example, the proportions of income deriving from fee income versus gift income varies substantially among major subfields for reasons that can be understood at least partially through the lens of benefits theory. Health care and education, for example, are more heavily financed by fees (including tuition and insurance payments) because their services are consumed by individual clients who can be charged directly or indirectly for the benefits they receive. However, educational institutions also receive a very substantial proportion of their income from charitable contributions and government, reflecting the public goods they produce (for example, research, and more informed citizens) as well as the collective benefits provided to alumni who wish to maintain or enhance the

Table 3.1   Aggregate revenue sources by subsector 2010. National Center for Charitable Statistics

Field (NTEE)	Contrib., gifts, grants (%)	Prog service revenue & contracts (%)	Investment income (%)	Other (%)
Arts, Culture	40.4	57.0	0.2	2.5
Education	29.2	63.0	3.6	3.8
Environment	76.2	19.8	0.5	3.4
Health	12.2	85.5	0.9	1.3
Human Services	36.8	56.6	1.9	4.7

reputations of their alma maters and support the education of future members of their group. The split reliance between charitable gifts and fee income is even more pronounced in the arts where attendees of arts performances or museums directly benefit as individuals and where arts lovers as a group (which clearly overlaps with attendees) also support the presence and enhancement of these institutions in their communities through gifts. Similarly, in the human services, consumers or clients benefit from the individual private services they receive in exchange for fees paid directly or possibly through governmental programs such as Medicaid in the U.S. In the latter case, society acknowledges the broad benefits of assisting its less fortunate members (called "redistributive" private goods; see below and Chapter 4). In addition, human service organizations receive gifts directly from more prosperous citizens who benefit from their pure or impure altruism as discussed above. Finally, Table 3.1 shows that environmental organizations are supported mainly by gifts, reflecting the broad benefits they confer to society with their conservation and advocacy efforts on behalf of the natural environment. Again, caring, concerned and nature-loving citizens receive the benefits of their gifts in the form of warm glow for having contributed and appreciation of the impact of their gifts on helping to preserve the natural environment (plus possible private benefits such as calendars or other tokens offered in partial exchange for such contributions, as discussed in Chapter 6).

The gross differential patterns of finance for alternative nonprofit subsectors, as displayed in Table 3.1 are only suggestive, of course. However, more rigorous research has confirmed the connection between mechanisms of finance and the public/private nature of the services and benefits provided by SPOs. Such research is challenging because SPOs rarely provide direct measures of the different kinds of benefits they offer. However, several alternative approaches have produced positive evidence that SPOs, nonprofits in particular, connect income sources with the nature of the benefits they produce. One study examined a sample of nonprofits according to their second level field designation in the National Taxonomy of Exempt Entities (NTEE) in the U.S. (one level more detailed than that used in Table 3.1) and classified each subfield as providing either public, private or mixed (public and private) benefits (Fischer, Wilsker and Young, 2011); it found significant positive correlations between reliance on earned (fee) income and provision of services offering private benefits; positive correlation between reliance on charitable (gift) income and provision of public benefits; negative correlation between reliance on earned income and provision of public benefits; and negative correlation between charitable income and provision of private benefits. A second study examined expenses devoted to alternative services provided by a national sample of Jewish Community Centers (Wilsker and Young, 2010). Again services were classified as public, private or mixed. Here, increases in expenses on privately classified services were found to be positively and significantly related to increases in earned income, and increases in expenses on services classified as public in nature were significantly and positively related to increases in government funding. (This study is discussed further in Chapter 11.) A third study directly examined the websites of a national sample of nonprofits, and programs of these organizations were coded independently by three researchers as providing individual private, collective group, general public or individual redistributive benefits (Young, Wilsker and Grinsfelder, 2010). (As discussed in the next chapter, group benefits are public benefits restricted to a limited targeted group of beneficiaries, and redistributive benefits are private benefits to individuals unable to fully afford them.) This study found that reliance on earned income was significantly and positively related to individual private benefits and significantly, negatively related to group, public and redistributive benefits, while reliance on charitable income was significantly negatively related to individual private benefits and positively and significantly related to redistributive benefits. These findings are all consistent with the basic idea of benefits theory that SPOs seek out the most "natural" financial foundations for the particular missions they pursue.

Moreover, research has begun to show that this finding is robust with respect to international context and different organizational forms of SPO. For example, Italian social cooperatives operating in particular service areas including education, health, social services and other fields derive very similar proportions of their income from alternative sources (fee revenues, grants and investments) as their American nonprofit counterparts (Bassi, Soh and Young, 2016). Similarly, the revenue mixes of Switzerland based International Nongovernmental Organizations are found to be best explained by the public/private nature of their beneficiary groups, confirming the expectations of benefits theory (Aschari-Lincoln and Jager, 2016).

As considered in more detail in Chapter 11, research on nonprofit income portfolios is also consistent with the notion that nonprofits intuitively seek a mix of income consistent with their missions. For example, benefits theory appears to explain the income portfolios of membership associations more effectively than traditional portfolio theory (Bowman and Bingham, 2015). While there are a number of other considerations that affect the balancing of income portfolios (such as risk management and growth strategy, discussed further in Chapter 11), according to one recent study that finds a trade-off between growth and revenue diversification as a stabilizing strategy:

> [A]n organization's 'natural' revenue mix – the revenue streams that emanate as a result of the nature of benefits conferred – and the revenue concentration strategy addressed here do not necessarily have to be at odds. Nonprofits' understanding of the benefits of the services they confer, and hence, why they are able to attract particular funding sources, may serve as an important precursor. That is, having achieved a revenue mix that is congruent with its mission and the services it provides, a nonprofit can then adopt a revenue concentration strategy from this mix, for financial capacity building purposes. (Chikoto and Neely, 2014, pp. 581–582)

The exposition in this book takes account of issues such as risk, growth and financial health in the synthesis of SPO income strategies, but with particular attention to the contribution that a benefits orientation makes toward achieving these goals by ensuring that SPOs fully exploit their benefits-related income potentials.

THE CHALLENGES OF EXPLOITING ALTERNATIVE FORMS OF INCOME

It is easy enough to give cavalier advice to SPO leaders to match income sources to their benefits and beneficiaries. However, the particular challenges of each form of income must first be acknowledged and its constraints appreciated. These will be scrutinized in depth in subsequent chapters. Here the intent is to provide an overview of some of the nuances of the benefits theory framework.

The challenges of pursuing various income sources can be understood in terms of economists' notion of "transactions costs," essentially the costs of doing business under various arrangements. These costs differ by type of income source, as do the skills required of the SPO to manage that source. This is significant for two reasons. First, an SPO must have the resources to establish the infrastructure required to collect income in a particular way. Second, an SPO must have the necessary skill sets within its workforce, or it must educate current workers or employ new people who have the requisite knowledge and experience. For example, an organization skilled in fund-raising is not necessarily adept at selling services in the marketplace. The issue of transactions costs is especially important for smaller or newer organizations whose management capacity is limited and heavily stressed (Searing, 2015).

For the pursuit of earned income, an SPO must be particularly adept at a diverse package of skills characteristic of profitmaking businesses. These include pricing and product quality decisions which in turn require an assessment of both market demand and costs of production and distribution. The skill set also includes strategic analysis of markets to assess where the SPO has a competitive advantage, and marketing expertise to promote services to the desired target audiences. Interestingly, the pricing skills required of an SPO go beyond those needed by a conventional business. In particular, business pricing practices are based on the premise of maximizing net revenues, hence setting prices so that at the margins, prices paid exceed the additional costs of service provision. For an SPO, however, mission may require servicing targeted clients who are unable or unwilling to pay the marginal cost. In such cases, the SPO manager must identify sources of subsidy in order to provide discounted or even free services, possibly by undertaking additional (more commercial) services priced to generate profits. This leads SPOs to consider both who benefits from the organization's mission and who *could benefit* from services that the organization is capable of offering at a profit. In any case, an SPO that depends on earned income requires a sophisticated set of business skills and the ability to adapt those skills to a social rather than purely commercial mission. In addition, the SPO must have the organizational capacity to sell to the general public, including appropriate collection technology (credit card processing, bill collection, and so on), financial controls and accounting procedures. And, if memberships are considered a form of earned income, which they would be for membership organizations and cooperatives, as well as for certain kinds of conventional nonprofits such as YMCAs and Jewish Community Centers, then still other transactions costs and skill sets will be involved. One interesting issue here again relates to pricing. Memberships can often usefully be viewed as a form of "package pricing" in which multiple services are sold for a single price. The design of service packages and their associated prices and membership eligibility levels, as well as the recruitment of members themselves, constitute additional sets of transactions costs and skill sets associated with streams of earned SPO income. Complicating matters further, memberships often fall within the category of charitable rather than earned income, where membership in such institutions as arts or social service organizations are essentially honorific and serve as an inducement to further giving. In these cases, the skills and transactions costs associated with philanthropy are equally relevant (see below).

Finally, the borderline between fee and gift income is also blurred in the case of so-called "social procurement" wherein consumers or institutions purchase goods or services from suppliers that they favor because of their social missions (Barraket and Weissman, 2009). This would apply to fair-traded goods, for example, or products made by SPOs that employ marginalized or challenged workers. For example, a company may decide to cater its events by contracting with an SPO that employs workers with developmental disabilities, or use the courier services of an SPO that employs low income women. In such cases, the buyer is not seeking the best price but rather is looking to support the SPO contractor, in effect making a contribution through its purchase, if indeed the price is higher or the quality lower than market price and quality. For the SPO that sells such services, transactions costs include appropriate marketing of its products as well as management systems that ensure desired product quality, safety and branding. The practice of social procurement also blurs the distinction between fee income and government support. In particular, governmental procurement programs commonly include preferential provisions to favor needy and deserving populations or organizations serving or employing these groups. To take advantage of such policies, SPOs must be knowledgeable about opportunities for government contracts and have the capacity to secure and manage them.

Pursuit of charitable gifts, a second major source of SPO income, entails still other transactions costs and skill sets. Gift income differs from earned income largely because of the so-called *free rider problem*. Gift income is usually raised to support services which are public in character, hence not easily withheld from beneficiaries who decline to pay. While that same public goods character inspires altruism, SPOs have limited strategies for compelling beneficiaries of these kinds of goods and services to pay for them at a level that fully reflects the benefits they provide. Unlike earned income, for which SPOs can withhold private benefits from non-payers, gift income requires appealing to donors to volunteer their resources through various kinds of incentives, social pressure and informational strategies. This requires a different set of transactions costs and skill sets customized to targeted audiences of potential donor groups. To appeal to large numbers of individual donors, the SPO must become adept at marketing its appeals through such avenues as direct mail, social media, Internet sites, and broadcast media. To appeal to major individual donors yet another set of skills and resources is needed, to identify and cultivate prospective donors through relationship building, engagement in organizational activities, hosting special events and the like. To appeal to institutional donors such as foundations and corporations, grant writing skills and capacities are of special value. While many SPOs, especially large nonprofits including private universities, social service federations and arts institutions, have developed highly complex, multifaceted and sophisticated "development" capacities, they are unlikely to fully capture gift income entirely commensurate with the benefits they generate for targeted groups; that is the nature of the free rider problem. In one way, however, gift income strategy does resemble that of earned income strategy. SPOs must be careful not to overspend on their development efforts to the point where their transactions costs at the margin exceed the gift income they receive in return. Indeed, it makes good sense for SPOs to view their development arms as profit-seekers, trying to maximize the difference between their transactions costs and their returns (Young and Steinberg, 1995). But, as discussed in Chapter 6, this is a great challenge, with dangers at both ends of the spending spectrum: SPOs often spend too little on fund-raising because they may be chastised by oversight groups to keep their fund-raising cost ratios low as a matter of propriety and "good practice"; yet SPOs can also spend too much on fund-raising in efforts to chase down every last donor or out compete their charitable rivals even if that costs more than it brings in. Special fund-raising events, for example, should never lose money unless they are intended to provide some other social benefit than net income support for the organization.

The issues for generating volunteer capacity for SPOs are similar to those of charitable fund-raising. The free rider phenomenon obtains here as well. Collectively speaking, fewer people volunteer than the number who benefit directly or indirectly from SPO services, and volunteers offer fewer hours than would be commensurate with the value they receive, yet volunteers or potential volunteers cannot be compelled to contribute. However, the transactions costs and skill sets for this source of (in-kind) income are different from those of other sources. Volunteers must be skillfully recruited, managed and rewarded, and assigned to tasks where they can be most productive, including appropriate positioning vis-à-vis paid staff (Leete, 2006). Here too, decisions must be made as to how many of what types of volunteers are appropriate, and how much to spend on volunteer administration.

Similar observations apply to other (material) types of in-kind gifts to SPOs. Such income is again quite diverse, ranging from donation of real estate to artwork to used cars to clothing, food and household goods. Here too the transactions costs and skills are different and specialized. Not only must SPOs be skilled in making sometimes complex transactions (as in real estate or the art world) but they must also determine market versus organizational value so as to decide whether to utilize gifts for internal purposes or sell them for cash. In some cases, in-kind donations constitute the life blood of the organization – such as art for museums or grocery items for food banks, and sometimes they constitute the key source of money income as for Goodwill Industries which sells its donated items in its thrift stores. (See also the cases of the Atlanta Community Foodbank and MedWish in Chapter 6.) Negotiating these various markets for in-kind goods requires specialized skills and capacities different again from administering other sources of SPO income.

The third major source of income for NPOs is government, which also entails unique transactions costs and requires special skill sets. Government funding, discussed further in Chapter 7, is also multifaceted, comprised of grants, contracts, reimbursement schemes, tax incentives and other mechanisms, or "tools" (Salamon, 2002). Government can be an effective source of funds to address the free rider problem as its programs generally focus on public goods which it can support with tax revenues. However, securing government grants and contracts, or qualifying for reimbursement funds through programs such as Medicaid in the U.S., can be resource intensive, requiring considerable skill and labor for applications, reporting and other administrative work. Moreover, the degree to which government can be relied upon to cover the full costs of the services for which it contracts with SPOs may vary considerably (Boris et al., 2010). Frequently, SPOs assume substantial obligations to supplement government funds with other sources in order to remain solvent. Moreover, SPOs with government grants and contracts are often under pressure to spend their funds within the current fiscal year so as not to lose them, posing additional management challenges.

Political realities can further complicate the subject of transactions costs for government funding. For example, in the case of corruption, public officials and favor-seekers can take the notion of exchange quite literally. Corruption is a too common problem wherein exchange takes place between citizens who require the help of government and public officials who abuse their positions of authority to line their own pockets or those of family and friends. More generally, the provision of goods and services through government often entails rent-seeking behavior by constituents who secure benefits through programs supported by taxes that are imposed well beyond the benefitting group (Buchanan and Tullock, 1971). For example, if a majority of citizens approves a program counter to the wishes of a large minority, they will pay only a fraction of the cost. Or if logrolling behavior takes place, coalitions of minority groups may seek their own rents by supporting each other's programs at general taxpayer expense. SPO leaders may not be political actors per se, but they need to be aware of the politics behind various sources of government support; thus, their transactions cost can include negotiating the political environment in which government allocations decisions are made. In short, SPOs must enter transactions with government with their eyes wide open, and with the requisite knowledge, capacity and political sensitivity to successfully navigate governmental systems of funding allocation, reporting and oversight.

A fourth important source of SPO income is returns on investments. As considered in Chapter 8, this is especially important for large capital intensive nonprofit institutions in higher education and the arts, and of course for grant-making foundations (which can be viewed as SPOs that outsource their programming to operating SPOs). Here too it is clear that special skill sets and transactions costs are involved. These include both particular expertise and capacity to manage portfolios of financial investments, as well as the aforementioned skills of soliciting major capital gifts from private donors. Such skill sets can be secured in various ways including internal staffing, reliance on governing board members or contracting with investment firms. Each of these involves its own variants of transactions costs, including those of negotiating the terms of engagement, monitoring the work and paying for the services involved. While some SPOs, such as top universities like Harvard, Yale and Stanford, have proven themselves to be skilled long-term investors and securers of capital, other institutions such as the New-York Historical Society (Guthrie, 1996), Drexel University (Paul, 2008) or the New York City Opera (Levy, 2015) have been known to fritter away large endowments. Interestingly, endowments for generating investment revenue can be assembled in different ways. The most common is through capital gifts from major individual or institutional donors; however, it is also possible to build endowments through retained net earnings. For a variety of reasons, the latter is uncommon, at least for conventional nonprofit organizations, partly because these SPOs tend to stretch current spending as far as possible to address pressing mission-related imperatives. Indeed, SPOs funded by certain institutional sources such as government or some foundations may want to avoid realization of substantial net earnings so as to more easily justify their requests for future grant allocations. As a result most nonprofits do not even build sufficient reserve funds to hedge against risks (see Chapter 11). In any case, it is again clear that investment revenues require yet another, different set of transactions costs and skills than other forms of SPO income.

An interesting variant of investment income pertains to the growing practice of "mission-related investing" pioneered by the Heron Foundation (Miller and Johnson, 2015). In this framework, returns on investment are considered in terms of both financial gains and mission impacts. (An element of mission-related investing is the Program-Related Investment (PRI), as noted in Chapter 2.) Mission investing was conceived to help grant-making foundations leverage the corpuses of their endowments to achieve social goals in excess of what they could achieve by allocating grants from investment returns alone. Conceptually, however, this idea applies to any (endowed) SPO having resources to invest. In essence, such an SPO has two ways to support its mission: one is to generate money income for operations through conventional investments; the second is to invest in mission-focused activity and reap the gains directly in terms of mission impact. This is not so different from an SPO choosing between spending on a commercial venture whose profits are used to subsidize a mission-impacting activity versus allocating operating funds directly to a mainstream mission-related program that pays for itself or runs a small surplus. However, thinking this way about investment of funds by an operating SPO is a step further than the "socially responsible investing" commonly undertaken by well-endowed universities or health care institutions in their efforts to avoid socially undesirable investments in tobacco producers, soft drink makers or companies engaged in discriminatory or exploitative labor practices. In essence, it requires assessment of the value of the direct mission impacts versus the alternative prospective financial returns from conventional investments. In sum, mission-investing is a new approach to investment income generation involving a variety of potential financial instruments including grants, PRIs, bonds and equity, and requiring new protocols and guidelines for asset allocation, due diligence, investment fees and monitoring – all of the transaction costs of managing ordinary investments and more, but potentially worthwhile in terms of net mission impact.

Finally, to complete the spectrum of income sources for SPOs one must further consider capital funding, especially for types of SPOs that allow market participation by owners. Conventional nonprofit organizations do not have financial investors in the traditional sense because they must adhere to the "non-distribution of profits constraint." However, other SPO forms, such as cooperatives, and various types of profitmaking social businesses, do indeed look to outside financial investors for capital funding. Here, a special challenge is to find investors that share the dual goals of social impact and financial reward in various proportions, presuming that programming decisions may entail some sacrifice of the latter for the former. This too requires a different set of transactions costs and skill sets, likely entailing interesting mixes of the capacities required for seeking traditional donors, recruiting members, managing investments and selling products in the marketplace. Legal costs also enter the picture in circumstances such as the Ben and Jerry's case (Page and Katz, 2011) where management and investor perspectives may differ.

As discussed in Chapter 10, capital funding is a frontier area of social purpose organization finance for which the skill sets and transactions costs are yet to be fully understood or perfected. Indeed, there are many different dimensions along which the possibilities for capital financing of SPOs vary, including the mix of social and financial returns to capital, the combinations and variations of debt and equity involved, the life stage of an organization or project for which the capital is intended, the duration over which capital is provided and repaid, the level of financial risk versus return offered to investors, and the individual, collective or institutional source of funds and their intermediaries (For a full discussion see various chapters in Nicholls, Paton and Emerson, 2015; also Mook et al., 2015, Chapter 9).

Table 3.2 is a rough summary of different sources of SPO capital funding and their corresponding applicability to different types of SPOs. In this display, SPOs are divided roughly into four categories – nonprofits, cooperatives, social purpose businesses and sustainable businesses (see further discussion of this categorization below). Different types of capital funding instruments are more or less accessible to alternative types of SPOs because of the latter's differential ability to appeal to the predilections of various types of capital providers – individual and institutional donors, government, individual and institutional investors and various types of financial institutions, entrepreneurs, volunteers, members and so on. For example, sweat equity is accessible to all types of SPOs albeit for different reasons (for example, social impact versus future financial reward) and from different parties (for example, volunteers versus entrepreneurs). In contrast, traditional sale of equity is essentially confined to for-profit SPOs while conventional foundation grants target nonprofits. As noted above, retained earnings may be more difficult for nonprofits to generate and hence exploit as a means for accumulating capital. Debt is available from one source or another to all kinds of SPOs and certain hybrid sources such as PRIs and mezzanine funds (a form of capital combining elements of debt and equity) allow capital providers to balance their social impact and financial goals or their risks and financial returns, respectively. Overall, the diverse array of capital funding instruments and strategies, as well as the complexity of many of them, require SPOs to do their homework and to acquire or delegate the capacity to manage whatever sources of capital funding they pursue.

In sum, an overarching benefits theory of SPO finance must account for the fact that organizations may differ structurally in their abilities to cultivate certain income sources that may correspond to the services and benefits they produce. This adds substantial nuance to the simple notion that SPO income portfolios should faithfully mirror the benefits they offer to their various beneficiaries as a result of pursuing their social missions. That said, however, organizational forms can be adapted so that appropriate sources of operating income or capital funding may be pursued more easily.

Table 3.2 Major sources of capital for social purpose organizations

	Nonprofits	Cooperatives	Social businesses	Sustainable businesses	Returns to capital
Sweat equity	Volunteers, social entrepreneurs	Members, volunteers	Social entrepreneurs	Owners	Social impact; possible financial reward
Small gifts	Annual donors, crowd-funding	Members, donors	Crowd-funding		Social impact
Grants/Major Gifts	Foundations, government, major donors; capital campaigns	Foundations, government, members			Social impact
Retained Earnings		Net sales, member fees	Profits	Profits	Social or financial return
Debt	Bank loans, bonds	Bank loans, PRIs, bonds, member loans	Bank loans, bonds, crowd-funding	Bank loans, bonds	Financial return; possible social impact
Equity		Share capital	Sale of stock or ownership shares; crowd-funding	Sale of stock or ownership shares	Financial return; possible social impact
Mixed Types	PRIs from foundations		PRIs, mezzanine capital	Mezzanine capital	Financial and social returns
Comments	Non-distribution of profit constraint	Social coops similar to nonprofits	Limited profits distribution; possible subsidy	Profitable	

VARIATIONS BY FORM OF SOCIAL PURPOSE ORGANIZATION

As suggested above for capital funding, the fact that SPOs manifest themselves in various legal forms raises interesting questions for resource development strategy. While benefits theory provides generic guidance on where resources can potentially be sought, the legal forms impose various constraints and advantages to pursuing different types of income. Some of these issues will be considered further in Chapter 10. Here the intent is to offer an overview of the comparative advantages of different legal forms for cultivating alternative sources of income so as to provide the necessary nuance to benefits theory as a strategic frame of reference for all SPOs. While the focus is on sources of income for which each form may be handicapped, it is also important to understand that alternative forms of SPO may be adopted or integrated in various ways to overcome limitations to income development.

Traditional nonprofit organizations have demonstrated their considerable flexibility in drawing from all of the major types of income sources – earned income, monetary and in-kind gifts, volunteering, government and investments. The one major limitation for nonprofits is their ability to attract capital investments through sale of equity because of the non-distribution of profits constraint. Investors interested in monetary returns can loan money to nonprofits but they cannot take an ownership share or receive dividends from them. This is a principal reason for recent innovations in legal forms, such as Community Interest Companies in the U.K. and L3Cs and benefit corporations in the U.S. Nonetheless, some nonprofits have been creative in forming partnerships or conglomerate arrangements involving for-profits so as to attract investors to supply growth capital or generate profits that can be used for that purpose. In particular, nonprofits can own for-profit enterprises (along with conventional investors) so long as they pay appropriate taxes (for example, Unrelated Business Income Tax) and so long as such substantial business enterprises are separately governed and devoid of conflicts of interests for nonprofit managers or trustees. Moreover, with the participation of government as paymaster, private investment can be secured through innovations such as the Social Impact Bond which rewards investors with bonuses or dividends (and repayment of principal) only when the nonprofit succeeds in achieving pre-specified results (see further discussion in Chapter 10).

For-profit forms of SPO are, of course, well-positioned to attract private investment capital so long as they can offer a competitive financial return to their investors. These organizations may also be attractive to government funders if they can deliver designated public services efficiently or achieve desired results. For example, in the 1990s the U.S. government turned to a private company – Lockheed Martin – to be prime contractor for new services required by welfare reform legislation. For-profit SPOs are much more limited, however, in their capacities to attract gifts or volunteer effort. The problem here is mainly that of trust. Donors are reluctant to donate their monetary resources or time to entities that can exploit such gifts to the private benefit of their owners or managers. For-profits can overcome this limitation to some extent by establishing their reputations as good corporate citizens and creating separate nonprofit mechanisms to draw in charitable resources. For example, businesses can create charitable foundations to which individuals may be urged to contribute, and they can sponsor events such as local races through which participants and their sponsors may support a specific cause. Still, an SPO in for-profit form is less likely to be reliant on charitable contributions to finance its programming.

Cooperatives offer a kind of intermediate mechanism that allows for investment by members (share capital) and private benefits paid back to members. Indeed, traditional consumer and producer cooperatives are intended in large part to produce material benefits for members, if not in cash directly then certainly in such terms as lower prices for purchases or greater profits for items sold in the marketplace. However, share capital normally does not accurately reflect market value, given restrictions on sales and limits to how much share capital must be retained by the cooperative itself (a so-called asset lock). Moreover, the new breed of "social cooperatives" such as those in Italy are organized as nonprofits and have no share capital as such. Overall, given their collective and democratic nature, and possible broad social goals, many cooperatives can attract substantial volunteer effort and gift income directed toward achieving broader social purposes beyond member benefits. Again, the issue is trust for which cooperatives may have some advantage over traditional businesses because of the more direct involvement in governance by their members. At the same time, cooperatives may have the same disadvantages as nonprofits in attracting investment capital if they cannot share financial surpluses with outside investors.

To a degree, organizational form poses a "chicken and egg" problem for social entrepreneurs and SPO leaders. Benefits theory provides guidance on the best prospective combination of income sources, which in turn can inform the choice of organizational form that may be best suited to engage those sources. For example, if philanthropy is a major prospect, the nonprofit form may be the best choice. Alternatively, existing organizations will want to pursue their best income possibilities without necessarily contemplating a change of legal status. In this case, they will have to cope with the constraints imposed by their legal structures. It is not out of the question, however, that an SPO would choose to convert its legal status in order to pursue its best revenue strategy. For example, the for-profit classical radio station WCLV in Cleveland, Ohio converted to nonprofit status to maintain its social mission as desired by its aging founders. Conversely some nonprofit health care organizations in recent years have converted to for-profits in order to gain access to equity capital.

While conversion of legal form may be a radical long-term approach to aligning mission with income potential, it is certainly not unusual for SPOs to adapt or augment their legal structures in the shorter run, in order to take fuller advantage of the income potential to support their particular missions. Even in the public sector, governments create "friends" organizations, for example, Friends of the Library or Friends of the Park, in nonprofit form to augment government support with philanthropy. Corporate foundations and sponsored charities in nonprofit form allow profitmaking companies to pursue charitable goals and tap into community largesse. Nonprofits own profitmaking companies to generate earned income, and advocacy organizations not eligible for tax deductions create charitable arms in order to augment gift income for favored social causes (combinations of 501(c)(4) and 501(c)(3) nonprofits in the U.S.). Thus corporate form can be viewed as a means to achieve an SPO's mission and if this requires legal changes or augmentations in order to realize full income potential there are numerous ways to do that. Benefits theory is premised on the primacy of mission and is thus widely applicable to all forms of SPO with the understanding that legal forms can be adapted over time. Indeed, adjusting legal form to income potential can be viewed as an important long-term transactions cost.

SUMMARY

Benefits theory stipulates that SPOs are most effectively financed by income sources that correspond to the types of public and private benefits they generate through their services. Those services in turn derive from an SPO's social mission, or in the case of an SPO with mixed goals, its particular focus and balance of public and private objectives. While the matching of benefits with income sources is the central tenet of the benefits approach, a number of moderating factors can also influence an SPO's income strategy in any particular environment or organizational setting. These include the organization's administrative capacity and expertise to pursue different forms of income, its particular legal form, as well as the market and political environments in which the organization operates. Existing data and research suggest that SPOs intuitively pursue benefit strategies of finance. However, without explicit recognition and understanding of this way of thinking, it is likely that SPOs are not generally taking full advantage of all possible means of supporting their missions. The latter requires a more complete understanding of the economic nature of the services that they offer as well as a deeper appreciation of the challenges and nuances of each alternative source of prospective income. The next chapter continues with an explication of the variety of public and private goods and services and the financing mechanisms to which they are amenable.

REFERENCES

James Andreoni, 1990. "Impure Altruism and Donations to Public Goods: A Theory of Warm-Glow Giving", *Economic Journal*, 100, pp. 464–477.

Jessica Aschari-Lincoln and Urs P. Jager, 2016. "Analysis of Determinants of Revenue Sources of International NGOs: Influence of Beneficiaries and Organizational Characteristics", *Nonprofit and Voluntary Sector Quarterly*, 45(3), June.

Jo Barraket and Janelle Weissman, 2009. "Social Procurement and Its Implications for Social Enterprise: A Literature Review", Working Paper No. CPNS 48, Brisbane, Australia: The Australian Centre for Philanthropy and Nonprofit Studies, Queensland University of Technology, December.

Andrea Bassi, Jung-In Soh and Dennis R. Young, 2016. "Applying the Benefits Theory of Nonprofit Finance to Social Cooperatives", draft paper presented to the International Society for Third Sector Research, Stockholm, Sweden, July.

Elizabeth T. Boris, Erwin de Leon, Katie L. Roeger and Milena Nikolova, 2010. *Human Service Nonprofits and Government Collaboration: Findings from the 2010 National Survey of Nonprofit Government Contracting and Grants*, Washington, DC: Center on Nonprofits and Philanthropy, The Urban Institute, October.

Woods Bowman and Brianna Bingham, 2015. "Toward a Theory of Membership Association Finance" draft paper presented at the Association for Research on Nonprofit Organizations and Voluntary Action, Chicago, IL, November.

James M. Buchanan and Gordon Tullock, 1971. *Calculus of Consent: Logical Foundations of Constitutional Democracy*, Ann Arbor, MI: University of Michigan Press.

Grace L. Chikoto and Daniel Gordon Neely, 2014. "Building Nonprofit Capacity: The Impact of Revenue Concentration and Overhead Costs", *Nonprofit and Voluntary Sector Quarterly*, 43(3), pp. 570–588.

Robert L. Fischer, Amanda L. Wilsker and Dennis R. Young, D. 2011. "Exploring the Revenue Mix of Nonprofit Organizations: Does It Relate to Publicness?", *Nonprofit and Voluntary Sector Quarterly*, 40(4), pp. 662–681.

Kevin M. Guthrie, 1996. *The New-York Historical Society: Lessons from One Nonprofit's Long Struggle for Survival*, San Francisco, CA: Jossey-Bass Publishers.

Laure Leete, 2006. "Work in the Nonprofit Sector", Chapter 7 in Walter W. Powell and Richard Steinberg (eds), *The Nonprofit Sector: A Research Handbook*, Second Edition, New Haven: Yale University Press, pp. 159–179.

Reynold Levy, 2015. *They Told Me Not to Take That Job*, New York: PublicAffairs Books.

A. Page and R.A. Katz 2011. 'Freezing Out Ben & Jerry' Corporate Law and the Sale of a Social Enterprise Icon', *Vermont Law Review*, 35 (Symposium issue), pp. 211–249.

Clara Miller and Toni Johnson, 2015. "Mission-Aligned Investing: More Complex Than It Seems", *Stanford Social Innovation Review*, https://ssir.org/articles/entry/mission_aligned_investing_more_complex_than_it_seems, June 4.

Laurie Mook, John R. Whitman, Jack Quarter and Ann Armstrong, 2015. *Understanding the Social Economy of the United States*, Toronto: Toronto University Press.

Alex Nicholls, Rob Paton and Jed Emerson, 2015. *Social Finance*, Oxford: Oxford University Press.

David A. Paul, 2008. *When the Pot Boils: The Decline and Turnaround of Drexel University*, Albany: State University of New York Press.

Thomas Piketty, 2014. *Capitalism in the Twenty-first Century*, Cambridge: Harvard University Press.

Lester M. Salamon (ed.), 2002. *The Tools of Government: A Guide to the New Governance*, New York: Oxford University Press.

Elizabeth A.M. Searing, 2015. *Beyond Liabilities: Survival Skills for the Young, Small, and Not-for-Profit*. Doctoral dissertation, Atlanta: Georgia State University.

Richard Steinberg, 1991. "Does Government Spending Crowd-Out Donations? Interpreting the Evidence", *Annals of Public and Cooperative Economics*, 62, pp. 591–617.

Amanda L. Wilsker and Dennis R. Young, 2010. "How Does Program Composition Affect the Revenues of Nonprofit Organizations? Investigating a Benefits Theory of Nonprofit Finance", *Public Finance Review*, 38(2), pp. 193–216.

Dennis R. Young (ed.), 2007. *Financing Nonprofits: Putting Theory Into Practice*, Lanham, MD: AltaMira Press.

Dennis R. Young, 2015. "Financing Social Innovation", Chapter 3 in Alex Nicolls, Rob Paton and Jed Emerson (eds), *Social Finance*, Oxford: Oxford University Press, pp. 96–122.

Dennis R. Young and Richard Steinberg. 1995. *Economics for Nonprofit Managers*, New York: The Foundation Center.

Dennis R. Young, Amanda L. Wilsker and Mary C. Grinsfelder, 2010. "Understanding the Determinants of Nonprofit Income Portfolios". *Voluntary Sector Review*, 1(2), pp. 161–173.

4. The nature of benefits and their financing

INTRODUCTION

Chapter 3 made a general distinction between public and private benefits produced by social purpose organizations. This chapter further differentiates within and between these broad categories in order to account for the myriad combinations of SPO finance. In brief, it is argued that the better that an SPO understands the nature of the benefits it provides, the more successful it can be in generating the necessary economic resources to support its operations and achieve its mission.

Traditional microeconomic theory focuses on markets and is concerned primarily with "private goods." Public goods come into play in this theory to describe conditions of "market failure" where, without some form of modification through public policy or alternative mechanisms of resource allocation, markets will not by themselves allocate resources efficiently. A wide variety of mechanisms, including subsidies, regulation, taxes, direct government provision, or the engagement of alternative quasi-public organizations, may then be considered to correct market failures.

This book is not focused primarily on conventional for-profit businesses and markets but rather on organizations that address social goals. Therefore, the generation of public benefits is viewed as a strength to be exploited through appropriate market and non-market mechanisms. Moreover, private benefits are seen to play an important role, either as direct desired outputs of SPOs, where public and private goals may coincide, or as means to generate market support for social goals.

VARIATIONS OF PRIVATE AND PUBLIC GOODS

In the terminology of microeconomics a private good is a good or service that has two basic characteristics – *excludability* and *rivalry*. These characteristics are both necessary for competitive markets to allocate resources *efficiently* – that is, to allocate goods and services to their most highly valued uses as judged by society's willingness to pay for them (Young and Steinberg, 1995).

Excludability is simply the feasibility of excluding individuals from consuming a good or service if they do not pay for it. Many common goods have this characteristic – food, clothing, shelter, entertainment in a theater, medical care, air travel, and so on. For-profit providers are able to charge for such goods and services by withholding them from those who refuse to pay their stipulated prices.

Rivalry is a bit more subtle. A good or service is rival if a unit of its consumption by one individual precludes its consumption by another. Again, many common goods have this characteristic – shoes, food, paper products, individual counseling or health services, clothing, a reserved seat in a theater or airplane, and so on. However, goods that are not fully rival may be sold profitably by suppliers; the problem is that such sales may not be economically efficient. For example, a museum may charge a price for entry. In doing so, it may exclude people who are willing to pay something less than the asking price even though it would cost the museum almost nothing to admit them (assuming capacity has not been reached). A profit-seeking firm in this situation may charge a price that excludes many such customers, thereby forgoing prospective economic benefits that could be enjoyed by (sub-marginal) consumers. In such a situation, "market failure" can be addressed by subsidizing low income consumers, policy regulation requiring lower prices for certain groups, or provision by nonprofit providers who may be driven to maximize net social benefits rather than financial profits.

Combining the two dimensions of private goods together offers four possible variants of private and public goods, as follows:

1. *Rival and Excludable*: these are classical *private goods* or services underlying the basis of efficient markets.
2. *Excludable and Non-rival*: these are goods that can usually be produced by private profit-seeking firms in markets but perhaps inefficiently because consumers who are willing to pay less than the asking price are excluded even where the marginal cost of serving them is less than what they would be willing to pay. These are called *Toll Goods*. Examples of such goods include toll roads, theaters, private parks, and other goods and services where exclusion is possible but not necessarily efficient.
3. *Rival but Non-excludable*: This is the case of a common resource that is overused because consumers do not share consumption of common units, yet for-profit providers have no incentives to increase supplies because they cannot exclude and charge a price. These are

called *Common Pool* goods which include water supplies, below ground oil reserves, grazing areas on public lands, and other examples where exclusion is difficult and the supply is degraded by use and not renewed through ordinary market processes. This type of good embodies the famous "tragedy of the commons" (Ostrom, 1990).

4. *Non-rival and non-excludable*: Goods and services with these characteristics lead to market failure because for-profit suppliers cannot charge a price and consumers have little incentive to offer to pay a price because they can share in others' consumption of the good. The result is that, left to the market, such goods will not be produced at all, except through voluntary acts by magnanimous individuals or groups (philanthropists). Economists call these *Pure Public Goods* where the classical expectation is that they must be produced by government, which can impose taxes and mandate desired levels of provision. Examples include public safety, national defense, justice, environmental conservation, and public health.

It should be noted that this 2x2 taxonomy is really a two-dimensional continuum in the sense that both rivalry and excludability are often matters of degree rather than binary discrete categories. For example, rival goods such as music files or use of an automobile or private apartment can be shared once secured by one individual. Similarly, people can be excluded from certain nominally excludable goods such as fire protection or the use of a very large public park though only by costly means such as ignoring the burning house of a non-subscriber or building a fence around Yosemite National Park. Indeed, the nuances in classifying private and public goods are what create the opportunities for social purpose organizations to contribute to social good, by discerning the niches where markets alone, or indeed government, cannot efficiently do the job. Thus SPOs are active in providing every type of public and private good or service in our taxonomy. Moreover, particular variants of these categorical goods are especially amenable to SPO provision and financing. These variants and how they are connected to different modes of SPO finance are considered next.

THE CASE OF PRIVATE GOODS

Social purpose organizations produce a variety of essentially private goods. How then is the provision of such goods connected with an SPO's social mission? This question has at least four answers. First, SPOs may choose to provide private goods for profit much as commercial firms do.

In the case of SPOs that do not have a strict non-distribution constraint, such as cooperatives or various forms of social business, the production of private goods can enable the generation of earned income that results in profit that can be shared with owners in the form of dividends or increased equity. Even for SPOs with a strict non-distribution constraint such as conventional nonprofit organizations, the production of private goods may be undertaken to generate profit that may be used to subsidize mission-related goods and services that take some form of public goods. Second, an SPO may produce private goods that are directly mission related and for which the SPO enjoys a particular advantage over conventional for-profit businesses. In particular, for certain kinds of private goods which are difficult for the consumer to evaluate, such as day care for children or counseling for the mentally disabled, SPOs may engender greater public trust than conventional for-profit businesses, giving them a market advantage and positioning them to provide such services more efficiently than business sector counterparts. Such private goods may be called "trust goods." Trust goods may or may not be sold at maximum profit, depending on whether the SPO considers it important to expand sales past the profit-maximizing level in order to enhance its mission impact. For example, an SPO may decide that the more children in day care the better, and design its price schedule accordingly to include families that would not be able to pay a competitive market price. Alternatively its counseling services may be directed to middle class insured adults for whom paying the market price is not a critical issue. Third, certain kinds of private goods, which society may deem essential, may not be affordable for low income consumers. Affordable housing, basic health care and food fit this description. SPOs may produce these private goods by supplementing fee income with other sources. These kinds of private goods may be labeled "redistributive" private goods. To the degree that society as a whole or large groups within society decide that provision of such goods benefits everyone and should be provided as a matter of fairness or societal stability, redistributive goods have a quality resembling public goods. Finally, some private goods may not be completely private (that is, fully rival and excludable) in the sense that they are associated with what economists call "externalities." In particular, the consumption of such goods by an individual may indirectly impact others in a way that resembles a public good. There are two variations of such goods – those which produce "positive externalities" and those which involve "negative externalities."

Consider positive externalities first. When children are inoculated against disease, not only do these children and their families benefit directly but the inoculations also reduce the risk of contagion to others. SPOs may choose to provide such private goods because ordinary businesses may not produce them in sufficient quantity since consumers are willing to pay only for their own benefits; hence revenues will not reflect the greater public good. SPOs can supplement fee revenues from other sources (including reduced profits) to ensure that a socially efficient level of the good is provided.

Alternatively, SPOs may conceivably choose to provide private goods with negative externalities so as to reduce the level of externalities that would ordinarily be produced in the commercial marketplace. For example, the production of various manufactured goods such as plastics or energy pollute the environment. An SPO might choose to provide such goods in a manner that is less harmful, perhaps appealing to consumers to purchase their higher cost brand as an act of social responsibility or perhaps by subsidizing its price from other sources. For example, SPOs can produce energy from clean sources or plastic products from recycled materials. (Alternatively, an SPO might instead view the reduction of negative externalities as a public good through the pursuit of better laws and regulations.)

In summary, SPOs may be engaged in providing the following types of *private goods*, either wholly or partially financed with fees:

1. Conventional private goods, where SPOs seek to produce profits to compensate owners or subsidize other mission-related services.
2. Trust goods where the quality is difficult for the consumer to evaluate.
3. Redistributive goods which are essential but difficult for low income consumers to afford.
4. Mixed goods associated with positive or negative externalities.

THE CASE OF TOLL GOODS

SPOs produce various toll goods which can be supported at least in part through fee revenue because they are excludable. However, the fact that toll goods are non-rival, at least up to the point where they become congested or reach capacity limits, can cause conventional businesses to under-produce such goods in order to maximize profits. Alternatively, SPOs can choose to provide such goods at higher levels in order to expand access to consumers willing to pay a lower price. Examples include museums, parks and recreation areas, performing arts and education. Essentially, the marginal costs of such services are very low since allowing another individual into a museum gallery or lecture hall is negligible so long as capacity limits (or congestion that reduces the benefits to infra-marginal consumers because of crowding) are not reached, while the benefit as reflected in the marginal consumer's willingness to pay may be modest but substantial. Thus there is a net benefit to society of accommodating sub-marginal consumers. However, a conventional business attempting to maximize profit or to cover average cost will charge more than that consumer is willing to pay. Here is where an SPO can have a positive social impact by partially financing additional consumers from other sources. As discussed in Chapter 5, toll goods also offer an SPO the opportunity to engage in progressive pricing strategies such as price discrimination (sliding scales) and congestion pricing in order to both accommodate consumers below the margin and to use facilities more efficiently by spreading demand over time or among alternative locations.

A sub-category of toll goods of interest to some SPOs are so-called "associative goods" which provide benefits specifically to members of an organization, often supported by member fees or dues, as in the cases of health and social clubs (Bowman and Bingham, 2015). Some of the latter benefits (such as social status or networking opportunities) may derive specifically from the association with other members and vary with the degree of exclusivity of membership. Associative goods which depend solely on the interaction with other members are called "relational goods" (Bassi, 2010).

THE CASE OF COMMON POOL GOODS

As noted, common pool goods have the distinct drawback of easy consumer access and limited incentives for producers to replenish the common resource. Governments, of course, address this problem in various ways including assigning property rights to resources such as below ground water or mineral deposits, by regulating usage through controls or permits such as limits and licensing for hunting and fishing or emitting effluents from business operations, taxes on emissions into air, water and ground resources, or direct services such as sewers and waste management systems. Some of these policies essentially convert common pool goods into private goods by imposing excludability through legal means.

SPOs may also address the provision of common pool goods in various ways. Social businesses may become exemplars for best practices in production, for example, using clean energy or low carbon practices, which may give them market power to influence commercial competitors; or they may produce and distribute affordable products such as clean burning stoves or composting toilets that reduce degradation of common air and water resources. SPOs, for example environmental organizations, may also promote and facilitate voluntary agreements among affected parties so as to preserve grazing lands, rain forests or endangered species of animals and plants. While some of these strategies may permit the generation of earned income, they will generally require an SPO to engage philanthropic or governmental support.

Indeed, government is the natural steward of many common pool goods including libraries and water systems (Lohmann, 2016) and nature preserves such as national parks (Yandle, Noonan and Gazley, 2016). However, government is often limited in its capacity to fully protect these resources, leaving room for SPOs to contribute to their provision in one of two ways: Either as contractors to government, bringing to bear additional expertise and assistance, or as partners to enhance the total resources available for common pool stewardship. In the former case, it is logical for SPOs to look to government for financial support. In the latter case, SPOs can engage philanthropy to supplement government-derived resources. For example, Friends of the Park or Friends of the Library may be the SPO vehicles for leveraging gifts and grants to fund the benefits of common pool stewardship.

THE CASE OF PURE PUBLIC GOODS

Pure examples of goods and services that are neither rival nor excludable are rare. Some degree of rivalry and excludability are associated with most so-called public goods and services. For example, public education is clearly excludable since it usually involves admission to a school of some kind, and it is rival only to the extent that adding an additional student displaces another one, or consumes supplies and the time and attention of teachers and staff to the exclusion of devoting that attention to other students. Nonetheless, the societal benefit of an informed and productive citizenry is neither rival nor excludable.

Many so-called pure public goods have this character of attachment to an essentially private good, in the form of positive externalities or the prospective reduction of negative externalities. Inoculations, a private good, produces reduced contagion, a pure public good. Education produces positive externalities of economic productivity and good citizenship, both pure public goods. Production and consumption of various private marketable goods, ranging from automobiles to fast foods to guns, produce negative externalities such as pollution, climate change, reduced public safety, and obesity (and higher health care costs for all). These externalities can be addressed through SPO strategies such as conservancy, advocacy and public education programs that take the form of pure public goods. While many of these goods may be supported with various sources of government funding, they often require philanthropy and volunteer effort as well.

A BENEFICIARY-BASED TAXONOMY OF PUBLIC AND PRIVATE GOODS

In order to move from the foregoing generic classification of private and public goods to a simpler one that connects more directly with potential sources of finance for SPOs, the following refinement is offered:

1. *Private goods* saleable in commercial markets and supported by fees. Sale of such goods by SPOs presumes that they intend to generate profits to distribute to owners or to subsidize the provision of other goods. SPOs will offer such goods where they can compete successfully with conventional businesses because of some competitive advantage they enjoy. Provision of such goods also presumes compatibility with the SPO's social mission, that is, that they will not detract from mission impact. For example, health care organizations do not sell tobacco products. For an SPO to provide private goods presumes that it has identified specific beneficiary groups of consumers willing to pay for its products in the form of fees. An important subcategory of private goods produced by SPOs is "trust goods," also profitably sold in the marketplace and supportable by fees and likely to be directly mission-related. Absent the issue of consumer limits on willingness or ability to pay, or associated positive or negative externalities, provision of trust goods again presumes that the SPO has identified its beneficiary group of consumers willing to pay a market price for the services provided.
2. *Public goods.* This includes toll goods (with the exception of associative and relational goods) and common pool goods, as well as pure public goods, although the means for financing these variants may indeed differ. In all cases, there is a public benefit aspect that requires the SPO to examine where some or all of the income support could come from. Public goods with widespread benefits which impact a majority of citizens, especially pure public goods and common pool goods, would be logical candidates for governmental support in some form. Goods with more narrowly targeted benefits may look more toward philanthropy for their support (see group goods below). Moreover, toll goods have the advantage of excludability so that fees targeted to individual consumers (theater goers, museum visitors) may constitute a substantial portion of their financing.
3. *Group goods.* With the exception of associative goods (see below), such goods have the same characteristics as public goods except that their (non-rival, non-excludable) benefits are limited to a distinct, identifiable population that does not constitute a majority or controlling faction in

some political jurisdiction. This is not to say that SPOs providing such goods, such as research on a rare disease or disability that threatens a small, diffuse population, or preservation and promotion of early music, cannot secure government support under some circumstances, or find ways to sell associated commercial products, but rather that it is likely that they will have to depend substantially on voluntary contributions (charitable gifts, volunteerism) from members of their particular beneficiary groups. Group goods also include associative and relational goods which resemble toll goods because they are excludable but non-rival within the context of an identifiable group. For example, the benefits of membership in a club are confined to members of the club but shared simultaneously by all members. These include specific member privileges such as use of a common facility as well as status or satisfaction stemming from interaction with other members. Associative type group goods may derive support from membership dues since the benefits of membership are excludable.

4. *Redistributive goods.* As noted above, some goods and services have the characteristics of private goods (rival, excludable) but they are considered essential to, but hard to afford by, low income consumers. This opens up the financing of such goods to governmental and philanthropic support – governmental because their provision at some basic level derives from societal consensus, and philanthropic because some citizens are especially concerned about their provision to needy or deserving groups. For example, provision of food is supported by government through various programs such as food stamps and school lunch programs, while philanthropy supports soup kitchens and food banks.

5. *Exchange goods.* This is a variant of private goods (rival and excludable) whose benefits accrue to a few specific parties that are willing to support the SPO through various means including fees, gifts and grants, in-kind services and volunteering, in exchange for private benefits such as public recognition, or access to the SPO's services, clientele or expertise. Examples include corporate sponsorships wherein organizations provide material support to the SPO in exchange for public recognition and brand visibility, and volunteer arrangements that allow specific groups of participants (for example, docents) to enjoy the SPO's programming such as musical performances or displays of art.

This taxonomy of goods and services directly reflects the primary sources (beneficiary groups) and types of income on which an SPO may build its support. Table 4.1 summarizes this point.

Table 4.1   Types of SPO goods, beneficiary groups and sources of income

Type of good	Beneficiaries	Distinctive source of income
Private goods	consumers	Earned income, fees
Public goods	general public	Government grants and contracts
Group goods	limited communities of interest	Philanthropy and volunteering; membership dues
Redistributive goods	needy consumers	Fees plus government and philanthropy
Exchange goods	organizational partners and special supporting groups	Miscellaneous including fees, gifts, volunteering

As observed in examples throughout this book, SPOs produce individual services with various combinations of the characteristics of private, public, group, redistributive and exchange goods, as well as various mixes of services themselves. Table 4.2 shows that an SPO's income portfolio can be logically built on any of the different types of income as well as any particular mix of these sources. Specifically, the table illustrates a spectrum of possible SPO offerings and their logical combinations of income sources.

SOME INTERESTING CASES

A few cases will help illustrate how an SPO's mission, services, benefits and beneficiaries shape its finances. Every real life example exhibits nuances and variations particular to its circumstances, but general patterns and strategies are also clear. By recognizing the connection between mission and financing, an SPO can refine its strategies and better exploit its income potentials. The following three cases exhibit both the connections and the potentials for pursuing income streams consistent with mission, benefits and beneficiaries.

Tucson Botanical Gardens

Tucson Botanical Gardens (TBG) is a charitable 501(c)(3) nonprofit organization in Tucson, Arizona, whose attractions are spread over five and a half acres, including 17 specialty gardens (Mook et al., 2015). According to its mission statement "The Tucson Botanical Gardens promotes

Table 4.2   Prospective SPO income combinations based on corresponding benefits and beneficiary groups

Income combination	Example	Why?
Fees only	Tracing family tree	Consumer benefit only
Gifts only	Rare disease research	Benefits those afflicted or at risk
Gov't only	Offender rehab services	Increases public safety
Fees & Gifts	Performing arts	Private benefits to attendees; collective benefits to art lovers
Fees & gov't	Pre-school care	Private consumer and general public benefits
Gov't & gifts	Monitoring environmental quality	Benefits to outdoor enthusiasts and general public
Fees, gifts & gov't	University education	Private student, collective alumni, gen'l public benefits

responsible and appropriate use of plants and water in a desert environment through education and demonstration and provides a place of beauty and tranquility for Tucson residents and visitors" (TBG, 2016). TBG carries out its mission through an array of programs including general visitation of the gardens as well as tours, special evening and early morning programs; docent training and DIY (do it yourself) Desert Design classes; youth education which includes workshops and educational resources for teachers, as well as student field trips; horticultural therapy which includes community outreach, apprenticeships with local high schools, and training for staff working with people with disabilities in Guyana; two-week excursions to Australia; as well as a café and gift shop. These programs project a diverse array of private, public and redistributive benefits. Private benefits include the recreation, entertainment and learning enjoyed by visitors to the gardens, both local residents and tourists; consumers of café and gift shop products enjoyed by visitors; and the education enjoyed by teachers, local residents, and others who attend the workshops, classes, special events and excursions. These private benefits allow TBG to charge fees for many of its services. Redistributive benefits include visits and participation in programs by school children and less affluent individuals who may participate free of charge or at low cost. Public benefits include the general environmental and social impacts of TBG's efforts to educate people about conservation and to improve mental and physical health and community relations.

This mix of public and private benefits is reflected in TBG's sources of income. As may be anticipated, a substantial portion of its $1.7 million in annual revenues (48 percent) derives from fees, if memberships and special events are included. This reflects the fact that TBG charges fees for most of its services, though fee schedules may be designed to accommodate ability to pay and social benefits of many of its excludable activities. Moreover, some 46 percent of TBG's revenues derives from contributions, grants and in-kind support. TBG thus appears to do a good job of cultivating beneficiaries of both the private and public goods that it offers. Moreover, its gifts and grants revenue includes contributions from individuals, foundations, corporations and local governments, reflecting both the widespread environmental and social benefits as well as the particular values placed on TBG's programs by local citizens and businesses. In particular, larger gifts (over $10,000) derive largely from foundations, corporations and government, while smaller contributions are dominated by gifts from individuals and families.

Children's Aid Society

Founded in 1853, The Children's Aid Society (CAS) is one of the oldest and largest non-sectarian child and family welfare agencies in the U.S. Its mission is to help "children in poverty to succeed and thrive . . . by providing comprehensive supports to children and their families in targeted high-needs New York City neighborhoods" (The Children's Aid Society, 2016). CAS's services address every aspect of a child's life, from infancy through adolescence. These services include adoption and foster care; arts programming; summer camps and camps for disabled children; community social and recreational centers; community technology centers; counseling; early childhood education; community schools programming in partnership with public schools; after-school and weekend programming; health services including medical, dental, optometry, hearing, pediatric, adolescent, prenatal and well-baby care, mental health and other clinical services; transitional housing; employment training; mentoring; nutrition including food distribution; drug abuse prevention public policy and client advocacy; teen pregnancy prevention; and youth mediation and court diversion programming. The largest single area of expenditure is child welfare and family services (largely foster care and adoption services, representing approximately 40 percent of total expenses in 2015), with other programs for pre-school, school age, and adolescent children, and health and wellness services, each accounting for 13 percent to 18 percent of expenses.

CAS works in the five boroughs of New York City as well as Westchester County. In addition, CAS staff serve as technical assistance advisors for replications and adaptations of CAS's specialized services in teen pregnancy prevention and community school projects in cities throughout the United States. CAS focuses entirely on the needs of children and families from low income communities and/or those facing particular challenges such as educational achievement, involvement in the juvenile justice system, drug and alcohol abuse, teen pregnancy and physical, mental and learning disabilities.

CAS's annual expense budget was $107 million in 2015. Its operating revenues included approximately $11 million of investment income from its endowments. Government provides approximately two-thirds of CAS's operating funds. This compares to an average of more than 90 percent of government funding for New York State child welfare agencies over the period 2006–2010 (Marwell; Calabrese and Krauskopf, 2012). Approximately two-thirds of CAS's total government funding is comprised of revenue from New York City, which also includes pass-through funding from state and federal government sources. CAS receives the remaining portion of government revenue directly from state and federal sources, with federal awards comprising the smallest part of total government funding. The proportion of revenues from private, charitable contributions was 15 percent in 2015. This compares to an average of only 5 percent to 6 percent for other New York State nonprofit child care agencies (Marwell; Calabrese and Krauskopf, 2012). As a well-established nonprofit, CAS thus maintains considerable fund-raising capacity relative to its peers.

CAS's revenue from fees has declined in relative terms over recent years, from the 10 percent to 11 percent range in the first decade of the century to 5 percent in 2015. Fees are mostly derived from participants in CAS's early childhood education and summer camp programs. The remaining fee revenue is earned by providing technical assistance to other organizations replicating CAS's teen pregnancy prevention and community school programs. Part of the decline of fee revenue since 2011 may be attributed to the termination of fee-for-service initiatives located in a CAS-owned site in an affluent neighborhood. A similar CAS-owned site was put up for sale in 2013, with fee-based programs held at that location closing in 2014. The decision to sell the properties and thus terminate the fee-based programs was mission-focused, as CAS's mission does not encompass providing services to middle and upper-income children who are able to pay service fees or reside in the sites' upper-income neighborhoods.

Many of the services provided by CAS, for example, camps, health clinic services, adoption services, have the character of private goods since they benefit primarily individual children and families who could conceivably be charged fees. However, these services are redistributive in nature, going to needy recipients who lack a significant ability to pay and who would be excluded by fee requirements. Moreover, these services can be seen to benefit society as a whole as investments in future adult citizens, at least within the geographic scope of New York City and Westchester but even nationwide. Other CAS services are more explicitly public in character (for example, policy advocacy, drug abuse prevention), while still others (for example, employment training, foster care) have a mixed public/private character with significant public benefits (such as lower crime and a more productive workforce) as well as private benefits to recipients. Thus, it is not surprising that CAS would be funded primarily out of local government sources, supplemented by some fees from clientele and private contributions from donors who care about the welfare of low income and challenged children and families.

As an older nonprofit, CAS has the luxury of an endowment and reserve funds, which provide a financial cushion. Only 30 percent of New York nonprofit child care organizations have endowments in excess of $5 million and half of those have none at all (Marwell; Calabrese and Krauskopf, 2012). Still, CAS runs chronic deficits and given the semi-private character of some of its services, could conceivably reexamine its fee policies to search for additional earned income; and it could explore the possibility of exploiting some of its assets that may be underutilized (for example, camp facilities) in order to generate additional sources of commercial revenue. It is noteworthy, however, that CAS has decided to eschew services to children of higher income families. While this decision is driven by mission it may also be a lost opportunity for revenue generation to support its mission.

Finally, while private donations represent only a small portion of New York nonprofit child care revenues, CAS could conceivably explore enhancement of this source of funds. In particular, CAS has a long history to draw upon, including individuals and families who have benefitted from its assistance over the year (that is, its "alumni") and may be in a position to "give back." The design of any new giving program would have to be carefully researched and targeted to populations likely to understand and sympathize with CAS's mission.

Paolo Babini Cooperative (PBC)

PBC is a social cooperative in Forli, Italy founded in 1987 (Bassi, Soh and Young, 2016). Under Italian law it is a mixed type A and B social cooperative that provides a mix of welfare or care services (in social services and education) and integrates marginalized workers into the labor force. While it is governed democratically as a cooperative, it is organized as a nonprofit organization with no member dues. The mission of PBC is to support children and families in difficulty in its community, through effective services, by building community, and expanding public awareness. Its programs cover four areas – care, education, employment and citizen participation. PBC focuses on Mafalda Village a residential complex it established in the city of Forli in 2008, where most of its clients live. The organization embraces the culture of a supportive residential community with a focus on developing each individual to reach his or her full potential and ability to live autonomously. PBC's care services include three residential facilities for children, and additional facilities for teenagers, young adults, and mothers with children. PBC's education programs include a summer holiday resort center, three kindergartens, a youth center, two disability projects and a day center for the elderly. Its employment development program includes a centralized food service and a catering service that employs challenged workers. And its community building program includes projects to promote volunteering, as well as support for families involved with adoption, foster care and parenthood.

Overall PBC serves a range of vulnerable or troubled beneficiaries including children, young adults emerging from foster care, adults with mental health problems, families, and senior citizens. Moreover, its business enterprises offer food-related services to outside consumer groups and organizations.

The nature of benefits is largely private and redistributive, and public as well. Children, families, youth, troubled adults and seniors all receive private benefits though most are not in a position to pay much for them. Many would be otherwise eligible for government welfare and care services. Consumers of PBC's food and catering services receive private benefits for which they can pay. Additionally, PBC's work integration programs benefit the local economy and community at large through increased productivity and self-reliance of otherwise marginalized workers. Finally, PBC's community and family building programs benefit the Forli community as a whole through enhanced citizen participation, economic productivity and stronger families. More generally, PBC offers support for vulnerable populations of general concern to Italian society and the concern of government care and welfare programs.

The income structure of PBC largely reflects its benefits and beneficiaries. Of total annual revenues of approximately €3 million euros (approximately $3.3 million USD), government contracts constitute a two-thirds share while private fee and sales revenues account for one quarter, with the rest from private gifts and grants (8 percent). PBC also engages 200 volunteers who live in Mafalda Village and provide stability and guidance to its various residents. This pattern affirms the largely public and redistributive benefits provided by PBC as well as the value of the products and services it is able to sell in the marketplace. While philanthropy plays a minor role in PBC's support, volunteering is especially important as an unpriced but still valuable in-kind income stream. PBC's focus on its local jurisdiction necessarily circumvents its wider philanthropic appeal. Nonetheless, PBC considers gifts and grants as its most important source for capital projects to maintain and build its substantial physical infrastructure. This also makes sense, given its physical prominence in the city and hence its potential appeal to local citizen/donors.

Overall, these three cases illustrate how the missions of three diverse SPOs influence their sources of income. In the case of the Tucson Botanical Gardens, the balance of earned and gift revenue reflects the private benefits afforded to visitors and program participants with the public benefits that TBC provides for the local and regional jurisdictions. For Children's Aid Society, service to its vulnerable children and families is captured in strong government support, and continuing philanthropic support for its public and redistributive programming. For Paolo Babini Cooperative, its largely redistributive benefits are reflected in heavy governmental support as well, supplemented by sales revenues from consumers who receive private benefits from the products of the social enterprises that employ PBC's clientele. While these cases affirm the expectations from benefits theory, they also highlight prospective areas for income development stemming from a benefits theory perspective. For example, Children's Aid begs the question of why earned income is not further developed to reflect its substantial capacity to provide private benefits in its service programs by serving additional client groups who could pay for them, while PBC appears to lag in its cultivation of philanthropy, especially within its local community and perhaps among interest groups concerned with vulnerable families, troubled youth and adults, and senior citizens.

APPLICATIONS

Having covered the rudiments of benefits theory in this chapter and Chapter 3, and considered the above case studies, the reader should be able to begin diagnosing the financial support structure of any particular SPO. In this section two generic, hypothetical mini-cases are offered for consideration. Two general questions are suggested for analyzing the cases. First, how well are the sources of income aligned with the nature of benefits and potentially supportive beneficiary groups? Second, is the SPO missing opportunities by failing to exploit additional prospective sources of income consistent with its benefit offerings? The following cases use tables that capture the answers to key questions that should be asked in the process of analysis. The reader is invited to adapt such tables to other (real) SPOs. In the Appendix, a more comprehensive set of templates is offered for a deeper dive. Worksheets A.1, A.2 and A.3 pertain most directly to the discussion in this chapter.

Commuter Bicycle

Commuter Bicycle is a cooperative organized by commuters in a large metropolitan area where people suffer from traffic congestion and health issues stemming from sedentary lifestyles. *CB* allows its members to drive to commuter parking lots outside the city, and transfer to bicycles for their rides to and from work in the city, or alternatively to ride their own bicycles to the parking lots and catch trains and buses to their jobs. *CB* is also active in advocating for bike trails and lanes and rules of the road to increase bicycling safety. In addition, *CB* provides amenities to members including places to change clothes, emergency response to cyclists with troubles en route, repair services for members' own bicycles, and information for recreational cycling in the city. *CB* is funded by annual member fees and some local foundation grants, plus sales revenue for repair and tourist (bike rental) services for nonmembers. Table 4.3 summarizes *CB*'s benefit and income structure.

The chart suggests that *CB's* private benefits are appropriately captured by fee revenues and memberships in the cooperative, but that the more diffuse public and group benefits for the citizenry, bicycle enthusiasts and the bicycle industry are not fully realized by government support, philanthropy, or corporate sponsorships. The issue is the degree to which *CB* can invest in its capacity to administer the transactions costs of grant seeking, fundraising and/or solicitation and management of government or corporate funding. This analysis could set the stage for *CB's* further development to enhance its mission impact and maintain stable and robust finances.

Veteran's Theater

Veteran's Theater (VT) is a nonprofit theater company in a mid-sized city established by returning war veterans to provide their peers with the opportunity to participate in public theater, to learn acting and other skills, and to engage in theater as a therapeutic activity. *VT* also seeks to educate the community about veterans and improve their employment prospects. *VT* aims for professional quality productions of interest to the broader community, so as to attract general audiences in order to inform them about veterans' issues. As an innovative program, *VT* also hopes that its model will be replicated in other communities. *VT* is funded by donations from local citizens and businesses and modest box office revenues, and

Table 4.3   Commuter bicycle analysis

Services	Bike sharing; repair and emergency services; amenities; advocacy; recreational biking information
Benefits	Commuter cost savings, convenience and health benefits (private); lower traffic congestion and air pollution (public); improved bicycle safety (public); recreation benefits for tourists and local citizens (private); improved biking conditions for bike enthusiasts (group)
Beneficiaries	Commuters; general public; tourists and recreational bicyclists; bicycle enthusiasts; bicycle product retailers
Sources of Income	Member fees (90%); nonmember fees for repairs and other bicycle services (5%); foundation grants (5%)
Alignment?	Fees reflect private benefits; public benefits not well reflected in revenues
Opportunities?	Local government support and more gift income from bicycle enthusiasts and foundations promoting health and environment. Sponsorships by bicycle industry
Administrative Capacity and Transactions Costs	Established capacity to solicit members and administer member fees and sales; limited expertise or capacity to secure grants or cultivate corporate sponsorships
Issues/recommendations?	Explore government support and greater philanthropic funding contingent on costs of acquiring grant seeking skill sets; explore business sponsorships

engages substantial volunteer participation by veterans and their families and fans of community theater. Table 4.4 summarizes *VT's* benefit and income structure.

The chart indicates that *VT* captures the private benefits of community theater attendance via fees and the group benefits of helping community veterans and strengthening community theater through local donations and volunteering. It falls short of exploiting the wider public benefits it can create through outreach and education to the broader public beyond the local community, but the latter would require investment in new skills and additional transactions costs associated with grant writing, lobbying government and working with the military.

The foregoing mini-cases are simply suggestive of how "benefits thinking" can shape the financial strategies of social purpose organizations. Readers are encouraged to expand on the analysis above and to consider how they raise or exemplify issues or shed new light on other SPOs of interest.

Table 4.4   Veterans' theater analysis

Services	Performances; group therapy; community outreach
Benefits	Therapeutic and skill development benefits for veterans (private); improved employment prospects and public understanding for veterans in the community (group); entertainment for theater goers (private); role model for helping veterans' in other communities (public); improved public relations/ image for military (exchange)
Beneficiaries	Veterans, individually and as a group; theater goers and fans of community theater; the military establishment; local community
Sources of Income	Local donations (40%); volunteer effort (40%); box office fees (20%)
Alignment?	Current funding captures private benefits to theater goers and group benefits for the local veterans' community and theater fans. Broader public benefits outside the community or public relations benefits for the military are not exploited. Private (redistributive) benefits are received by some participating veterans who attend programs free of charge or at reduced cost
Opportunities?	Participating veterans may be willing to pay for premium services such as extra therapeutic programs or counseling or mentoring sessions. Consulting services might be offered to other communities seeking to organize veterans' theater. Military services and associated organizations, and foundations dedicated to veterans' issues might be approached for sponsorships
Administrative Capacity and Transactions Costs	*VT* is adept at volunteer recruitment and management, box office revenue management and gift solicitation in its community. Grant writing, consultation services and outreach beyond the community would require investment in new skill sets
Issues/recommendations?	Explore possibilities for additional services to local veterans for which they would be willing to pay. Weigh the costs of acquiring grant writing capacity to seek additional foundation grants to support outreach on veterans' issues, and to seek sponsorships from military organizations

CONCLUSION

The present chapter has delved into the nature of benefits and how they relate to different sources of income. Subsequent chapters will expand on the subtleties and variations of alternative income sources and their admixtures in greater depth. The key points of this examination of benefits may be summarized as follows:

- SPOs produce a variety of goods and services corresponding to their diverse missions which may be characterized in terms of the classical definitions of private and public goods and mixtures and variants thereof.
- The different types of goods, given their intrinsic natures, call for different types and mixes of financing including fees income, charitable gifts, and government support.
- For purposes of analyzing SPO finances, a variation of the classical public goods classification is a four-fold schema that includes private goods, group goods, public goods and exchange goods – each of these corresponding to particular sources of income – fees, gifts, government support and direct exchange of benefits between institutions.
- Particular mixtures of these four categories are especially important. These include redistributive goods that are essentially private in character but which incorporate the societal goal of ensuring access by audiences unable to pay full market prices, and private goods with externalities that generate both private and public benefits.
- The finances of any particular SPO are likely to reflect the special mixture of public and private benefits deriving from its mission and the chosen strategies employed to address that mission.
- While most nonprofits may implicitly connect their mission and benefits to their income strategies, without explicit analysis of this connection they are likely to miss income opportunities that fully exploit the benefits they offer or could offer.

REFERENCES

Andrea Bassi, 2010. *La mosaïque coopérative. Stratégies de réseaux de la coopé-ration sociale à Ravenne*, in Xabier Itcaina (ed.), *La politique du lien, Les nouvelles dynamiques territoriales de l'économie sociale et solidaire*, aux Presse Universitaire de Rennes, pp. 109–126.
Andrea Bassi, Jung-In Soh and Dennis R. Young, 2016. "Applying the Benefits

Theory of Nonprofit Finance to Social Cooperatives". International Society for Third Sector Research, bi-annual conference, Stockholm, July.

Woods Bowman and Brianna Bingham, 2015. "Toward a Theory of Membership Association Finance", draft presented to the Annual Conference of the Association for Research on Nonprofit Organizations and Voluntary Action (ARNOVA), November.

The Children's Aid Society, 2016. "Financials", retrieved on December 13, 2016 from www.childrensaidsociety.org/about/financials.

Roger A. Lohmann, 2016. "The Ostroms' Commons Revisited", *Nonprofit and Voluntary Sector Quarterly*, 45(4S), August, pp. 27S–42S.

Nicole P. Marwell, Thad Calabrese and James Krauskopf, 2012. "The Financial Health of New York's Child Welfare Nonprofits", New York: Center for Nonprofit Strategy and Management, Baruch College School of Public Affairs, retrieved on December 13, 2016 from www.baruch.cuny.edu/spa/researchcenters/nonprofit-strategy/documents/COFCCAReportFINAL_TheFinancialHealthofNewYorks ChildWelfareNonprofits.pdf.

Laurie Mook, John R. Whitman, Jack Quarter and Ann Armstrong, 2015. *Understanding the Social Economy of the United States*, Toronto: Toronto University Press, pp. 255–256.

Elinor Ostrom, 1990. *Governing the Commons*, New York: Cambridge University Press.

Tucson Botanical Gardens (TBG), 2016. www.tucsonbotanical.org; includes Tucson Botanical Gardens, 2013. *Community Report 2012–2013*.

Tracy Yandle, Douglas S. Noonan and Beth Gazley, 2016. "Philanthropic Support of National Parks: Analysis Using the Socio-Ecological Systems Framework", *Nonprofit and Voluntary Sector Quarterly*, 45(4S), August, pp. 134S–155S.

Dennis R. Young and Richard Steinberg, 1995. *Economics for Nonprofit Managers*, New York: The Foundation Center.

5. Fee-reliant SPOs

INTRODUCTION

Earned income plays a major, often dominant, role in the financing of many nonprofit organizations, and even more so in some of the new forms of social enterprise such as for-profit social businesses. Indeed earned income is the mainstay of nonprofits in the U.S. in health care and a principal financial pillar in sectors such as education and the arts. Following benefits theory, one would expect the missions of earned income-reliant SPOs to be centered on the provision of private goods. However, important nuances to this connection, especially links between earned income and public, group, redistributive benefits and exchange benefits, are also explored in this chapter.

VARIETIES OF EARNED INCOME

Earned income is a broad concept that includes many variations of revenue derived from exchange in the marketplace. It is thus important to examine the varieties of earned income in order to analyze basic issues such as the pricing of services, use of an SPO's assets to generate earned income, and the different ways that earned income impacts an SPO's mission and overall income. In addition, examining these variations allows an appreciation of both the purposes of earned income generation, and the blurred boundaries between earned income and other sources of funds such as philanthropy and government support. Broad subcategories of earned income include fees for services, memberships, commercial sales, royalties and license fees, rental income, and special events.

Fees for Service

This is the prototypical variety of earned income – the exchange of an SPO's mainstream services for fee payments. Examples include museum entry fees and tickets for shows in the performing arts, school tuitions, fees for office visits and lab tests in health and mental health services, and

fees for activities at community recreation centers. Fees may be intended
to fully or partially offset costs or possibly to generate net income (profit).
(Note, the term 'profit' is used here generically to connote net operating income or financial surplus, whether or not an SPO is intendedly
profitmaking; in the case of nonprofit organizations, profit may not be
distributed to those who benefit from or control the organization; this is
the so-called *non-distribution of profit constraint*.)

Fees may manifest themselves in different forms including out of pocket
payments and insurance reimbursements as in many health services. In
some cases, fees are paid through government programming such as
school vouchers for charter schools or Medicare or Medicaid reimbursement for health services. Since the latter derive from government they will
be examined further in Chapter 7 on government funding. One reason
for distinguishing such reimbursements from ordinary fee income is that
government usually sets prices rather than responding to the market; hence
SPOs may have little discretion in setting prices or even determining the
precise volume and nature of services.

Memberships

Memberships or subscriptions are fees for bundles of services, rather than
a la carte charges for individual services. Examples include health and
recreation club memberships that allow consumers to engage in a cluster
of activities without separate charges for each, colleges charging by the
year or semester rather than for individual courses, and subscriptions to
seasons of concert and theater performances rather than single shows.
As discussed below, SPOs can sometimes generate more income or have
a greater mission impact, or both, by offering bundled services with
appropriate pricing schedules than to offer individually priced services a
la carte. Membership income also shares a fuzzy border with charitable
contributions in some instances. For example, memberships in museums
or in environmental organizations do not offer a substantial quid pro quo
of payments for private benefits provided. In such cases, memberships are
really honorific designations, usually tax-deductible and better understood
as gifts. However, the border can be extremely blurred, as when museums
provide members with substantial discounts on goods in their gift stores or
free admissions to their special exhibits.

Royalties and Licensing Fees

Many SPOs have property rights to their intellectual capital such as publications, patents and artistic images. These are assets that the SPO may not

seek to exploit directly, for example, through commercial sales of derivative products, but which nonetheless constitute value that can generate an income stream in the marketplace through the sale or leasing of rights to private interests. For example, recordings of performances by orchestras such as the *Chicago Symphony* or the early music group *Apollo's Fire* belong to those organizations but can be sold to others for private listening or sanctioned rebroadcast. Although less tangible, many SPOs also have considerable 'reputational capital' which can be exploited in exchange for a stream of earned income. For example, the logo of a well-regarded SPO such as the *Sierra Club* or *National Public Radio*, has market value that can be leased to the sellers of products bearing those logos. An SPO's lending of its reputational value to commercial interests can of course be fraught with challenges as reputation is often an SPO's most important asset. For example, endorsement of particular medical devices by health care associations such as the American Medical Association (Weisbrod, 1998), or marketing of particular insurance retirement plans by AARP, are damaging if such arrangements raise the specter of mission compromise (Pear, 2008). Recent revelations that health research nonprofits undertaking studies on the benefits of physical fitness were funded by the Coca Cola Company raised suspicions that these SPOs were instruments of Coca Cola to divert attention from the damaging effects of sugary beverage consumption (Editorial Board, 2015). As such, the credibility of those SPOs, having sacrificed their reputational capital, was seriously undermined.

Rental Income

SPOs also possess various other assets capable of generating earned income through appropriate means. SPOs with performance venues may have attractive spaces that are not in constant use which they can rent to external parties for meetings and conferences. Botanical gardens have beautiful grounds for photoshoots of weddings and other celebrations. Schools have expert faculties who may have time available for paid public speaking engagements. Orchestras, botanical gardens, museums, and libraries have specialized research and teaching capacities that can be engaged by educational institutions seeking internship opportunities for their students, museums have artworks in storage that can be leased for exhibition elsewhere, and so on. One clear approach for an SPO to explore new earned income strategies is to examine its special assets, assess whether they are fully utilized in the provision of its mission, and ask whether these assets are marketable in ways that produce net income without inhibiting the pursuit of mission.

Special Events

This category of earned income includes athletic events such as walk-a-thons, luncheon and dinner programs, golf tournaments, auctions and other such "fund-raising" initiatives periodically undertaken by SPOs, particularly charitable nonprofits, to generate net income from entry fees, sales, and donations, as well as to celebrate the organization's work and honor its supporters. Special events straddle the border between earned income and charitable funding. However, such events are usefully thought of as earned income strategies if only because most SPOs would not undertake them if they did not lead to a net increase in operating income or funding for capital projects. Still, it is not uncommon for special events to "lose money" especially where SPOs fail to conceptualize them as earned income ventures that should be appropriately designed, priced and marketed to yield a profit, although such calculations can be complex, possibly requiring projection of future net increases in charitable contributions.

Commercial Income

This refers to income intended to generate profits from commercial sales of goods and services peripheral or incidental to an SPO's mission impact. In the U.S. commercial income unrelated to mission is technically subject to unrelated business income tax (UBIT). However, there are exceptions and nuances involved in distinguishing commercial income from ordinary fee income. For example, do Girl Scout cookie revenues constitute commercial income? Although cookie sales are certainly intended to generate profits, they are also said to be integral to the Girl Scout mission of advancing the education and character development of girls. Whereas ordinary fee income may be intended only to partially offset costs in many cases, commercial income is intentionally profitmaking and not necessarily integral to mission achievement. As discussed below, this distinction affects how commercial services are priced and the role they play in an SPO's financial portfolio and specifically its earned income strategy. Still, the distinction is subtle. As the case of Girl Scouts cookies suggests, it is entirely possible and legitimate for an SPO to make a profit on a service impacting its mission. As another example, an adoption placement organization may profitably place displaced infants with well-to-do prospective parents, using the surpluses to fund other aspects of its child welfare mission. Similarly, a university may profit from its executive education program in order to help support its undergraduate program. In contrast, a university's sponsored cruises for alumni to exotic ports of call or a health charity's sponsored credit card program are more explicitly intended to be profitmaking without substantial aspirations for direct mission impact.

As the discussion here suggests, commercial income is a somewhat broad and vague category that melds with several classes of earned income, including fee income from mission-related services, royalties and licensing fees, rental income and special events. It also blends into gift income in some cases, such as corporate sponsorships or donations associated with memberships or special events. In the discussion of pricing later in the chapter, commercial income may be understood as essentially earned income streams that are driven primarily by the desire to maximize profit.

WHEN TO UNDERTAKE A COMMERCIAL VENTURE

While the distinction between commercial and other types of earned income can be elusive, it is useful to outline the general parameters under which purely profit-maximizing activity, unrelated to mission, should be considered by an SPO. Here is a brief summary of considerations that flow from the benefits theory framework:

- Benefits theory revolves around mission. Thus, the first question to ask is how any proposed earned income venture relates to mission. There are three legitimate possibilities here: First, profit-generation may indeed be a part of an SPO's mission, as would be the case of various forms of social businesses or cooperatives that explicitly balance mission impact and financial returns. Second, it may be the case that profit-maximizing actually contributes simultaneously to mission. For example, an enterprise in a competitive industry such as a bakery or restaurant set up as a for-profit social enterprise that employs challenged workers should, within the constraint of its hiring policies, try to maximize profits since teaching the workers to run a successful business is the principal goal. Third, a commercial venture may simply be intended to maximize profits that would be plowed back into the social mission. This was the case of New York University's pasta company (see below) or indeed *Newman's Own* if the latter corporation is viewed as part of a larger structure to support its selected charities (Newman's Own, 2016).
- Assuming that one of these mission-related justifications holds, the next issue is whether the SPO is well suited or well-advised to carry out the venture. Here, a series of questions should be asked:
  - Does the SPO have a competitive advantage in the marketplace that would allow it to succeed in running a profitable

venture? For example, a botanical garden may simply be the most beautiful place in town to cater a wedding, fully able to compete with other venues. Alternatively, a restaurant run by a social enterprise may have difficulty competing with existing restaurants in its local market area, hence unable to provide the promised private benefits required to make a profit.

- Is there a risk that the venture could have a negative mission impact? For example, might commercialization of the botanical garden space detract from its main purpose to serve and educate visitors or promote horticulture? Would a sponsorship arrangement with a corporation with a dubious record of environmental or labor practices damage the SPO's reputation and hence mission-effectiveness? Could the pursuit of commercial patents by a university impinge on its basic mission to develop and disseminate scientific knowledge? What public, group or redistributive benefits could be lost in these instances?

- Does the venture entail a risk of "mission drift"? For example, will a nonprofit theater's financial success in offering popular musicals divert its attention from its basic mission of supporting local artists and new works, hence reducing the public and group benefits associated with that mission?

- Does the SPO have the administrative capacity and expertise to successfully run or oversee the venture? As noted in Chapter 3 and elsewhere, transactions costs are an important consideration in diversifying to additional sources of income. Without the proper understanding and staff capacity in marketing, accounting, billing and so on, a commercial initiative may be ill-advised.

- What are the "opportunity costs" associated with the investment required to undertake a commercial venture? What mission-related benefits might be forgone by investment in the commercial venture rather than another program? For example, what group, public or redistributive benefits might be lost by renting a social service agency's meeting space to outside parties?

These questions are, of course, relevant to all earned income projects, though brought into stark relief for purely commercial initiatives.

Commercial and other earned income opportunities often stem from the malleability of private/public goods distinctions, as well as the associated assets that SPOs can bring to bear, which allow them to think creatively about their potentials to generate earned income. In particular, the ability to generate earned revenue revolves around the issue of property rights and nuances of the tax code, as well as ownership of physical and intellectual assets. For example, a nonprofit educational or research institution may essentially provide mission-focused public goods but also accumulate intellectual property, reputational capital, physical plant or tax credits which it can sell or lease in various ways that can yield commercial income. The documentation and examination of underutilized assets of various types can be a good starting point for developing ideas for potential commercial income generation initiatives.

The Basics of Pricing

All of the various subcategories of earned income have in common the charging of prices in exchange for private (excludable, often rival) benefits to individual or institutional purchasers. Fundamental to all such transactions is the design of appropriate pricing strategies tuned to the particular goals of an SPO's earned income development activities (see Seaman, 2010). Because many SPOs produce goods and services whose benefits are private in nature, they are able to charge fees for their services. The types and levels of service pricing must, however, be sensitive to the organization's mission which may require that fees be designed to minimize exclusion of important target audiences. Thus, in comparison with purely commercial enterprises, SPOs do not generally design their fees schedules to maximize net revenue. Rather they may seek to follow a number of different pricing rationales consistent with the goals of particular services. For example, they may choose to only partially offset costs, given externalities (public benefits) associated with the private good; or they may seek to cross-subsidize one group of service recipients with profits from another. Similarly, SPOs may choose to undertake commercial ventures ancillary to their missions, with the understanding that their surpluses will support the organization's general operations or its accumulation of growth capital. Accordingly, a variety of SPO pricing strategies are explored here.

WHEN TO CHARGE

SPOs make explicit decisions about which services they offer for free, and which they offer without charge. For example, a study of Jewish Community Centers (Wilsker and Young, 2010; see Chapter 11 for further discussion) found that JCCs generally charge for programs such as religious education, camping, early childhood programs, swimming lessons, community theater and general access to fitness facilities through membership, but offer community lecture and meeting programs, day care and transportation for the elderly, youth groups and mentoring programs without charge. There are many situations, of course, where it is technically feasible or at least conceivable for SPOs to charge for services, but which are not easily amenable to the implementation of pricing. One possibility is that administration of a pricing regime might be too expensive, that is the "transactions costs" associated with putting in place and running a price-based system may outweigh the potential income return. For example, a nonprofit such as Park Pride in Atlanta (see Chapter 10) which helps neighborhoods develop their parks and recreation facilities is in no position to cordon off an improved park area in order to restrict it to paying customers. Even if legally and physically feasible it would probably be too expensive or aesthetically or morally objectionable. Similarly, collecting fees assumes a certain administrative infrastructure that may not be available to an organization of modest internal capacity. For example, many universities can potentially offer fee-based executive education or community lectures; such services are rival and excludable and colleges and universities can draw on the expertise of their faculties to offer programs with unique information and character. But not all such institutions have conference centers and staff trained to market programs, collect and expend the revenues, and carry out the various business functions necessary to run an efficient, secure operation at a profitable scale.

Cultural barriers may also inhibit SPOs' decisions to price a service. Some services are conceived as free from the outset, as an intrinsic aspect of social mission, and charging for them can create substantial organizational and community distress. For example, the Free Clinic in Cleveland was established to provide free urgent care to low income and homeless residents who lack health insurance. The Clinic is supported by contributions and volunteer effort. To begin to charge fees would be a seismic shift for the culture of the organization and the manner in which it operates. Nonetheless, it will be interesting to see what decisions are made in the future, especially given the uncertainty of universal health coverage under the Affordable Care Act.

Such examples occur in various other fields as well, including education and the arts. For example The Cleveland Museum of Art (see Chapter 8) was established by its founders in the early 20th century with the explicit stipulation that its collection be available to members of the community without charge. To this day, admission to the museum and viewing of its permanent collection remain free, although CMA has found other strategies for generating earned income including its gift shops and charges for special exhibitions. In the field of education, Cooper Union College offers another telling example (see Chapter 8). Again, based on the intent of the founder, and generous philanthropic funding, both undergraduate and graduate education in science and the arts were offered tuition-free for over a century, with students admitted solely on their merits. This changed in 2013 when the institution, under financial stress, decided to implement a tuition schedule sensitive to ability to pay. In a strictly economic sense, this should not have caused an uproar among students, faculty and alumni – higher education clearly exhibits the characteristics of a private good (with positive externalities) that enables the common practice of institutions of higher education charging tuitions as one of their most important income streams. But for Cooper Union, the prospect of tuition ran against the historical and cultural grain, raising fears of lost organizational identity and possible drift from its mission of serving the most talented students without regard to ability to pay.

ALTERNATIVE PRICING POLICY GOALS

The cases of institutions such as the CMA and Cooper Union suggest how important it is to be clear about the purpose of charging fees, in order to set prices for any particular good or service. Typically an SPO will offer more than one good or service, and the goals for alternative offerings may be very different. For example, CMA may intend for its gift store to generate profits to help support its general operations, while it may seek broad community attendance of its special exhibits, perhaps within certain cost constraints. Similarly, Cooper Union could offer special executive education programming for corporate executives with the intent of earning extra net income, while it prices its regular degree programs to ensure that it serves the most talented possible student body in arts and sciences.

In fact, there are at least four general reasons for an SPO to consider charging for its services. The first is obviously to generate revenue to help offset costs of a mission-related service. A second is to generate net profits which may be used to subsidize free or reduced priced services for target groups or to support or expand mission impact in other ways (see James and Young, 2007). The third is more subtle – to enable a more efficient use of scarce resources. In particular, SPOs want to allocate their limited resources and services to their most highly valued uses, for example, by serving those who put the most value on the benefits and services they are receiving, and by ensuring that the organization's assets (for example, space, expertise) are used as efficiently as possible. Pricing strategies can often help to achieve these goals. Fourth, pricing of services can sometimes directly enhance mission effectiveness, for example by increasing consumer or staff commitment to services which they pay for. Accordingly, pricing strategies can be sorted into the following goal-related categories: (a) pricing to maximize profit; (b) pricing to maximize mission-related social benefits; (c) pricing to improve the efficiency of internal resource allocation and use of assets; and (d) pricing to enhance motivation or commitment of clients and staff.

Pricing for Maximum Profit

Some SPO services are simply intended to raise net funds to support general operations or other mission-focused activities. These services differ little from commercial business in their intent or the manner in which they should be run. Museum gift shops are a common example; although they may serve an ancillary purpose of distributing items that reflect great art or advertise the museum's name and logo, they are essentially meant to generate profits and would not be maintained if they lost money. Fund-raising special events, for example marathons, walk-a-thons, and golf tournaments are meant to generate profits. These activities may entail elements of cultivation for future donors and promoting awareness of the organization's work, but these goals are usually ancillary to the primary revenue-generating goal. Finally, SPOs may choose to own and possibly directly administer businesses unrelated to their missions, for which they presumably will pay a tax on profits, such as the U.S. Unrelated-Business Income Tax (UBIT). Indeed, the origins of UBIT stem from New York University's ownership of the Mueller Macaroni Company which generated large tax-free profits for the university in the first half of the twentieth century but which caused resentment over "unfair competition" by other pasta makers. The UBIT law now requires that nonprofit organizations pay tax on profits from such operations in order to "even the playing field." However, many nonprofit commercial enterprises remain untaxed because they can demonstrate a relationship between those activities and mission. For example, Girl Scouts do not pay taxes on their cookie sales and museums avoid taxes on their gift shop sales. Nonetheless, within broad parameters, these activities are intended to run at a maximum profit, within some constraints such as the purposive engagement of community volunteers or restriction to key locations that can be associated with the mainstream museum exhibits (such as in-house stores or website operations).

A good example of pricing for profit is provided by Goodwill Industries which runs a very successful thrift store operation. These stores sell donated goods which are deemed of sufficient quality to justify commercial sales, and they train and employ qualified staff and price their merchandise for maximum financial return. These stores are not considered supported work programs wherein employees with handicaps operate in protective conditions. Rather, the mission of Goodwill is "to put people to work." Its programs are designed to help unemployed, challenged and low income citizens to move into productive jobs in the broader economy. The thrift shops constitute a key earned income strategy for Goodwill to support its other work training and placement programs, thus requiring it to price its goods to sell as profitably as possible. Admittedly, the attraction for consumers to shop at Goodwill is not only low prices, the variety of recycled goods and the friendly service, but also the understanding that profits are used to support Goodwill's job-generating mission-focused programs. That does help provide Goodwill with a competitive advantage but it does not change its intent to maximize its profits from thrift shop sales. Hence, thrift shop sales are priced accordingly.

The actual specification of price schedules to achieve profit maximization obviously requires market research and experimentation. Standard economic texts emphasize the principle that prices should be set where the marginal cost of selling the next unit of a good or service is just offset by the marginal revenue that it brings in (Young and Steinberg, 1995). In the case of competitive markets, as is likely for thrift shop sales, cookie sales, executive training, and so on, SPOs should research the prevailing market price and expand their sales so long as the extra (marginal) cost of doing so is less than the price received. In cases where the SPO may have some "market power" because of its special brand name or customer loyalty (such as Girl Scout cookies) some experimentation may be worthwhile, because raising or lowering the price has two effects: an incremental price increase leads to fewer units sold but at a higher price; similarly, an incremental price decrease will sell more units at a lower price. The question then becomes whether the increase or decrease in volume will lead to higher or lower profits. The answer depends on what economists call the "price elasticity of demand"; if demand is price elastic, meaning that a 1 percent decrease in price will lead to more than a 1 percent increase in demand, then the best policy is to lower the price. Similarly if demand is price inelastic, that is, a 1 percent decrease in price will lead to less than a 1 percent increase in demand, then the best policy is to increase the price. SPOs can experiment at the margin with their prices to determine the price elasticity of demand, or they can rely on market studies or other sources of information. In any case, if the goal is profit-maximizing for a particular good or service, an SPO should behave like a conventional profit-seeking business in setting its price.

Pricing to Maximize Mission Impact

As discussed in Chapter 4, SPO services must often take into account both "externalities" and "redistributive" considerations, consonant with the SPO's mission. For example, providing a superb education to excellent students presumably results in general social benefits over and above what may be reflected in students' own willingness to pay, such as intellectual and technological innovations leading to better health, productivity, and environmental and cultural advancements, or generation of new wealth that can be taxed to support society's less fortunate members. These externalities suggest that pricing take into account community-wide (group or public) benefits implied by the SPO's mission. Similarly, an SPO's mission may reflect the notion of fairness and equal opportunity, regardless of direct social benefits; if an SPO intends that consumers not be excluded because of inability to pay, pricing policies must reflect that intent. If there are such mission-related social benefits associated with the consumption of certain SPO services, then pricing policy should reflect these benefits. For example, providing pre-school programming, especially in low income communities, may be associated with long-term educational, public health and safety, and productivity benefits that would not be fully accounted for in consumer (parent) demand. Hence pricing solely for profit would exclude consumers who may be "profitable" from a social point of view but not from the SPO's purely financial point of view. In theory, in this case, the SPO should lower its prices beyond the profit-maximizing level so as to accommodate additional consumers who are otherwise excluded by the price. There are various ways of approaching this issue: The SPO could lower its price to the point where it simply breaks even on the stipulated service. Or, it could lower the price even further (by subsidizing the program from other sources – for example, grants that reflect the public benefits) to a level where it is satisfied that it is doing the most it can to maximize the total of social and private benefits. Or, it could try to develop a more sophisticated differential price schedule that brings in more revenue as it extends services to lower paying consumers. Consider each of these strategies in turn:

Lowering the price to reflect mission
This is a straightforward strategy premised on the assumption that the social benefits of providing additional services past the point of profit maximization outweigh losses of profit. In this case, the SPO can lower its price (and concomitantly expand its output to meet the additional demand) up to the breakeven point where total revenues equal total costs of providing the service; or if funding is allocated from another source,

it can lower its price (and expand output) until its losses reach the level of available subsidy. An SPO with greater analytical sophistication might try to go one step further, by estimating the value of the social benefits it provides (per unit of consumption) and then setting its level of subsidy accordingly.

For example, an SPO that provides inoculations against infectious diseases can assume that charging a fee well below the profit-maximizing level would be socially worthwhile because the benefits associated with reducing the risks of contagion are commensurate with the private benefits of preventing infection for those choosing to be vaccinated. Thus a decision to set a price that would maximize the number of inoculations subject to breaking even, or even subsidizing the price further from other sources (perhaps even providing the service for free) could very well make good sense. Similarly, in higher education, students rarely pay the full sticker price, and indeed the sticker price itself is set well below the profit-maximizing price. This is particularly the case in public universities where the state pays a substantial portion of the cost (in recognition of the public benefits ascribed to a college educated citizenry) and universities are expected to make up the difference through (below market) tuitions and fees. The case of private universities is somewhat different. While they usually draw on philanthropy rather than government to underwrite tuitions, their sticker prices are closer to profit maximizing values. However, as nonprofit organizations with social missions to educate the public and increase knowledge, they too are motivated to account for social as well as private benefits by holding down tuitions. However, they tend to do so in a more complex way – both by holding down the sticker price (for example, through subsidies from philanthropy and investment income) and also by offering discounts (scholarships) to students according to their families' abilities to pay. Differential pricing can serve a number of different objectives, including accommodation of consumers with limited abilities to pay and generation of additional revenues by charging more to those who can pay.

Differential pricing

When an organization sets a single price for a given service, the prospective consumers of that service fall into two broad categories – those who are unwilling to pay the price and choose not to purchase it, and those who value the service at least as much as the stipulated price. The dividing line between these two groups is defined by those consumers at the margin whose valuation is just equal to the price they pay. This situation, which is reflected in the conventional downward sloping demand curve in microeconomic theory, sets the stage for two kinds of opportunities for

SPOs. First, the SPO can try to generate additional revenues by charging higher prices to the second group; next, it can try to provide additional benefits by offering lower prices to the first group. This approach is called *price discrimination* in the for-profit realm and often dubbed *sliding scales* in the nonprofit world. However, for-profits and nonprofits usually engage in differential pricing for different reasons. Generally, businesses are trying to increase profits by "milking the demand curve," converting consumer surplus into additional profits. In contrast, nonprofits often use sliding scales to accommodate low income members of their target groups while drawing additional revenues from those willing to pay more. Still, SPOs also can use differential pricing to maximize profits where this is appropriate, in which case they would again imitate the behavior of conventional businesses.

The general problem with differential pricing is the difficulty of identifying what each consumer is actually willing to pay, or finding criteria that correlate well with such propensity. Asking consumers directly does not work unless there is some coercion involved, since there is little incentive for consumers to report their willingness to pay accurately if they believe this will lead to being charged more or being disqualified from lower prices. Thus, in the for-profit world, firms use proxies such as age (such as, seniors, children) and residential location to set differential price schedules. SPOs may also do the same. For example, museums may set discounted prices for children and seniors. However, SPOs can often go further, for example by insisting on verifiable information on family income (for example, copies of tax returns) prior to determining charges for a social service, health care or education. This is common practice in private higher education where, as noted, few students pay the sticker price, and financial assistance is determined on an individual basis. Note too that SPOs (as opposed to profit seeking businesses) may have an easier time asking well-off customers to pay more. For example, parents of preschoolers may feel that their children will benefit from exposure to a diverse set of classmates from different ethnic and economic backgrounds and that the SPO will use their fee premiums to pursue this goal. As a result, they may be willing to pay more in order to ensure that less wealthy families can pay prices affordable to them.

Again, it is important for SPOs to be clear about the goals behind a differential pricing strategy. A sliding scale intended to increase net revenues will be different from a sliding scale intended to accommodate a low income target group. Moreover, these objectives can be combined in various ways to generate a net profit, breakeven or limit net loss, through suitably designed differential pricing schedules.

Finally, SPOs must be aware of the various challenges to designing and implementing differential pricing schemes. Finding ways to accurately identify who is willing to pay what is probably the biggest challenge overall. In addition, one must be sure that products sold at lower prices to some groups cannot be resold to others who would not qualify for discounts. Since most SPOs offer services that cannot be transferred from one client to another, this is usually not a great problem. However, there are exceptions. For example, age-specific price setting in areas such as the arts can be problematic unless one is willing to check IDs at the box office.

A more serious problem may be resentment or stigma associated with paying different prices for the same services. Those who are asked to pay more may question why they must do so, and those who receive substantial discounts can be stigmatized if proper precautions for anonymity are not taken and an SPO's reasons for differential pricing are not made transparent. Students in private colleges and universities will compare notes on what they are paying, but informed and enlightened parents will generally understand why such a policy is desirable.

The following stylized example illustrates how differential pricing can serve alternative SPO goals and how such a policy, if it can be practically implemented and accepted, can be superior to a single price scheme.

Suppose that a community center such as a YMCA or a JCC offers swimming lessons for children. Also assume that instructors are hired by the hour and that there is plenty of room in the pool and time in the schedule to accommodate children without limit. As a nonprofit organization the community center may have various goals in offering this service. The management of the center may view it simply as a profitmaking initiative, ancillary to its primary mission as a venue for community activities and recreation. Or managers may see it as a mainstream service for which they would like to maximize participation. And they may be especially concerned that children from low income families have the opportunity to take the swimming lessons.

Further suppose that the center has assembled the following information, as summarized in Table 5.1: Swimming lessons require individual one-hour sessions and instructors cost $20 per hour. From a market study, the center has determined that there are 100 children from high income families in the community willing to pay $50 per lesson, another 100 children from middle income families willing to pay $30 per lesson, an additional 100 children from low income families willing to pay $10 per lesson, and numerous additional children wanting lessons from very poor families but who cannot afford to pay anything.

As Table 5.1 illustrates, under a single price scheme, if the goal of the program is just to make money (in order to support the organization and its other programs) it can charge $50 per lesson, make a profit of $3000

Table 5.1   Pricing swimming lessons

	Price ($)	Revenue ($)	Cost ($)	Profit/Loss ($)	Children served
Max profit, one price	50	5000	2000	3000	100
Max service, one price	30 or	6000	4000	2000	200
	10	3000	6000	−3000	300
Max profit, multiple prices	30	3000	2000	4000	200
	50	5000	2000		
Max service, multiple prices	0	0	3000	0	450
	10	1000	2000		
	30	3000	2000		
	50	5000	2000		

and serve 100 children. Or if its goal is to maximize service under a single price scheme, it could choose among two options depending on its preference to run a profit or sustain a loss and serve more or fewer children: in particular, it could charge $30, serve 200 children and run a profit of $2000, or it could charge $10, serve 300 children and run a loss of $3000.

However, introducing a sliding scale allows the organization to do better, no matter its goal. A two-price scheme ($50 and $30) could increase profit to $4000 with service to 200 children, and a four-price scheme ($50, $30, $10, $0) would allow the center to serve 450 children and breakeven. In other words, differential pricing can facilitate either increasing profits or increasing service or both. The main problem with a multiple level price policy of course is to implement a system for identifying the families who can pay the alternative prices. One approach to allow the community center to do this without excessive cost or stigma, would simply be to ask applicants to voluntarily select the charge that applies to them and charge them accordingly, counting on their understanding and goodwill to participate honestly. Alternatively, the nominal price could be set at $50 and applicants could be asked to apply for discounts of $20, $40 or $50 by certifying their eligibility.

Pricing to Improve Efficiency

Pricing itself can be a mechanism for improving an SPO's own efficiency, that is, its mission and financial performance can be enhanced by using prices in a manner that provides better incentives for efficient use of resources, services and assets. In this category, we can consider such pricing

Table 5.2   Yoga classes: uniform versus congestion pricing

Prices	Demand at A	Demand at B	Total revenue	Profit	Users
$10/$10	40	10	$300	$100	30
$15/$5	20	20	$400	$200	40

strategies as the bundling of services into packages (such as memberships or subscriptions) or congestion pricing to make better use of facilities, for example, by spreading demand over time or among alternative venues.

In general, prices serve as incentives to change the behavior of consumers. SPOs can exploit this understanding to improve the effectiveness with which they address their missions and the efficiency with which they are able to use their resources, through pricing strategies such as congestion pricing and package pricing.

Congestion pricing
The idea behind congestion pricing is to "spread out" service demands over time or space so that the SPO can limit its costs while continuing to meet its mission obligations. The success of this strategy depends on creating incentives for customers or clients to change their patterns of consumption, based on the nature of their individual demands. For example, some Sunday museum goers might be willing to visit on Wednesdays when the museum is less crowded, especially if the admission charge was lower on Wednesdays. This in turn would enable the museum to limit its extra staffing on Sundays, make better use of its core staff on Wednesdays and avoid costs of capacity expansion to accommodate peak Sunday crowds. A stylized example of how this can work is given in the following example, sketched in Table 5.2.

Suppose a health center runs two facilities in alternative locations and offers yoga classes in each. (Different times of day or different instructors can be substituted for alternative locations for the two facilities in this example. The concept of congestion pricing is broadly applicable in this respect.) Suppose further that the capacity at each facility is 20 and expansion (additional classes) at either facility is not possible because of other constraints. As the table shows, the classes at facility A are in higher demand, perhaps because of accessibility, ambience or staffing. If the organization charges a single price for a yoga class, it will be oversubscribed at A (requiring 20 potential users to go unserved) and underutilized at B (10 empty slots). Overall, 30 users will be accommodated and a net profit of $100 will be secured. However, if classes can be differentially priced by location (say $15 at A and $5 at B) demand is likely to shift from A to B, allowing B to run at capacity and A to avoid turning users away. The result in this hypothetical example is full accommodation of 40 users and doubling of profit to $200 (in addition to potential savings from avoiding facility expansion at A).

Consideration of congestion pricing may be appropriate in any circumstance where demand for a fee-based service varies over time, among locations or even among parallel offerings of the same service that may differ by quality characteristics. For example, universities might consider differential tuition levels among its alternative campuses, for alternative courses of varying interest and popularity or even among sessions of the same course featuring different instructors or offered at alternative times of the year or in different (intensive, traditional and online) formats. (Indeed, professional sports teams now vary prices of games, according to the popularity of their opponents, a practice called dynamic pricing.) Similar opportunities may present themselves to a wide variety of SPOs that charge fees for services with the excludability characteristics of private goods, including performing arts organizations, community health centers, counseling organizations, or recreational programs.

Package pricing

Package pricing or "bundling" is the practice of charging a single price for two or more services offered together. For example, performing arts organizations offer subscription packages for multiple performances, colleges charge by the semester rather than for individual courses, and community centers offer memberships that include access to clusters of their multiple activities and facilities. There are several possible advantages to package pricing. For one, package pricing can reduce transactions costs, that is, the extra costs associated with the collection of fees for many different services rather than just one membership or subscription fee. For example, it would be costly and logistically difficult for a YMCA to charge separately for use of its fitness machines, swimming pool, basketball court and locker room accommodations. A single membership or day usage fee is more practical and less costly. Similarly, it would be costly and disruptive for an orchestra to charge separately for listening to different pieces in a concert program. The cost of moving people in and out of the concert hall, and collecting separate fees for each feature, would likely outweigh any revenue advantage.

Moreover there can be mission-related benefits associated with package pricing. Few members of a health club are likely to take advantage of lectures on nutrition or stress reduction if priced separately from their memberships but they might well try these services if they are included in the membership fee. If the SPO's mission is to improve community health, it may achieve a greater impact by including such classes in its package pricing scheme. Similarly, an orchestra whose mission is to advance public appreciation of classical music may choose to include avant-garde selections or the work of unfamiliar composers in its concert subscription packages, so as to expose its audiences to art that they may not have chosen to purchase a la carte. For example, mixing some Schoenberg or Philip Glass in with pieces by Beethoven and Mozart can educate audiences to a fuller range of musical composition than they might have had otherwise.

The art of package pricing hinges on formulating packages and prices that are more favorable to consumers than a la carte purchasing. This is possible when alternative groups of consumers each value the components of service packages at different levels. Without package pricing, they would buy various a la carte combinations. With package pricing they may each purchase the package, with consequent increases in the benefits they experience and the revenue secured by the SPO. Consider another stylized example. Suppose a community center offers two general types of services – those which are child-focused such as playrooms, kiddie pools, team sports and day camps, and those which are more adult-focused such as lap pools, workout equipment and fitness training. Further suppose that there are two kinds of families who are potential members, with 100 such families in each category – family type A with young children who put a high value on child-focused programs but would also like to take advantage of adult health services; and family type B consisting of two or more adults and older children who prefer the adult health services but would also occasionally like to accommodate visiting friends and relatives with younger children. Table 5.3 estimates the (annual) value that each of these family types may put on each of these categories of services. The question is whether the SPO should price these services separately or as a single membership package.

Assume that the SPO would like to maximize its revenues and provide as much service as possible to each of these groups of families. Under an a la carte strategy it could charge $600 for child-focused services and $300 for adult-focused services. As a result, the 100 child-oriented families would

Table 5.3   Valuations of alternative services by family type

	Child recreation services	Adult health services
Family Type A: child-focused	$600	$300
Family Type B: adult-focused	$250	$500

purchase the former, yielding revenue of $60,000 and both family types would purchase the adult-focused services yielding an additional $60,000 for a total of $120,000.

Consider now, a package price of $750 for both types of services. Each of these family types would derive at least $750 in value for the package, yielding a total revenue of 200 x $750 = $150,000. Thus the package price increases both revenue and utilization of the SPOs services and provides maximum access for both types of families.

PRICING TO IMPROVE PARTICIPATION

Paying for a service can enhance the commitment of clients who consume the service and staff who provide it. This often applies to services provided to needy groups where the desire to maximize access is in tension with the tendency of both consumers and providers to take free services less seriously and hence produce or consume them less effectively. One issue here is that the effectiveness of many SPO services depends as much on the effort and commitment of clients and consumers as it does on the efforts of the organization itself. Social service and mental health clients, students in educational programs, and participants in job training or community lecture programs, cannot be well served if they don't show up or if they don't invest enough of their own time and effort. In some cases, the charging of a fee can enhance rather than limit participation because price may serve as a signal of value or it may preserve the dignity of prospective consumers who don't want to be viewed or treated as charity cases. In any case, clients may be more motivated if they have "some skin in the game." Similarly, if an SPO serves both paying clients and recipients of free service, its staff may tend to take the latter's needs less seriously or give them less attention out of concern for retaining paying customers or out of belief that nonpaying consumers aren't as worthy.

In these various cases, the presence of a fee is more important than its level. For example, elderly residents may be more likely to use a special bus service to a community center if they are charged a nominal fee than if it is offered with no charge, simply as a matter of preserving their dignity. And school children from poor families are less likely to feel stigmatized if they pay a small fee and are not openly identified as receiving free lunches. Finally, *charging in advance* for the provision of a service can increase participation because clients are likely to feel obligated to use services for which they have already paid. Educational institutions interested in increasing participation in community lecture programs or associations wanting to draw attendance at conferences for members are well-advised to collect fees in advance. While such behavior contradicts the idea that making participation decisions on the basis of "sunk costs" (nonrefundable fees paid before the event) is irrational (Young and Steinberg, 1995), this is how people often actually behave.

SOME INTERESTING CASES

The Fox Theatre

The Fox Theatre in Atlanta earns almost all of its income through box office sales. It is an entertainment venue in a beautiful renovated Art Deco theater that was rescued from demolition in the 1970s (Fox Theatre, 2016). The Fox's offerings are generally commercial fare including Broadway shows such as Wicked or Jersey Boys, popular music groups such as the B-52s, and celebrity entertainers such as Neil Young and Yanni. Indeed, the Fox does not lay claim to providing or preserving classical cultural art like traditional orchestras, community theaters, or art museums do. It clearly provides a private good, with ticket prices designed to fill the house and make a profit, with limited concession to potentially excluded consumer groups such as school children or low income citizens. Still, it operates as a charitable nonprofit, following the rules of non-distribution of financial surpluses and it is governed by a board with community-oriented sensibilities. Given the nature of its services, however, it is not surprising that the Fox's income is predominately fee revenue. What is perhaps surprising is why it operates as a nonprofit. The answer lies in two other streams of benefits that it produces, which are of a more public nature. First, it preserves an historic theater venue that would have been lost to demolition had community efforts not saved it. Second, the Fox became a model for historical theater preservation and now works with such theaters at risk in other cities through its Fox Theatre Institute. A further nuance is that the management of the Fox purposely avoids seeking charitable contributions because it is so capable of relying on earned revenue and does not wish to compete for donations with other local nonprofit institutions, hence implicitly supporting other kinds of public goods. The Fox does, however, accept corporate sponsorships for which they offer public recognition in exchange for sponsorship fees. An example is the Coca Cola Summer Film Festival which it hosts. A risk associated with this source of support is the potential alienation of other such sponsors. For example, Delta dropped its long-term sponsorship of the Fox when it hosted a show for Qatar Airways (Atlanta Journal Constitution, 2016).

Famicos

Famicos is a community development corporation established in 1970 following the Hough riots in Cleveland. The mission of the Famicos Foundation is "to improve the quality of life in greater Cleveland through neighborhood revitalization, affordable housing and integrated social services" (Famicos, 2016). Its direct beneficiaries are elderly, low income, and disabled residents in that part of the city where it operates. Clearly it offers services that can be characterized as redistributive goods – essentially private goods such as housing, and a cluster of integrated social services which require subsidy in order to be affordable to its target group. Famicos also provides services with the character of public goods. In particular, it rehabilitates and refurbishes historic buildings and promotes the economic development of its district, reducing blight and crime, encouraging (retail) business enterprise, and preserving the city's architectural heritage.

Given the nature of its clientele and its provision of public and redistributive goods, one might expect Famicos to rely primarily on government funding. However, the organization has developed an interesting income strategy that allows it to generate almost 60 percent of its revenue from fees, with 30 percent from government and another 10 percent slice from charitable gifts. A portion of the fee revenue is easy to appreciate; as a provider of affordable housing it charges rent within parameters that accommodate residents' abilities to pay. But another portion derives indirectly from government because Famicos qualifies for tax credits for its affordable housing and historic preservation activities, credits that it cannot use directly, given its tax exempt status, but which it can sell to private developers. In fact, Famicos conceives itself as a property manager and has developed a sophisticated income strategy reflecting a multifaceted approach to its affordable housing mission that includes historic preservation, retail development, new construction and rehabilitation, lease-purchase homeownership opportunities, affordable rental options and homes for market rate sale. Famicos has also taken on large-scale development projects that offer affordable homes for more than 1,000 families and individuals.

Famicos recognizes that almost everyone can pay something for housing at long as such cost does not overwhelm one's personal budget. Thus its policy is to limit rent to 30 percent of individual or family income. This produces a substantial income stream without excluding members of the target audience it is designed to serve. Famicos also engages in historical preservation by buying, renovating and using or selling architecturally significant older buildings in its district. Both its historical preservation activity and its affordable housing policies qualify Famicos for the tax credits that it sells to private developers, converting the public benefits it produces into a private commodity to generate another earned income stream. One may argue, of course, that, as benefits theory would stipulate, Famicos is essentially receiving income from government for its provision of public and redistributive goods. However, the sale of credits shows up as fee income on Famicos's books and represents a creative earned income strategy based on the fact that the tax credits, once earned, are rival and excludable, and marketable to private real estate developers.

Madi Apparel

Another, very young, SPO that relies on earned income is *MADI Apparel*, an LLC for-profit company in Kansas City which maintains a nonprofit subsidiary called MADI Donations (MADI Apparel, 2016). MADI has the unusual mission of contributing women's underwear to charitable institutions such as domestic violence shelters, disaster relief organizations, and hospital rape crisis centers. It was founded in 2012 by Hayley Besheer who learned from a family member, once a victim of domestic violence, that underwear was the most needed and under-donated item to organizations that help vulnerable and victimized women. MADI Apparel manufactures and sells women's underwear, following fair labor and environmental sustainability practices, and donates one item to its foundation for each one that it sells in the private marketplace (a practice developed by other socially focused companies such as Tom's Shoes). The foundation also allows MADI to receive charitable gifts to support its distributions operation. In 2015, the foundation received approximately $42,000 in income, composed mostly of cash donations but also including sales of tickets to, and items sold, in a silent auction of externally donated items. Overall, MADI utilizes an interesting business model based largely on earned income through underwear sales. These sales support the business (LLC), and allow profit to the owners, but also underwrite the charitable purpose through donation of goods to the nonprofit which then executes the mission-related programming. The nonprofit itself supplements this support from the LLC with monetary and in-kind gifts from external donors. MADI is able to compete in the underwear market because of its special appeal to customers, not only because of the intrinsic quality of its product but as importantly its connection to a larger social purpose. In addition, the LLC's pricing policy reflects social goals rather than profit maximizing, as it essentially sells its items at two for the price one to support its social purpose.

Famicos, the Fox Theatre and MADI Apparel are just three of many examples of SPOs that have found ways to generate reliable earned income streams from activities consistent with their social missions. In each of these cases, pricing is a critical issue. For the Fox, prices need to reflect a profit maximizing mentality, with some acknowledgment of community sensitivities; for Famicos, pricing must accommodate social goals more explicitly while generating sufficient earned income to sustain the organization; for MADI prices must be high enough to cover the expenses of the LLC, including some profit, while accommodating the two for one policy in a competitive marketplace. All SPOs seeking to generate earned income face these kinds of tensions though in varying proportions.

SUMMARY AND PERSPECTIVE

Many SPOs depend on earned income as their primary source of financing, and many others rely on it for a substantial proportion of their income. Securing earned income depends on SPOs' provision of services that have the character of private goods – those which can be withheld from individuals if payment is not received (excludable) and whose benefits are substantially individual (rival) rather than simultaneously shared with others. Earned income reflects a quid pro quo of revenue for services received and individualized benefits provided. That said, earned income is often tied to goods and services that are not entirely private in nature, for example, involving redistributive elements or positive externalities, hence requiring supplementation from other sources of finance.

Within this generic framework, earned income exhibits a wide variety of forms, including direct fees for mission-related services, commercial venture profits, membership packages, licensing fees, rental income, and special events. In some cases, the prices of services offered for a fee by SPOs may be set externally or determined entirely in competitive markets. In these instances, SPOs have no control over price and must simply decide how much of what kinds of service to offer. For example, earned income generated to capture insurance reimbursements or government vouchers for schools or housing, is based on externally determined rate schedules. In many other cases, SPOs have discretion to set prices as well as quantities of services offered.

In all cases it is critical for SPOs to be clear about the goals served by their earned income (price and quantity) strategies. These goals may include revenue generation for the purpose of offsetting costs of mission-related services, net profit generation, maximal service provision within a breakeven constraint, maximal service provision given a stipulated level of subsidy from other sources, improving efficiency by structuring prices to influence consumer behavior and use of assets such as space and time more efficiently, and motivating consumers to participate and staff to be more conscientious.

While some SPO earned income initiatives are solely intended to generate net revenues, most are associated with providing social (group, public, redistributive) as well as private benefits. Consequently, earned income strategy must be coordinated with the generation of income from other sources such as philanthropy or government support. Thus prices may be contingent on the availability of charitable or government funds, in order to ensure that groups targeted by an SPO's mission are fully served (as in the case of affordable housing) or that consumption generates the desired level of external benefits (as in the case of education).

Finally, the generation of earned income entails transactions costs and requires certain expertise and skills and costs associated with the effective marketing of services, the proper collection and administration of payments, and a culture consistent with market transactions. Thus, while an SPO may generate, or potentially provide, considerable private benefits it is not always sensible to pursue earned income to reflect those benefits. For example, a small nonprofit organization solely supported by volunteer efforts and charitable gifts may not be ready to pursue an earned income project. An institution that has been historically committed to free service may find it costly to change. Even a larger, sophisticated SPO may not have particular expertise in market-based provision. In sum, adding earned revenue, or expanding its role in an SPO's income portfolio requires a deliberate assessment. Nonetheless, over the long term it makes eminent sense for an SPO that provides goods and services with private goods characteristics to cultivate earned income to reflect the private value it offers, or can potentially offer, to consumers of its services.

REFERENCES

Atlanta Journal Constitution, 2016. Retrieved on December 13, 2016 from www.ajc.com/news/business/delta-exec-on-fox-theatre-spat-not-trying-to-threa/nrQmx/ May 20.

Editorial Board, 2015. "A Defense of Sugary Soda That Fizzled for Coke", *New York Times*, p. A22, December 5.

Famicos, 2016. http://famicos.org/mission/.

Fox Theater, 2016. http://foxtheatre.org/the-fox-story/.

Estelle James and Dennis R. Young, 2007. "Fee Income and Commercial Ventures", Chapter 5 in Dennis R. Young (ed.), *Financing Nonprofits: Putting Theory Into Practice*, Lanham, MD: AltaMira Press, pp. 93–199.

MADI Apparel, 2016. www.madiapparel.com/pages/our-story.

Newman's Own, 2016. www.newmansown.com/charity/.

Robert Pear, 2008. "AARP Orders Investigation Concerning Its Marketing", *New York Times*, p. A18, November 18.

Bruce A. Seaman, 2010. "Pricing Strategies", Chapter 10 in Bruce A. Seaman and Dennis R. Young (eds), *Handbook of Research on Nonprofit Economics and Management*, Cheltenham, UK and Northampton, MA, USA: Edward Elgar Publishing, pp. 142–155.

Burton A. Weisbrod, 1998. "The Nonprofit Mission and Its Financing: Growing Links between Nonprofits and the Rest of the Economy", Chapter 1 in Burton A. Weisbrod (ed.), *To Profit or Not to Profit?*, New York: Cambridge University Press, pp. 1–22.

Amanda L. Wilsker and Dennis R. Young, 2010. "How Does Program Composition Affect the Revenues of Nonprofit Organizations?: Investigating a Benefits Theory of Nonprofit Finance", *Public Finance Review*, 38(2), 193–216.

Dennis R. Young and Richard Steinberg, 1995. *Economics for Nonprofit Managers*, New York: The Foundation Center.

6. Contributions-reliant SPOs

INTRODUCTION

Many SPOs produce group goods whose benefits are shared collectively by particular beneficiary groups, for example alumni of a university or sufferers of a disease on which research is being carried out, or art lovers of one genre or another. Such organizations may not be able to charge for all of the benefits they provide nor attract society-wide support through government, but may be able to support themselves substantially through philanthropy. This chapter explains the rationale for philanthropy as a key source of SPOs' income as it relates to their missions and circumstances, and also offers examples of organizations that are primarily philanthropy dependent.

Contributions income tends to be concentrated in certain fields of social endeavor. For example, while contributions account only for approximately 13 percent of the revenues of reporting public charities in the U.S. overall (McKeever and Pettijohn, 2014), they account for 69 percent of the revenues of international and public affairs public charities, 45 percent of the revenues in arts, culture and humanities, 49 percent in environmental and animal charities, 20 percent in human services, 17 percent in education, and only 4 percent in health care (Roeger et al., 2012). Benefits theory suggests that these proportions roughly reflect the ratios of public or group and private benefits associated with the services provided by SPOs in these various broad fields of activity. However, the phenomenon of private giving is much more nuanced than that. First, there are many different sources and varieties of gifts and contributions income; second, the motivations of donors and the mechanisms available to solicit their support are also manifold. This background is prerequisite to understanding the strategic place of gift income in the income portfolio of any particular SPO.

THE BASICS

The fundamental challenge to raising gift income is that there may be no explicit quid pro quo associated with donor giving. Thus raising gift income requires an understanding of why donors give and what they expect to receive in return, what incentives can be created to encourage their giving, and what sorts of activities donors are likely to support, given their preferences and propensities.

While there is such a thing as "pure altruism" – technically defined by economists as giving that takes places solely to advance the provision (increase the output) of a valued collective good, without any personal reward or private benefit – in fact, donors do benefit in personal, if not tangible ways. To begin with, donors may themselves be part of the group that receives the group benefits to which they contribute. For example, arts lovers contribute to museums and orchestras and benefit from the presence of these institutions in their communities over and above what they pay for ticketed performances or subscriptions, and donors contribute gifts to their own religious congregations and alma maters. Alternatively, donors who care about other particular groups of people – sick children, refugees, homeless people, victims of natural disasters, disadvantaged youth, and so on – may simply value on their own terms the (redistributive and collective) benefits provided by the SPOs to which they give. The problem, however, with these forms of donor benefit is that donors (or prospective donors) are not compelled in any extrinsic way to give in support of those benefits, at least not at levels that reflect their full valuations. This is what economists call the "free rider problem" – meaning that beneficiaries will rely on others to pay for the services they value while continuing to enjoy those (non-excludable, non-rival) benefits.

As Andreoni (1990) and others have explained, the free rider problem is not entirely pervasive because donors often receive private benefits in the form of "warm glow" when they give. Warm glow, however, does not fully compensate for the free rider problem. Indeed, other forms of private benefits (or costs) must be engaged in order to generate gift income closer to the full value that actual and prospective donors place on group and public goods. Mancur Olson (1965) classified these benefits and costs into three categories: selective incentives, social pressure and coercion.

Coercion is usually associated with government: if collective goods are not fully funded on a voluntary basis then government can use the power of taxation to compel such support. As discussed in Chapter 7, government is indeed an important source of funding for SPOs in the social services, the environment, higher education, health care and many other areas of social impact involving collective benefits. It is also involved in creating private incentives for donors through the tax code (part of Olson's selective incentives category). However, for SPOs, the art of raising income through gifts relies not on coercion but on Olson's other two strategies – selective incentives and social pressure.

Social pressure may be the oldest strategy for overcoming the free rider problem through voluntary means although it can sometimes border on coercion. Passing the plate in church, responding to "asks" from fellow board members of a community organization, or being solicited to contribute to your employer's charitable campaign, can be difficult to resist. Social pressure also comes into play when SPOs publish lists of donors on their websites or in annual reports, or more dramatically on donor walls in their lobbies. While this is a form of donor recognition (a selective incentive) it also may entail an element of guilt or embarrassment to some who have not contributed but may have been expected to do so. Social pressure is most effective in small groups whose members know each other and where social disapproval or ostracism is a real threat. But social pressure can work on a large scale as well. If you are part of the 5 percent of employees in a large organization who have not contributed to the campaign, you may be embarrassed into doing so. Or if Ira Glass calls you up on public radio as a result of your friend's reporting that you listen to public radio but fail to contribute, you may be similarly initiated.

In recent years, SPOs have become particularly adept and creative, however, at generating gifts through the use of a variety of selective incentives that lead people or businesses to contribute by providing private benefits tied to donations. Again, this takes a variety of forms including discounted admissions to performances or exhibitions in arts organizations, special items such as coffee mugs, entries into lotteries for significant prizes, special receptions or previews for donors, citations in organizations' programs, annual reports, donor recognition walls and website pages, and for large gifts – naming rights to buildings, scholarships, professorships, centers, laboratories, libraries, various service programs, gardens, and so on. Another example of selective incentives used on a large scale to stimulate donations is the practice of including inexpensive special gifts – coins, calendars, note pads, address labels, postage stamps, tote bags, and so on – with charitable solicitation letters in order to prod the recipient to give. This form of incentive puts some additional psychological pressure on the recipient either to receive (or dispose of) a gift without reciprocating with a donation, or to respond with a gift. It is unclear how cost-effective psychological pressure (essentially guilt) applied in this way actually is, but charities seem to find it effective. For institutional donors, the inclusion of corporate logos on SPO materials such as special events tee shirts, hats and water bottles, printed programs, or explicit connection of SPOs with corporate activities such as credit cards that generate a percentage of sales revenue as gift income, constitute additional examples of Olson's selective incentives.

An important growing phenomenon is the exploitation of social media for purposes of generating contributions to SPOs. An interesting example is the "Ice bucket challenge" campaign which raised significant funds for research on ALS, demonstrating that social media has the potential to generate considerable social pressure (or incentives) to give, even where prospective donors are numerous and unknown to one another. According to one account: "The ice bucket challenge went viral in 2014 partly because it was so much fun to watch videos of celebrities or friends dump ice water on their heads. . ..The ALS Association says the ice bucket challenge raised $115 million in six weeks" (Kristoff, 2015). Remarkably, although the ALS Association was the beneficiary of the ice bucket challenge, it did not initiate it. Rather, it was started by an individual who wanted to bring awareness to the disease by challenging people to contribute or have ice dumped on their heads. The videos went viral on social media and people who googled ALS found the Association as the first listing. By contrast, *Kickstarter*, one of the largest crowd-funding platforms, manifests a very intentional, strategic effort to mobilize funding through social media. *Kickstarter* is itself an SPO, a U.S. public-benefit corporation that mediates the funding of creative projects in the arts, technology, food-related and other fields, claiming almost $2 billion in pledges from almost 10 million parties to fund a quarter of a million projects to date (Wikipedia, 2016).

In general, it remains unclear how significant "crowd-funding" will become as a mechanism to overcome the intrinsic challenges of free-ridership in generating gift income (Lehner, 2015). Research on this subject is still in its infancy, but it is clear that the Internet and social media have greatly amplified the ability of SPOs to increase prospective donors' awareness of the public and group goods that they provide, the unique benefits they can offer to donors, and the social pressure they can bring to bear to increase giving. In part, this seems a result of the proactive nature of social media, where prospective donors can find opportunities of interest through active search rather than reacting to volumes of solicitations they have not sought. Social media giving is also premised on one-to-one interactions among solicitors and prospective donors, reflecting long-standing evidence that "being asked" is a strong motivator of charitable giving (Schervish, 1997).

VARIETIES OF GIFT INCOME

There are two main sources of SPO gift income – individuals and institutions. The latter includes business corporations and charitable foundations. (Government grants are discussed separately in Chapter 7). Institutions provide monetary gifts in the form of formal grants, large and small, as well as in-kind (goods and services) donations. Gifts from individuals may range from small financial or in-kind donations to large multi-year commitments known as major gifts, and may come from living donors or in the form of bequests from the estates of deceased individuals. Gifts in-kind include donations of art work, used cars, food and clothing, real estate, securities and other products or assets. One of the most important forms of philanthropy is the gift of time through volunteering. The work of volunteering also comes in a variety of forms including staff level volunteering, trusteeship and pro bono volunteering by professionals in disciplines such as law and accounting.

Overall, giving by individuals outweighs giving by institutions. In the U.S. approximately 71 percent of charitable gifts come from living individuals and another 9 percent from bequests. Foundations account for 15 percent and corporations for 5 percent (IUPUI, 2015). Note that many foundations are "family foundations" essentially run by individual donors or their immediate relatives, thus tilting the picture toward individual giving even more. Monetary giving outweighs gifts-in-kind. In particular, non-cash material donations constitute about 20 percent of all gifts by those who itemize their charitable deductions for income tax purposes, and volunteer hours can be estimated in value as roughly half as much as charitable monetary giving (McKeever, 2015). (In addition, "social procurement" as discussed in Chapter 2, can be considered a form of giving although such revenue would more likely be recognized as fee income, as considered in Chapter 5.)

Each type of donor and gift poses special challenges and unique potentials for supporting the work of SPOs. Not surprisingly in-kind gifts are better suited for SPOs in some fields of service more than others. For example, food-related SPOs such as food banks receive more than 60 percent of gift-in-kind donations compared to 19 percent for environmental organizations and 10 percent for arts and cultural organizations (Roeger et al., 2012). The efficacy of raising monetary versus in-kind income depends on both the motivations of donors and the ability of the SPO to make effective use of non-monetary resources. For example, food banks can make direct use of properly collected grocery items. Alternatively, Goodwill Industries has become adept at processing used clothing and other household items for resale. Substantial differences in motivations and potentials for non-monetary gift giving distinguish individual and institutional donors. For example, corporations are motivated to give away product as part of their marketing strategies and to have their employees volunteer as part of their human resource development and public relations strategies. Alternatively, art collectors may be concerned with finding a good home for their collections.

Finally, it is well to observe that nonprofit intermediary institutions commonly broker the space between individual and institutional giving. In the U.S., individuals give to federated fund-raising organizations such as United Way, the Combined Federal Campaign and other workplace giving programs, religious federations such as Catholic Charities or Jewish community federations, community foundations, Kiwanis and Rotary clubs, local churches, and voluntary giving circles, which then direct or reallocate funds to specific charitable service organizations. These arrangements allow a mix of "donor choice" and undesignated giving, wherein the donor may earmark gifts to particular recipient organizations or contribute to a general fund to be allocated by the intermediary. In recent years, emphasis has moved in the direction of donor choice in many of these intermediary institutions. Thus, SPOs must understand both individual donor preferences as well as institutional goals in order to effectively solicit support from these intermediaries.

MOTIVATIONS FOR GIVING

Understanding donor motivations is important because charitable income is raised by educating donors about the benefits that SPOs can offer in exchange for gifts. As suggested earlier, donors vary in what they value as a result of gift transactions. And there are important differences between individual and institutional donors, although there is a gray area separating these categories. In particular, many institutional donors are essentially organizational manifestations of individual philanthropists, most notably family foundations – especially if the donors are still alive or their families have retained foundation control from one generation to another. Moreover, many foundations are simply mechanisms for major donors to park their charitable resources, receive immediate tax benefits, and distribute their gifts over time in a manner that suits them better than giving directly to recipient SPOs. Similarly, so called "donor-advised funds" are administered by community foundations, charitable federations or securities firms such as Fidelity, in a manner that allows donors to receive tax benefits and retain control of their gift giving.

A substantial body of research and theory suggests that individual donors are motivated by both the public and private benefits that an SPO may confer (Vesterlund, 2006). The bulk of traditional empirical economic studies, based on analysis of the phenomenon of "crowd-out" (the degree to which giving is displaced by other forms of revenue such as government funding) indicate that the stronger factor is private benefits conferred in the act of giving, while more recent results of experimental economic studies suggest a more equal balance of public and private motivations. Benefits theory argues that it is the collective (group or public) aspects of an SPO's services that define the arenas in which SPOs may productively seek support through gifts and grants. That is, without a collective (or redistributive) dimension to an SPO's mission there is no underlying rationale for seeking charitable support. However, while necessary, collective benefit is not a sufficient condition for successful fundraising. As discussed above, private incentives or social pressures are often required, which may take a wide variety of forms including mechanisms of acknowledgment and status recognition, material gifts, discounts and other economic incentives, or various kinds of social strategies which impose private costs on non-givers or enforce behavioral norms to which groups of people subscribe. In the case of bequests, as well as major gift giving over one's life time, salvation or the quest for a degree of immortality through permanent forms of recognition may come into play. Further, tax incentives (deductions) enhance the private benefits dimension of giving, amplifying the level at which donors are willing to contribute once they have made the choice to give to a particular organization or cause.

Why people say they give may differ from the motives discerned from their actual behavior. Nonetheless, for purposes of segmenting donor markets and shaping appeals, SPOs are well advised to understand the multifaceted nature of individual donor psychology. For major donors, Prince and File (1994) suggested the following stereotypes based on analysis of extensive survey data: communitarians who believe that giving (and volunteering) is a sensible way to help their communities; the devout who are motivated by religious values; investors who believe that philanthropy is good for their businesses, especially in view of tax benefits; socialites who derive pleasure from their involvement in fund-raising; altruists who give out of selflessness and empathy without regard to recognition; repayers who want to give back to organizations that have helped them in the past; and dynasts who have inherited wealth and carry on family traditions of philanthropy. Prince and File found that communitarians, followed by the devout, were the most common types and that dynasts were the least common. In this classification scheme one can of course discern various mixes of response to public and private benefits of giving. However, it is important to note that the various motivation types may be differently attuned to SPOs with alternative missions. For example, Prince and File found that the devout not surprisingly gave primarily to religious institutions while repayers gave heavily to medical charities and educational institutions. This again is consistent with benefits theory which connects the nature of received benefits with the sources of SPO income.

In motivational terms, the border between institutional and individual donors is indistinct. Thus, analysis such as that of Prince and File is likely to apply to family foundations, donor advised funds within community foundations and securities firms, and even very large independent foundations such as the Gates Foundation, the Skoll Foundation and the Rockefeller Family Fund, where the original donors or their descendants are actively involved. However, many of the larger philanthropic foundations such as the Ford Foundation, the Carnegie Endowment and the Ewing Marion Kaufmann Foundation have long since professionalized and moved beyond their founders' specific guidance. Nonetheless, these institutions are far from homogenous in their motives and styles of giving. Again, stereotypes from the research literature can be helpful (Cordes and Sansing, 2007; Young, 2001). Young proposed the following foundation models based on the concept of "organizational identity" (see Albert and Whetten, 1985): General Altruist foundations that profess broad support for a given community or area of interest (say health care or education); Mission-driven foundations which focus on their own specifically articulated mission and seek to support those SPOs that can advance that mission; Problem-Solving Catalyst foundations that concern themselves with particular social issues or problems and are receptive to supporting SPOs with alternative solutions; and Venture Capitalist foundations that seek to invest in SPOs in a variety of fields that promise substantial social returns to their investments in an ultimately self-sustaining way. From the perspective of benefits theory, these various types of institutional funders require exchange or trade benefits of different characteristics. Mission-driven foundations are looking to outsource their missions to SPOs whose programs align with their goals, as if a foundation were itself an operating SPO. General Altruists want to see that promised activities are carried out and funds are usefully and properly spent; Problem-Solving Catalysts want to see that they have stimulated collaborative solutions and that recipient SPOs have helped to generate specific results that alleviate the problem. Venture Capitalist foundations want a strong hand in managing their recipient SPOs and require that their efforts ultimately become self-sustaining and impactful.

Given these various approaches, and the fact that philanthropic institutions, while often quite visible and more easily accessible than individual donors, constitute a small slice of overall gift income, it is well to appreciate that these institutions often seek leverage well beyond their size. Thus, long-term grants are relatively rare from any of these categories of institutions and SPOs are generally well advised to look to foundations for growth capital or to fund an innovation or startup of a new program rather than ongoing operational support.

The fuzzy border between individual and institutional philanthropy also applies to giving by profitmaking businesses and corporations. This is most apparent for small businesses, privately held by families or individual proprietors. In particular, Prince's and File's "investor" type of donor also describes a small business institutional donor driven by a desire to succeed in business by strategically giving to community causes. Similarly, even the leaders of large corporations have outsized influence on the philanthropy of their organizations, especially for maintaining amicable community relations in localities where corporate headquarters are located.

There is a considerable history to corporate philanthropy (Burlingame and Young, 1996; Esparza, 2014). Once thought to be the domain of individual discretion by community-minded corporate chief executives, the legality of corporate giving was challenged as a violation of shareholders' rights to have all corporate income directed toward profit-maximizing ends. Thus, until the 1950s corporations were required to justify their charitable gifts specifically as strategic business expenses. Even now, corporate philanthropy is usefully understood as strategic, intended to fund causes that will burnish corporate image, build the customer base and enhance long-run profitability. This has resulted in a variety of approaches ranging from numerous relatively small gifts and grants that nurture good community relations to fewer, larger strategic partnerships between corporations and selected charities, such as product sponsorship arrangements, capital projects with naming rights, and other initiatives that associate corporations with the good names and reputations of particular SPOs. A dramatic example of the latter is the adoption of the University of Oregon football program by the Nike Corporation under which a large gift by the founder of Nike built the university's Football Performance Center and helped transform the university into a football powerhouse in exchange for the university's embracing a close identification with the corporation (Bishop, 2013). While such relationships are fraught with risks to the SPO's reputation, they illustrate, perhaps in the extreme, the opportunities for SPO funding that may align with corporate interests.

Many corporations have automated their small grant application processes through their websites in place of applicants' direct engagement with corporate giving officers. Larger grants, of course, necessarily involve more intensive personal engagement. According to the Foundation Center (2015) the largest giving program by a corporate foundation is the Novartis Patient Assistance Foundation which provides approximately $450 million in annual assistance to patients without insurance or the means to afford medical costs. Other large corporate giving programs are the Wells Fargo Foundation which gives more than $180 million in a cluster of community-focused areas related to their business including affordable housing and foreclosure prevention, financial education, minority business development and environmental stewardship; and the Wal-Mart Foundation which gives in excess of $180 million for causes related to their customer, supplier and employee concerns including hunger relief and sustainable agriculture, women's economic empowerment and career development.

The strategic connections between most corporate giving and business interests are generally clear. An emerging exception may be that of so-called "sustainable businesses" which seek to operate in a manner that is profitable but also mindful of environmental and social costs, and even intentional in providing net social benefits (Jäger and Sathe, 2014; Mook, Quarter and Ryan, 2012). Historically such corporations as *Ben & Jerry's, The Body Shop, Patagonia* and *Newman's Own* have led the way. However, even sustainable businesses are not typically focused on external grant-making to SPOs outside their own specific areas of interest. In the *Newman's Own* case, the corporation gives all its profits to selected chari-ties. Even more dramatic are companies that have been wholly donated to social ends, for example by placing their shares in trust and stipulating how they should be run and what social and environmental goals they should serve. This idea has a long history (Quarter, 2009). Examples include the *Zeiss* and *Bosch* companies in Germany, and the *John Lewis Partnership* and the *Bader* company in the U.K.

VOLUNTEERING AND GIVING IN-KIND

The motivations for volunteering and giving in-kind are similar to those described for monetary giving but with interesting nuances (Gray, 2007; Preston, 2007). Again, individuals are the prime source of these gifts but institutions, especially businesses, also participate for strategic reasons. For example, businesses often donate their own products and services, which can help promote their products, reduce their inventory costs, and improve their public images. Similarly, businesses often engage their own employees and leaders in corporate volunteering programs that can enhance company morale as well as provide valuable work experience to their staff and visibility in their communities. So-called *pro bono* volunteering is one manifestation of volunteering primarily undertaken by professional law, marketing and consulting firms, where the firms' as well as individual volunteers' motivations come into play.

Non-cash, material donations are estimated to constitute approximately 20 percent of total giving by individuals who itemize their tax deductions in the United States (Roeger et al., 2012). This is an exaggerated figure, however, since 40 percent of the latter is given in the form of financial securities including corporate stock. Corporations give more than half their gifts in-kind (IUPUI, 2015). And volunteering is estimated to be worth approximately half as much as monetary giving in the U.S. (about $179 billion dollars in 2014; McKeever, 2015). All told then, in-kind giving and volunteering are important sources of income for many SPOs (Leete, 2010; Gray, 2007).

Nonprofits in the U.S. are highly differentially dependent on gifts-in-kind and volunteering. Not surprisingly food-related nonprofits are most reliant on in-kind gifts which represent more than half of the gifts they receive; international charities and medical research institutions follow with a third and a quarter of their gifts received in-kind, respectively. Religious institutions receive the largest proportion of volunteering in the U.S., roughly a third, followed by education and youth-serving organizations which garner about a fourth of U.S. volunteer effort. Nonprofits utilize volunteers for a variety of tasks including, most prominently, social services and care giving and administrative and office support (McKeever, 2015).

Gifts-in-kind can be fraught with difficulties for SPOs. There are basically two ways that gifts-in-kind can be productive – if they can be effectively used directly in the SPO's operations or if they can be easily sold for cash income. If neither of these options are viable, or if they cost more than they yield, then an SPO is wise to avoid them. Gifts of real estate, small businesses, race horses, art work, library collections, and other difficult to manage assets often fit this description. While SPOs may be tempted to accept them in order to please donors, they require due diligence prior to acceptance. The experience of the New-York Historical Society is just one egregious case where the maintenance of donated items for its collections far outran its ability to manage them or convert them to income (Guthrie, 1996).

While there are similarities in the motivations of individual money donors versus volunteers, some differences are worth noting. Both altruism and warm glow also drive volunteers, but the primary difference between donors and volunteers is the personal benefits that may motivate volunteers. These may encompass social and career-related benefits including networking opportunities, work experience and skill development, and free or discounted consumption of an SPO's goods and services. A distinction is worth making between volunteers who do work that paid staff could otherwise do, and volunteers involved in the governance of an organization. Volunteer directors may also benefit from leadership experience and special recognition associated with trustee status in well regarded or prestigious social institutions such as hospitals, universities and symphony orchestras. Even more than for monetary donations, the securing of volunteer services as a source of resource support may be understood as a transaction in which the benefits to the organization are exchanged for the benefits to the volunteers.

This follows for institutional volunteering as well, which manifests itself in different ways. Pro bono volunteering bridges individual and institutional volunteering. Pro bono volunteers donate their specialized skills episodically and often receive credit for their work from their employers. In turn, professional firms that allow or encourage pro bono volunteering require some level of recognition as well as a degree of control to ensure that critical employees give priority to their regular work agendas. Firms that allow their employees to volunteer on a pro bono basis also benefit from the experience those employees receive in the process, and from the good relations they build for cultivation of future business. Finally, many corporations also have general employee volunteer programs. For example, Bank of America claims that its employees logged 2 million volunteer hours in 2013, and it gives recognition to some of those employees on its website (Bank of America, 2015). This program, and many others like it, helps the corporation motivate its workforce, and improve public relations in the communities where its workers live.

Finally, it is worth noting the connections between giving and volunteering. For example, corporate giving is often focused on communities and SPOs where their employees volunteer. And research indicates that people who volunteer are much more likely to give and to give more (Havens, O'Herlihy and Schervish, 2006). SPOs seeking to expand their contributed income and volunteer support should consider how these sources may be cultivated in tandem.

TRANSACTIONS COSTS

Given its diverse nature, the skills and capacities for SPOs seeking to cultivate gift income must be matched to the forms of gifts that are sought. Cultivating small versus major gifts from individuals, from foundations versus corporations, and in the form of money versus volunteering or in-kind contributions, each require different capacities, skill sets and investments in staff, board members, and systems. Sizeable efforts to solicit money income will require a development (fund-raising) staff while reliance on volunteers calls for skilled volunteer administrators. Solicitation of small gifts from individuals calls for solicitation systems varying from direct mail, to telephone campaigning, to parsing the Internet for crowd-funding opportunities, and maintaining and expanding donor databases. Solicitation of grants requires personal networking by SPO leaders as well as skills for searching and applying for grants online, and administering them once received. In addition to regular staff, other resources may need to be engaged, including private consultants and fund-raising firms, as well as the assistance of the Foundation Center or other management assistance providers. SPOs that seek major gifts from wealthy donors must be prepared to engage their board members and executive leaders in personal outreach and cultivation efforts and be able to demonstrate their own commitments before obtaining pledges from outsiders. Certain forms of gift income require even more specialization. SPOs that seek funds through planned giving must be capable of offering advice and assistance with estate management. SPOs that accept gifts-in-kind such as real estate must have capacity to manage or sell such assets. Gift income generated through special events requires expertise in event planning. And so on.

A key principle for SPOs seeking to initiate or expand gift income is to weigh the additional transactions costs against the prospects for income identified through a benefits theory approach. This requires a continual inquiry "at the margin": how much more income can be generated for a given increment of investment in fund-raising capacity? While it seems incompatible with gift giving, the raising of contributed income must be viewed as a profit-maximizing activity – that is, the maximization of net income once transactions costs are accounted for. Thus, fund-raising events should generate as much *net* income as possible, as should capital campaigns, direct mail operations and annual giving programs. This is more subtle than it sounds, however, because investments made in one year may only pay off in future years. And there may be public relations and other benefits generated by fund development initiatives that should be accounted for as well – for example, community visibility gained from fund-raising events or additional volunteers. Managerial judgment will be required, but the principle of achieving net earnings for gift income is important to bear in mind.

SOME INTERESTING CASES

The *Georgia Justice Project*, the *Atlanta Community Food Bank* and *MedWish* are interesting examples of important social purpose organizations whose finances are built mainly on gifts and grants. While different in composition and rationale, these organizations demonstrate the connections between the sources of this income and the private, redistributive, group, public and exchange benefits they provide.

Atlanta Community Food Bank (ACFB)

The *ACFB* is a $100 million operation 95 percent of whose income derives from grants and charitable contributions, with the remainder from fee and investment income. ACFB's stated mission "is to fight hunger by engaging, educating and empowering our community" (Atlanta Community Food Bank, 2015). Its core work is food distribution through its 600 partnering organizations in a 29-county service area, though it also administers seven related programs: Its Product Rescue Center engages volunteers to inspect, sort and pack food contributions. Its Kids in Need program offers free school supplies for low income students in 17 school districts. Its Community Gardens program also engages volunteers and offers gardening expertise, tools and seeds for local community gardens which produce fresh produce for local families in need. Its Mobile Food Pantries works with agencies in 17 counties to deliver food to local households. Its Building the Capacity of Our Partners program provides partner organizations with grants to purchase equipment such as freezers, coolers and trucks. Its Atlanta Prosperity Campaign helps eligible families to qualify for food stamps and Medicaid benefits. Its Education & Advocacy program works to raise awareness about hunger and encourage advocacy and volunteering through its Hunger 101, Youth Summit and other outreach events.

In all, ACFB utilizes more than 1,700 volunteers a month, over 150 staff members, a large fleet of trucks and a 129,000 square-foot facility to procure and distribute food and grocery items received from hundreds of donors. In-kind donors include manufacturers, wholesalers, retailers, brokers, restaurants, food drives, gardens and individuals. Donated produce is accessed by partner agencies which place orders online to arrange for pick up or delivery from ACFB and then deliver the food to needy individuals and families.

Not surprisingly, roughly 80 percent of ACFB's contributions come in the form of in-kind gifts, mostly food products. Its list of 300 food product donors reads like a cross-section of the local food-related economy, including supermarkets, restaurants, hotels, food processors and supply companies, farmers' markets and various other establishments. In addition ACFB's financial sponsors include more than a hundred mostly local corporations, some 250 charitable foundations, a small handful of local governments, two dozen religious organizations, some 50 corporations, nonprofits and government agencies that incorporate ACFB into their workplace employee giving programs and an equal number that offer matching gifts for their employee contributions, and more than 2000 individual donors who give more than $500 annually.

It is interesting to note that while ACFB's income is extremely dependent on contributions, it is highly diversified within this broad category. Its services can be described as public or redistributive goods serving the entire Atlanta metropolitan region, though it draws in only limited fashion on the resources of government. No doubt ACFB's successful strategies of charitable support leverage the altruistic motives of many citizens of Atlanta who admire its work and sympathize with its goals to reduce hunger of the region's most vulnerable people. This is made vivid to them by solicitations that identify the number of meals or recipients that can be served for donations of varying amounts. But it is also clear that ACFB engages the direct private interests of many of its donors and volunteers. Food-related businesses gain recognition and help in managing their inventories and product surpluses, reflecting the major role that in-kind donations play in ACFB's finances. Volunteers enjoy a social experience and learn gardening and advocacy skills. Warm glow is no doubt pervasive among both volunteers and individual financial contributors.

Given the broad focus and community-wide impact of ACFB, it may be puzzling that government support does not play a larger role (less than 10 percent of ACFB's income). Benefits theory suggests that the public and redistributive nature of ACFB's services justifies greater governmental support since healthy children and families are a general public concern, although the actual recipient target groups for ACFB's services clearly constitute a minority of the population. ACFB recognizes the important role that government must play in addressing its basic mission, by engaging in public education and advocacy so that governmental programs such as food stamps and Medicaid are better funded and more effectively applied. At the same time, minimizing government funds for itself may allow ACFB greater leeway in pressing an independent viewpoint than if it were dependent on government support. In any case, ACFB focuses on needs of the indigent population not sufficiently addressed by government but compelling to many of the area's more prosperous citizens. Its success in generating gift income draws on the altruism of these citizens as well as the diverse private benefits felt by its various individual and institutional donor groups. The latter helps to address the considerable "free riding" among citizens who sympathize with ACFB's work but require additional stimulus to donate.

Georgia Justice Project (GJP)

The *Georgia Justice Project* is a much smaller operation than ACFB but equally as intriguing. GJP's annual revenue is approximately $1 million, derived almost exclusively from private contributions. The mission of GJP is to strengthen "our community by demonstrating a better way to represent and support individuals in the criminal justice system and reduce barriers to reentry. GJP promotes innovative change through direct legal representation, policy advocacy, education and coalition building" (Georgia Justice Project, 2016). GJP's program is multifaceted, including high quality legal defense provided at no charge to qualified candidates who meet GJP's criteria for commitment to changing their lives. GJP also offers counseling, training, cash assistance and referral services, assistance to incarcerated individuals, services for individuals with criminal records, including help with employment and records expungement, and policy advocacy on matters involving the criminal justice system. Three aspects of GJP's financial support are especially noteworthy. First, the organization receives no governmental support, nor does it seek such funding. Second, GJP engages substantial legal talent on a pro bono basis. Third it provides its services without charge.

Given that GJP clearly provides public and redistributive services that benefit the entire community it is again perhaps surprising that it avoids government funding. In some ways, its work is similar to public defense lawyers employed by government to defend indigent clients. However, GJP reasons that public support of legal services for the indigent is inadequate and requires targeted supplementation. Moreover, such representation often involves helping clients navigate the criminal justice system or indeed trying to change the system itself. These require a level of autonomy, additional resources and innovative and holistic strategies not available to public defenders or through government funding.

Given the poverty-stricken clientele that it serves, it is no surprise that GJP offers its services without charge. Interestingly, however, GJP did experiment with an earned income initiative in years past. For many years leading up to the great recession of 2008–2009 GJP's programs included the New Horizons landscaping company which provided grounds mainte- nance services to local companies, nonprofit organizations and individuals. New Horizons employed people with criminal justice system involvement as a means to reintegrate them into the world of work and to provide them with economic support. New Horizons was profitable for the years prior to the recession but began to lose money thereafter. However, NH was never conceived as a profit-center per se, but rather as a work integra- tion strategy. And it was a difficult strategy because potential customers resisted employing people with criminal records to service their homes and businesses. When its operation proved costly, GJP closed it in favor of supporting other programs to achieve this goal.

No doubt GJP draws on the altruistic and warm glow sensitivities of its donors. Much of this support comes from the legal community in Atlanta both directly through pro bono work and through financial contributions.

Half a dozen local law-related organizations provide GJP with in-kind and pro bono services, and three times that number also contribute financially. In addition, another two dozen other local independent, community and corporate foundations and trusts support GJP. While individuals also contribute to GJP the bulk of its support stems from various sources of corporate philanthropy and the legal establishment. In general, GJP appeals to the strategic interests of these parties, whose gifts signal their standing as responsible members of the community and the legal profession.

Given its particular clientele, it is understandable that GJP faces a daunting free rider problem if one considers that the entire general public benefits from a lower crime rate and rehabilitation of criminally-involved individuals into productive citizens. In fact, a relatively small part of the public is particularly sensitive to the benefits provided by GJP – most notably the legal community which sees the problems at close range and also understands the need for an independent organization to work with, but operate outside, government. GJP depends on both the altruistic motives of this part of the community, as well as the private benefits associated with pro bono work to generate its base of gift income.

MedWish

MedWish International was established in 1993 as a charitable nonprofit organization based in Cleveland, Ohio. Its mission is "repurposing medical supplies and equipment discarded by the health care industry with the objectives of providing humanitarian aid in developing countries to save lives and reducing waste to save our environment" (MedWish, 2016). The organization views itself as a link between medical surplus in the United States and medical scarcity in the developing world. In 2012 MedWish collected surplus supplies and equipment from some 69 hospitals and corporate product donors, including prominent institutions such as the Cleveland Clinic and Nationwide Children's Hospital, and sent 252 shipments to hospitals and clinics in 50 countries around the world, most prominently to Haiti, as well as Peru, Guatemala, Nicaragua, Ecuador, Ghana, Honduras, Syria, the Philippines and Nigeria. Shipments included bandages, hospital beds, surgical gowns, gloves, crutches, walkers, wheelchairs and other medical necessities. While the supplies themselves are free, MedWish charges a fee for the labor and materials necessary for packaging and preparing them for overseas recipients. Recipients are also responsible for paying shipping and receiving charges. In addition, MedWish collects a $7500 fee from sponsors for each container that is shipped.

MedWish runs a sophisticated multi-step logistical operation which involves soliciting and collecting supplies and equipment from U.S. health care providers, screening and sorting these donations into its inventory system, receiving and evaluating requests for equipment and supplies, assembling customized packages for shipment, and shipping orders to the receiving medical institutions abroad. In addition, MedWish runs a "medical brigades" program that sends volunteers to Central American countries to offer local wellness clinics, deliver supplies and assist with patient care. Volunteers include doctors, nurses, translators and other skilled individuals. MedShare also engages autistic children in its "building careers" program to provide them with skills training in its distribution center.

Various groups benefit from MedWish's work. Health care providers benefit from disposal of their excess (but still serviceable) supplies and equipment. Recipient medical institutions abroad benefit by receiving needed supplies that they could not otherwise secure or afford. Communities in the U.S. benefit from reduction of environmental costs associated with disposing of medical materials. Volunteers benefit from the skills and experiences they gain in the process of carrying out MedWish's programs. And institutional sponsors from the health care industry and elsewhere benefit from their association with a worthy cause.

MedWish's benefits and beneficiaries are reflected in its sources of income. MedWish separates product donations from other income in its budget calculations. In 2012, of its total nonproduct income of approximately $1.1 million, some 83 percent derived from contributions, including foundation and corporate grants (15 percent), individual donations (7 percent), income from special fund-raising events (23 percent) and gifts and services in-kind excluding product (38 percent). Fee revenue accounted for only 23 percent of operating income. By contrast, the value of product donations was some $5.6 million in 2012, five times the operating budget. Further, noncash income appears to be volatile from year to year: for example, more than twice the latter amount (almost $13 million) was received in 2014. This volatility is most likely a result of variation in surplus inventories of product donors. Overall, excluding product, MedWish ran a small operating deficit of approximately 5 percent (56 thousand dollars) in 2012.

MedWish attracts a long list of institutional donors which includes virtually all of the major medical institutions in Northeast Ohio as well as other major firms and businesses including the Jones Day law firm, CVS drug stores, the Jay Auto Group and Toshiba, and some local family foundations. Volunteers come from a wide array of associated local educational institutions, employers, churches, charities, service groups and honor societies. Product supply donors include many local and regional health care institutions and corporate providers of medical products.

While MedWish is highly reliant on both cash and in-kind donations more than any other source, it provides an interesting mix of public, private, redistributive and exchange benefits. The citizens of Ohio receive public environmental benefits associated with less medical waste disposal. Volunteers receive private benefits in the form of skills development and personal satisfaction and schools and colleges receive exchange benefits in the form of educational opportunities for their students. Recipients of care in developing countries receive redistributive benefits associated with improved care at little cost. Health care providers in those countries are the conduits of the latter benefits as they receive their supplies and equipment free except for payments for processing and shipping and handling. Corporate sponsors receive exchange benefits in the form of recognition for their support, and most importantly, product donors receive exchange benefits associated with reduction of their surplus inventories, marketing of their products, and creating goodwill for their brands.

MedWish's income profile recognizes all of these benefits and beneficiaries, though it is weighted toward contributed income of various kinds. Opportunities for fee income are intrinsically limited but exchange benefits seem well-cultivated. Two areas that MedWish might further develop in the future include individual donations, only a modest part of the current revenue stream, and government funding, which has not been realized to date. In particular, the environmental and redistributive benefits of MedWish's work transcend its location in Ohio and indeed are worldwide. Thus, its work should be appealing to donors elsewhere who are concerned with health and poverty in developing countries. Similarly, agencies of the federal government have relevant interests relating to international aid, environmental conservation, and health care management. As a small organization with a modest budget and staff (15 people in 2012), MedWish has focused appropriately on local private institutional donors but its growth may require expanding that view.

CONCLUSION

Giving and volunteering reflect the core spirit though usually not the primary source of income for most substantial social purpose organizations. People give and volunteer for SPOs largely because they believe in their social missions and wish to support them. However, giving suffers from free riding as not all who benefit from an SPO's work feel compelled to contribute at levels that reflect the value they receive. This is what differentiates gift income from earned income and what requires a different set of strategies. For earned income, benefits can be withheld if payment is not made. This is only partially true for gift income.

The strategies for overcoming free riding discussed here are of two types – private benefits tied to the contributions made to support public and group benefits, and social pressures brought to bear on those who are expected by others to give. The variety of specific tactics along these lines attests to the broad creativity of SPOs to convince people to give. The science of giving is not yet fully advanced and we can expect solicitation strategies to continue to evolve as technology advances and culture changes from one generation to the next.

Still it is interesting that many SPOs manage to thrive by building their business models primarily around giving and volunteering. For example, this is common for small and mid-sized churches in the U.S., especially given the constitutional separation of church and state. (Other countries have state churches that receive government support and funding programs for non-state churches. U.S. churches do often have membership fee structures, however, and they may charge extra for participation in programs such as day care or religious school instruction.) ACFB, GJP and MedWish are just three examples of substantial SPOs in the social service and health care arenas that have found giving and volunteering to be a sustainable strategy. ACFB has identified a broadly appealing mission that taps the altruistic sensibilities of many people who are disturbed by hunger in their own community, but also exploits the benefits to businesses of managing their excess inventories and motivating their workforces. GJP is more specialized, targeting both the altruistic sensibilities of informed citizens and professionals, as well as the exchange benefits conferred to firms that accommodate pro bono volunteering and the warm glow satisfaction of individual volunteers who lend their time and expertise. MedWish resembles ACFB in the way it exploits product donations to serve its ultimate beneficiaries – those in need of health care in developing countries – while providing exchange benefits to its suppliers and opportunities for its donors and volunteers to contribute to the well-being of the planet and needy people around the world.

As will be discussed further in Chapter 10, gifts and grants are an important source of income for capital projects as well as operating income. Here the strategies of capital campaigns come into play with target levels, intense donor cultivation, and communications strategies intended to achieve the desired results. Additionally, gifts and grants play an important if secondary role in the portfolios of many SPOs dependent on other sources, as illustrated by examples in other chapters.

Finally, gift income and volunteering are especially appropriate for certain types of SPOs, particularly nonprofit charitable organizations which can offer tax incentives (for example, deductions from taxable income), assurances through a non-distribution of profits constraint that gifts will be used to advance the mission of the organization, and restrictions on gifts that guarantee their use for particular purposes such as scholarships or overseas aid in designated countries. Other types of SPOs, such as Community Interest Companies in the U.K. or various kinds of cooperatives can also offer such assurances through so-called "asset locks" that restrict asset distribution to specified uses, and impose limits on distribution of financial surpluses to owners or those in control of the organization. None of these mechanisms are absolutely necessary for an SPO to solicit gift income, but to the extent that an SPO counts on altruism to attract gifts, donors will want to know that their gifts do not provide special private benefits to individuals who control the recipient organizations. Moreover, SPOs must be vigilant in other ways to maintain trust with their donors. As many organizations, even icons such as the American Red Cross, United Way, the Susan G. Komen breast cancer organization, and Planned Parenthood, have experienced, bad publicity, whether from perceived mismanagement, leadership turnover or political controversy, can be harmful to fund-raising efforts. For gift income, trust is the essential commodity in which SPOs trade.

REFERENCES

Stuart Albert and David A. Whetten, 1985. "Organizational Identity", in Larry L. Cummings and Barry M. Staw (eds), *Research in Organizational Behavior*, Vol. 7, Greenwich, CT: JAI Press, pp. 263–295.

James Andreoni, 1990. "Impure Altruism and Donations to Public Goods: A Theory of Warm-Glow Giving", *Economic Journal*, 100, pp. 464–477.

Atlanta Community Food Bank, 2015. "Feeding a Healthy Future: 2013–2014 Annual Report", retrieved on December 13, 2016 from www.acfb.org.

Bank of America (2015). "Leadership and Service", retrieved on December 13, 2016 from http://about.bankofamerica.com/en-us/global-impact/leadership-and-service.html?cm_mmc=EBZ-CorpRep-_-Google-PS-_-volunteer%20programs-_-Leadership-General%20Leadership#fbid=yE2kZBVe2tm.

Greg Bishop, 2013. "Oregon Embraces 'University of Nike' Image", *The New York Times*, August 3, page D1; retrieved on December 13, 2016 from www.nytimes.com/2013/08/03/sports/ncaafootball/oregon-football-complex-is-glittering-monument-to-ducks-ambitions.html?_r=0.

Dwight Burlingame and Dennis R. Young (eds), 1996. *Corporate Philanthropy at the Crossroads*, Indianapolis: Indiana University Press.

Joseph Cordes and Richard Sansing, 2007, "Institutional Philanthropy", Chapter 3 in Dennis R. Young (ed.), *Financing Nonprofits*, Lanham, MD: AltaMira Press, pp. 45–68.

Nicole Esparza, 2014. "Diffusion of Corporate Philanthropy: Economic and

Institutional Effects on the Establishment of Company-Sponsored Foundations", retrieved on December 13, 2016 from https://ssrn.com/abstract=2889006, May 15.

Foundation Center, 2015. "50 Largest Corporate Foundations by Total Giving", retrieved on December 13, 2016 from http://foundationcenter.org/findfunders/topfunders/top50giving.html.

Charles M. Gray, 2007. "Gifts-in-Kind and Other Illiquid Assets", Chapter 10 in Dennis R. Young (ed.), *Financing Nonprofits*, Lanham, MD: AltaMira Press, pp. 227–241.

Kevin M. Guthrie, 1996. *The New-York Historical Society*, San Francisco, CA: Jossey-Bass Publishers.

John J. Havens, Mary A. Herlihy and Paul G. Schervish, 2006. "Charitable Giving: How Much, by Whom, to What, and How?", Chapter 23 in Walter W. Powell and Richard Steinberg (eds), *The Nonprofit Sector: A Research Handbook*, Second Edition, New Haven, CT: Yale University Press, pp. 542–567.

IUPUI, Lilly School of Philanthropy, 2015. *Giving USA 2015*, Chicago, IL: The Giving Institute.

Urs P. Jäger and Vijay Sathe (eds), 2014. *Strategy and Competitiveness in Latin American Markets: The Sustainability Frontier*, Cheltenham, UK and Northampton, MA, USA: Edward Elgar Publishing.

Georgia Justice Project, 2016. www.gjp.org.

Nicholas Kristoff, 2015. "Ice Bucket Slacktivism Pays Off", *New York Times*, September 3, p. A27.

Laura Leete, 2010. "The Valuation of Volunteer Labor", Chapter 16 in Bruce A. Seaman and Dennis R. Young (eds), *Handbook of Research on Nonprofit Economics and Management*, Cheltenham, UK and Northampton, MA, USA: Edward Elgar Publishing, pp. 238–248.

Othmar M. Lehner, 2015. "Crowd-funding in Social Finance", Chapter 16 in Alex Nicholls, Rob Paton and Jed Emerson (eds), *Social Finance*, Oxford: Oxford University Press, pp. 521–542.

Brice McKeever, 2015. *The Nonprofit Sector in Brief*, Washington, DC: The Urban Institute, October.

Brice McKeever and Sarah L. Pettijohn, 2014. *The Nonprofit Sector in Brief*, Washington, DC: The Urban Institute, October.

MedWish, 2016. www.medwish.org.

Laurie Mook, Jack Quarter and Sherida Ryan (eds), 2012. *Businesses with a Difference*, Toronto: University of Toronto Press.

Mancur Olson, 1965. *The Logic of Collective Action*, Cambridge, MA: Harvard University Press.

Anne E. Preston, 2007. "Volunteer Resources", Chapter 8 in Dennis R. Young (ed.), *Financing Nonprofits*, Lanham, MD: AltaMira Press, pp. 183–204.

Russ Alan Prince and Karen Maru File, 1994. *The Seven Faces of Philanthropy*, San Francisco, CA: Jossey-Bass Publishers.

Jack Quarter, 2009. *Beyond the Bottom Line*, Westport, CT: Quorum Books.

Katie L. Roeger, Amy S. Blackwood and Sarah L. Pettijohn, 2012. *The Nonprofit Almanac 2012*, Washington, DC: The Urban Institute Press.

Paul G. Schervish, 1997. "Inclination, Obligation and Association: What We Know and What We Need to Learn About Donor Motivation", Chapter 8 in Dwight F. Burlingame (ed.), *Critical Issues in Fund Raising*, New York: John Wiley & Sons, pp. 110–138.

Lise Vesterlund, 2006. "Why Do People Give?", Chapter 24 in Walter W. Powell and Richard Steinberg (eds), *The Nonprofit Sector: A Research Handbook*, Second Edition, New Haven, CT: Yale University Press, pp. 568–587.

Wikipedia, 2016. "Kickstarter", retrieved on December 13, 2016 from https://en.wikipedia.org/wiki/Kickstarter.

Dennis R. Young, 2001. "Organizational Identity in Nonprofit Organizations: Strategic and Structural Implications", *Nonprofit Management & Leadership*, 12(2), pp. 139–157.

7. Government-reliant SPOs

INTRODUCTION

Many SPOs, especially those in the social services where benefits are redistributive in nature, or in such fields as relief and development, criminal justice or environmental protection where benefits are widespread and public in character, depend heavily on government support through programs that have been enacted via a political process which in principle at least, reflects a public consensus. Such organizations may not be able to charge for their services because of their public goods character, and they may be hampered by serious free rider problems if they try to subsist on philanthropy. This chapter will illuminate the rationale for government-derived support and will offer examples of SPOs where a government-reliant income portfolio prevails.

Understanding the opportunities for government support requires an appreciation of the complex, multifaceted relationships between SPOs and government. Broadly speaking these relationships fall into three categories – supplementary, complementary and adversarial (Young and Casey, 2016). In particular, SPOs often supplement with their own resources the public services that might otherwise be provided by government. Alternatively, SPOs may work in complementary fashion to help deliver services that government pays for. Finally, SPOs may advocate for government to develop new programs and government may oversee or regulate services provided by SPOs. Each of these kinds of relationships reflects ways in which government can help finance the work of SPOs.

In the supplementary mode, government can encourage the financing of SPOs through tax policies. For example, charitable deductions from income tax liability incentivize donors to give more to charity. In some areas such as the arts or religious institutions, tax incentives result in additional contributed revenue to SPOs at a level commensurate with or greater than direct government funding (Rushton and Brooks, 2007). Clearly tax incentives in such fields of activity also have the advantage of arms-length support that avoids issues of church–state separation or government censorship, and allows SPOs to protect their autonomy. In addition, tax incentives can sometimes be converted to direct financial support, as in the case of the Famicos Foundation discussed in Chapter 5, which sells its tax credits for affordable housing and historical preservation.

The adversarial mode of government–SPO relations may also lead to significant government support. An example is the Rock and Roll Hall of Fame in Cleveland, where a considerable lobbying effort by advocates of the Hall ultimately led to government support of the project (see Chapter 10). While it is rare for a single SPO to create its own government funding stream through advocacy work, many government funding programs are the result of advocacy activity of coalitions and interest groups in various fields including social services, education and health care. Strategically, unless an SPO dominates a field of service in a particular jurisdiction, it is probably wiser to participate in umbrella and advocacy associations to support funding for the field than to pursue its own government line of funding, although political connections to secure "earmarked" funds sometimes bear fruit.

The complementary mode of SPO–government relationships is the one most directly related to government support of SPOs. This category includes government grants and contracts to SPOs in exchange for the delivery of public services, as well as consumer subsidy and insurance programs such as Medicaid in the U.S. which help fund SPO services through reimbursement mechanisms. These mechanisms can be complex, involving government contracts with approved providers who must adhere to stringent, detailed reporting and accountability requirements.

In general, benefits theory argues that SPOs may look to government funding for goods and services of a public goods nature (non-excludable and non-rival) of sufficiently wide benefit to garner the political support required to fund them through the political process. Moreover, government in a democracy is limited by a so-called "categorical constraint" that requires it to provide equal treatment under law (Douglas, 1983). This constraint helps account for the detailed and pervasive standards and regulations that government generally imposes on the private organizations to which it provides direct financial support.

However, there are many variations associated with these broad generalizations, complicating the assessment of the potential for government funding in any given case. These variations stem from important nuances in political decision-making in a democratic society. Political decision-making is not just a matter of majority voting. In particular, "special interests" can secure government funding through lobbying and log rolling, resulting in funding opportunities for various collective goods that may not offer society-wide public benefits. As discussed in Chapter 4, these "group goods" are more aligned with voluntary support (gifts, grants, volunteering), but they may also leverage public sector support through the (adversarial) political process. For example, a majority of citizens in a given jurisdiction may not care much about after-school programs or opera or bicycle paths but determined minority groups promoting each such program can coalesce around package proposals to secure public sector funding for their interests (Buchanan and Tullock, 1999).

In addition, there are some public goods for which direct government funding is problematic or inappropriate, for example arts organizations or religiously affiliated organizations for which government support may compromise their autonomy or integrity. Another case in point is the Georgia Justice Project discussed in Chapter 6, where government funding would have limited autonomy, credibility and leverage in advocating for criminally-involved individuals, despite the clear society-wide public benefits that GJP provides. Recent controversy over government funding of Planned Parenthood is yet another instance where hot button political issues can subvert governmental support of services despite widespread public benefits (Wikipedia, 2016).

These issues notwithstanding, direct government support is an important component of the income portfolios of many SPOs. Indeed in many cases, where the public goods or redistributive nature of the service prevails, government is the dominant source of funding. Even in these cases, however, the SPO–government relationship can be fraught with tension because of administrative requirements and differences in points of view of SPOs versus their government funders.

PARTNER OR VENDOR?

Following the Great Society and War on Poverty programs of the 1960s in the U.S., a great deal of concern was raised about the integrity and compromised autonomy of voluntary, nonprofit organizations that accepted government funding to support and expand their social services (Kramer, 1981). Generally speaking, social service nonprofits accommodated to the new environment of government funded social services without feeling that their missions had been compromised, although important issues were raised about the rights of publicly funded private organizations to discriminate in their client services and hiring practices (Young and Finch, 1977). In the decades since then, however, the debate has been reframed and focused more on the adequacy of government funding than the interference of government in SPO management. In fact, the intervening decades witnessed a movement for greater public support of so-called "faith-based" social services and loosening the constraints under which government funding could be secured (Gronbjerg and Salamon, 2012).

This development paralleled a conservative turnaround in government that generally favored greater reliance on voluntary support and earned income, and calls for limits on entitlement programs and direct financing of welfare-related services (Smith, 2006). Constraining and reforming "the welfare state" also became an issue in Europe and in developed countries elsewhere. Indeed, the movement toward "social enterprises" was precipitated in part by the view that other sources of funds, such as earned income ventures, were needed to supplement if not supplant government funding (Osborne, 2008).

In this contemporary environment, the question arises as to how much of the cost of a public service delivered through an SPO should be paid for by government. One emerging view is that government should shoulder the full cost of services for which it contracts with private organizations. There are obviously good precedents for this position. In defense spending, contractors are paid handsomely for their work, and in scientific research the federal government in the U.S. provides generous "indirect cost" allowances to universities and research institutes in their grants budgets. For charitable nonprofit organizations, however, the complaint has turned from concerns about their autonomy and independence to their fiscal needs. Recent studies of nonprofit contracting with government in the social services indicate that state and local governments do not cover full costs nor do they always pay in a timely fashion (Fyffe, 2015). Recent efforts by the National Council of Nonprofits in the U.S. have succeeded in securing government directives through the U.S. Office of Management and Budget to mandate full and timely payment (Electronic Code of Federal Regulations, 2015).

However, the debate over the appropriate level of government funding hinges on the larger question of whether SPOs that deliver government funded services are merely vendors of government or rather partners that share public goals and collaborate to address those goals. If the former, a strong case can be made for full government payment for purchase of services. If the latter, then SPOs must decide how to share in the burden of finance, given their missions and the particular benefits they offer in addition to what government is willing to support. Benefits theory suggests that they seek government funding for services with widely distributed public and redistributive benefits, and then supplement those services with other sources to the extent that their missions call for it.

Cases in point include SPOs that have been created by government through legislation, such as arts councils, universities and Community Future Development Corporations in Canada, and public universities and Community Development Corporations (CDCs) in the U.S. In the U.S., public universities were established by state governments to expand options for higher education, especially in the second half of the 20th century, and these were originally funded mostly by government. In Canada, universities were similarly established and funded. Over time, however, in both instances the levels of government support have been severely diminished and replaced by tuition revenues, external research grants and philanthropy. In the U.S., CDCs, community and neighborhood health centers, and battered women and youth runaway shelters have similar origins in government legislation and funding. Meanwhile, government support of SPOs in education and health care has increased in recent years – attributable to growing funding for charter schools and to the Affordable Care Act which expanded government supported health insurance for low income people through Medicaid – while levels of government support for SPOs in other areas such as child welfare services and the arts have generally stagnated or declined (Smith, 2016).

The foregoing trends aside, it is worth considering the question of full financing of government supported SPO services from the perspective of public managers responsible for allocating and administering government funding programs. These officials are agents of the general public (the ultimate beneficiary of government-supported programs) and their resource allocation decisions reflect public policy as determined through the political process. Especially in recent decades in the U.S., government budgets have often been severely constrained relative to public needs, putting officials in the position of trying to leverage private resources for public benefit, or in some cases trying to save taxpayer money at SPO expense. Moreover, new forms of "pay for success" contracting, which pay SPOs only when they meet certain standards or performance targets, reflect the mandate of public officials to secure the most impact possible for taxpayer dollars (Smith, 2016). These pressures favor engaging SPOs in a manner that brings into play the private resources that SPOs can attract to address common goals. Here is where the idea of partnership comes in and where SPOs may determine that partial cost reimbursement by government better fulfills their objective to maximize public good than provision entirely dependent on other sources. All this makes for a subtle dance between public agencies and nonprofit contractors. Much depends on trust. Are government funders trying to reduce their commitments by offloading their financial burden to SPOs or are they trying to leverage their necessarily limited resources to provide more public benefit?

Finally, it is worth noting that government support of SPOs is a "moving target." In particular, over time in the U.S. there have been important changes in the character of government funding (Smith, 2016): mechanisms have shifted from traditional grant or contract support to performance contracting and indirect subsidies to individual clients. The locus of funding has substantially devolved from federal to state and local levels, and indeed to the engagement of intermediary organizations (such as Managed Care Organizations (MCOs) in U.S. health-related services) and public/private partnerships (PPPs) to mediate the connection between government funding agencies and individual SPO providers. In addition, the expansion of government funding in health care has caused a shift in financing of social services, with SPOs in the latter field becoming more oriented to and reliant upon Medicaid funding (the so-called medicalization of social services). All this has added to the burden on SPOs to adapt to new circumstances and shoulder the transactions costs that accompany learning and mastering the changes in systems of government support.

TRANSACTIONS COST

As much as any other source of SPO income, government funding requires special skill sets and administrative capacity for successfully securing, managing and reporting on the use of funds. While there may be technical differences among varieties of government funding, the "red tape" requirements for government financing are generally likely to be more burdensome than for market-derived or philanthropic sources. For example, the differences between government grants and government contracts are less than these terms appear to connote. Substantial application and reporting requirements accompany government funding from almost every source – national, state and local, and across fields such as scientific research, social services, health care, education or the environment. Government paperwork and red tape have long been issues in the U.S. and elsewhere, and valiant attempts have been made to streamline or reduce it over the years. Still, the cost of doing business with government can be daunting and SPOs must invest in appropriate levels of capacity and expertise in order to succeed in securing and maintaining government funding. The danger of insufficient investment is not only the risk of running afoul of the law, or failing to secure renewals of funding from year to year, but also the more subtle transformations that an organization may face when it takes on this challenge. Social scientists employ the concept of "institutional isomorphism" to describe how organizations change in order to conform to their environments (DiMaggio and Powell, 1983). In the case of government funding, SPOs must to a substantial extent mimic and adopt the ways of their government benefactors. This inevitably leads to growth of an internal bureaucracy capable of holding its own in an environment of high regulation and accountability, bureaucratic complexity, as well as uncertainty associated with the political process. The transaction costs are manifested in terms of necessary investments in the professionalization of SPO staff, and the time and expenses of meeting reporting requirements for accountability and compliance with government regulations. Nor are these costs simply monetary. Government funding can reduce an SPO's flexibility, the autonomy of its professional staff to make decisions, the ability to advocate for alternative points of view, or to remain responsive to local community or client needs (Smith, 2016). While these effects are not inevitable, SPOs must be aware of the risks.

An instructive example is federal funding in the U.S. for universities. The fastest growing component of university costs is professional administration. This trend over the past few decades stems from various causes that reflect Douglas's categorical constraint. For example, abuses in medical school research have led to stringent requirements for approval of research protocols and the creation of Institutional Review Boards (IRBs) in every research university in the U.S., accompanied by substantial administrative staff overseeing this process for every field of university research. Other components of university bureaucracy have been implemented to address many other concerns deriving from governmental mandates including workforce diversity, sexual harassment, security awareness, student loans, gender balance in sports, and so on. The growth in university bureaucracy not only involves direct costs of additional administrators and staff but also the time of existing faculty and university officials, who must oversee the regulations and procedures that these new bureaucratic entities generate and who must comply with constraints on their own work (Deboer, 2015). All this is not to say that seeking government funding is not worthwhile, only that it often entails serious cost commitments that should be weighed in the process of seeking government support.

INTERESTING CASES

Good Shepherd Services in New York City (Good Shepherd Services, 2016), the Centers for Families and Children in Cleveland (Centers for Families and Children, 2016) and the Center for Child & Family Health in Durham, North Carolina (Spears, 2015) are illustrative of SPOs whose missions are best served by financing primarily through government and which have built the capacity to successfully engage such funding.

Good Shepherd Services (GSS)

GSS is rooted in the religious order of the Sisters of the Good Shepherd organized as the Good Shepherd Province of New York in 1857 to assist incarcerated women and girls in New York City. GSS was formally incorporated as a nonprofit organization in 1947 for the purpose of providing social services to needy populations in New York, especially in the field of youth development. Since 1980, GSS has worked in partnership with the New York City Department of Education, providing school-based social services. In 2002, GSS participated in the competitive New Century High Schools for New York City Initiative, supported by the Gates, Carnegie and Soros foundations, resulting in the establishment of the South Brooklyn Community High School based on a new model of standards-based instruction targeted to truanting and out of school youth.

Partnerships with government, foundations, and corporations characterize much of GSS's recent history. In 2005, GSS took over a 30 year old network of Bronx community-based programs operated by Pius XII Youth and Family Services, significantly expanding its reach from its historical base in Brooklyn and Manhattan. In 2012, GSS absorbed the programs of two smaller nonprofits – Groundwork which provided after-school and college readiness programs and a service center for families and children seeking help with public benefits programs, and the Edwin Gould Academy in Harlem which provided supported housing and other services for young people who had aged out of the foster care and juvenile justice systems.

GSS's programming has gradually evolved from traditional social services toward educational support services. In 2002, GSS classified its primary services according to the aggregate groupings of Neighborhood Family Services which accounted for a quarter of its annual operating expenses and Group and Foster Care and Adoption, which accounted for 54 percent. The former category included counseling and family support, collaborative schools, drop-out prevention and in-school support services, after-school programs, youth leadership development, and career exploration programs. By 2012, the emphasis between these major groups of services had reversed, with Neighborhood Family Services accounting for 45 percent of operating expenses while Group and Foster Care and Adoption accounted for 37 percent. Neighborhood Family Services now includes counseling and support for youth and families, multiple pathways to graduation, school-based support services, college access and retention, after-school programs and summer camps, beacon community centers, domestic violence services and information and referral.

Consistently, for at least the past half century, the direct beneficiaries of GSS's programming have been needy populations in New York City, initially in Brooklyn and Manhattan and ultimately throughout the boroughs of Brooklyn, Manhattan and the Bronx. While GSS started from a Catholic religious base, it has always been nonsectarian in its clientele and operations. As a nonprofit serving lower income groups, especially youth and their families, GSS benefits New York City as a whole, as manifested in support from the New York City school system and other parts of New York City and state government. In addition, as an innovator in educational programming for struggling and challenged students, GSS's programs potentially benefit youth and educational systems nationwide and beyond through model programming and new methods that may be applicable elsewhere.

Given the public-goods and redistributive nature of its services, it is not surprising that GSS has been primarily dependent on governmental sources for its operating expenses. In particular, government revenues represent on the order of 80 percent of its $75million total annual revenue, with the remainder primarily from philanthropic sources. However, GSS has succeeded in diversifying within its base of government support. For example, its 2012 Annual report cites 10 different agency sources within New York City government, five different sources of New York State agency funding, and two sources of federal funding. Still, GSS is a government funding based SPO which engages other sources for strategic purposes but maintains a strong administrative capacity to seek and sustain steady streams of government support. This is its business model, rooted fundamentally in the kinds of benefits it provides and the beneficiaries (low income youth and families) it serves, as reflected in its long-standing social service mission.

The Centers for Families and Children (The Centers)

The Centers is a merger of three prominent human services organizations in Cleveland, joined together in 2011: The Center for Families and Children (CFC), the West Side Ecumenical Ministry (WSEM) and El Barrio. CFC itself was a merger of five nonprofit human service organizations in 1970: the Family Service Association, the Day Nursery Association, Travelers Aid Society, Cleveland Homemaker Service Association and Youth Service, all with histories dating back to the mid-1800s. Originally called the Center for Human Services, CFC changed its name in 1993 to more precisely reflect its focus on families and children in need.

WSEM was founded in 1966 by members and clergy of five West Side churches to better address the needs of the community than they could as individual congregations. Over the years, WSEM expanded its services to include early learning, food distribution, and behavioral health care. In 2004, WSEM merged with El Barrio, giving it a stronger capacity in workforce development. El Barrio itself was founded in 1990 to meet the needs of a growing Hispanic population on the near west side of Cleveland. The agency provided a wide variety of basic services with a strong focus on workforce development and training. The merger with WSEM provided El Barrio with a bigger employment platform for job creation and development services, allowing El Barrio to evolve into a nationally recognized program.

The Centers now has a staff of approximately 500 employees and serves some 20,000 people each year with a wide variety of services through 18 locations and community outreach programs across the Greater Cleveland metropolitan area. As such, the Centers is the largest nonprofit social service organization in the Cleveland area with total revenues of approximately $35 million in 2014. Approximately 60 percent of revenues derive from government sources and 30 percent from philanthropy.

The Centers' programs are multifaceted, falling primarily into three broad categories: health, education and social services. The Centers is also engaged in programs of government relations and public policy advocacy, and consulting with employers on workforce issues. In the area of health care, the Centers puts substantial emphasis on mental health care, broadly addressed through counseling, case management, psychiatry, primary care, medication management and pharmacy services. The Centers also offers participation in wellness groups focused on topics such as social recreation, nutrition, and fitness.

In education, the Centers operates nine Centers for Early Learning, including part-time and full day programs at most of these centers. The Centers also provides an in-home early learning program which includes home visits by qualified teachers for families that cannot travel to one of its facilities. The Centers' social services programs include workforce development, youth services, family services, and food distribution. The El Barrio Workforce Development Center matches qualified candidates to companies looking for diversity in their organization. In youth development, the Centers' in-school and community-based services focus on prevention and behavioral health. In prevention services the Centers offers curriculum-based, structured group activities that educate youth to make healthy life choices; age specific group activities that contribute to pro-social development as an alternative to involvement in risky behaviors; and a program to connect youth and their families to community resources. In behavioral health services, the Centers works individually with youth who have challenges in their social, familial, or school life. In family services, the Centers oversees the Heights Family to Family Collaborative and the Fathers and Families Together program. The Heights Collaborative was established in 2007 as a network of agencies to assist families in need by identifying community issues, advocating for youth, families and communities, and consulting to strengthen and expand community networking and partnerships. In addition, the Collaborative offers emergency food, foster and adoptive parent and relative caregiver support groups, foster care recruitment, rent assistance, an Ohio Benefit Bank, utility assistance, connection to mental health and counseling services, parental support, job training and education, transportation, child care and/or respite help, assistance with landlord/tenant issues, and other services. The Collaborative has ongoing partnerships with a network of service organizations, schools, libraries and government and municipal entities and assists families that reside in nearby suburban communities. Finally, the Centers' Fathers and Families Together program offers workshops to help fathers become caring, committed and responsible parents.

The Centers also operates the WSEM Food Centers program, one of the largest food distributors to families in need on Cleveland's West Side. Its three main centers provide more than 750,000 meals a year and connect more than 14,000 community members to supportive services. The Food Centers program includes food pantries which offer emergency food to families on a monthly basis, outreach and advocacy services for families, food stamp application assistance, a resale shop selling clothing and household items, an evening hot meal program, health screenings and additional holiday food. In addition, Ease@work is a net revenue-generating program that offers employee assistance services to employers to strengthen their organizations' workforces by helping to resolve difficult employee-life problems, enhancing managers' effectiveness in handling workforce performance, providing expert human resource advisory teams, and assisting with talent management through executive coaching, mediation, succession planning, training, assessments, customized programming and related services.

Finally, the Centers' Government and Community Relations Department pursues government relations, public policy advocacy and community relations strategies for the purpose of maintaining and expanding government funding for client services, monitoring public policies that support the success of the organization and its clients, and creating linkages between the organization and community partners. The Centers undertakes advocacy in three broad areas of public policy – education, health care and human services.

In terms of its beneficiaries, the Centers is clearly focused on the welfare of troubled children and families in the Cleveland metropolitan area. This constituency is economically challenged; it includes individuals and families with mental health problems, children and youth requiring basic health and educational services, adults seeking gainful employment and English language proficiency, and families requiring assistance with day-to-day needs including food and proper nutrition. These populations are generally not in a position to pay for the assistance they require, and many qualify for government assistance programs. Accordingly, the Centers' assistance largely takes the form of redistributive benefits consumed by individual clients, as well as public benefits in the form of improvements in public policy, through its advocacy work, and in the general health and welfare of local communities, through impacts of its direct services as well as its educational and prevention programs. In addition, however, the Centers offers private benefits to local employers engaging its employment services for help with corporate workforce issues, and to consumers of its pharmaceutical services; as well as exchange benefits through its work with local partnering organizations in the Heights Collaborative and with schools and libraries.

The Centers is primarily reliant on government funding from various sources. These include county reimbursements for various social services, pre-Kindergarten funding from the state, reimbursement for school meals from USDA, reimbursement for health services through Medicaid, federal grants for health and wellness programming, and funds allocated to the Centers from local property taxes. While the Centers' portfolio of government funding is highly diversified, offering a degree of protection against risk, reimbursement rates for various programs have been flat for several years, and threats to various government programs continue, putting pressure on the Centers to look elsewhere for stability and growth.

Still, the nature of its programs requires that it be largely driven in its finances by government, and within this framework there is potential for growth. For example, the Centers could explore providing special programming for youth with behavioral problems or for pre-school children, in various school systems. Moreover, the Centers can look beyond the borders of the City of Cleveland or Cuyahoga County to engage surrounding communities, as it has already begun to do in its Collaborative program. And given the uncertainty of government funding of social services in the U.S., it must track ongoing changes in the content of government funding. For example, until recently at least the Affordable Care Act (ACA) seemed to offer new opportunities for government support as traditional sources of public support came under greater budgetary pressure. Given its strength in mental health care and preventive services, and its expertise in managing government funding, the Centers seems well positioned to pursue such a strategy.

Center for Child & Family Health (CCFH)

CCFH was established in Durham, North Carolina in 1996 as a collaboration of three universities – Duke University, North Carolina

Central University and the University of North Carolina-Chapel Hill to promote a comprehensive care model for sexually or physically abused children (Spears, 2015). Initial funding came from the Duke Endowment (a foundation devoted to children, health and education in North and South Carolina), the Chapel Hill Service League and the Durham-Orange County Medical Society. The presidents of the three universities appointed the first board of directors to this free-standing charitable nonprofit organization whose mission is "to define, practice, and disseminate the highest standards of care in the field of prevention and treatment of childhood trauma. . ." (Center for Child & Family Health, 2016). CCFH programs have evolved over time, with various shifts in emphasis among programs focusing on treatment, prevention, training of professionals, and information for families. Treatment programs include an outpatient mental health care clinic for traumatized children, psychopharmacology services, and early intervention services in local schools. Prevention programs include home visit programs for high-risk families and families with newborns, and a "strong fathers" program that works with fathers with histories of domestic violence. Training programs include certification courses for mental health care clinicians in the areas of evidence-based treatment of childhood trauma and parent–child interaction therapy, and for child welfare workers in trauma-informed care; as well as collaboration with a national program on PTSD for families of war veterans, and various other workshops and seminars for certification in evidence-based treatment. Informational "family resources" programs include legal information and referral services, as well as information and referrals for families with adopted traumatized children.

Several different groups benefit from CCFH's services. Private benefits are received by families and children enrolled in CCFH's various treatment programs. These are largely redistributive in nature as many families cannot afford to pay full price and are eligible for Medicaid. Families receiving mental health care services in the clinic are asked to pay what they can. Others covered by government programs such as Medicaid cannot be charged. Mental health care professionals also receive private benefits from CCFH's services, in the form of training that enhances their skills and career prospects. These benefits are shared with employers who pay the tuitions of many of these workers. CCFH's informational serves also provide private benefits to families in the form of legal and other kinds of information, as well as service referrals.

CCFH also provides group and public benefits deriving from its mission to reduce the incidence and impact of child abuse. These collective benefits conceivably appeal to individual donors sympathetic to this issue. However, relatively few potential donors are touched directly by this issue and their identification and targeting is difficult for fund-raising purposes, especially considering the stigma associated with child abuse and the existence of many other avenues donors have to help children in need. However, there are substantial sources of institutional philanthropy and government support that benefit from CCFH's impacts through its education of care workers, and improvement of methods for prevention and treatment. These include foundations with stated interests in child welfare, and government agencies responsible for the care of families and children, the policing and adjudication of incidents of abuse, and the schooling of children.

Interestingly, the sources of revenue for CCFH's roughly $5 million annual budget (in fiscal year 2014–2015) reflect much stronger support for collective benefits compared to support for private benefits. Combined federal, state and county-level support constitutes almost 71 percent of revenues, compared with 21 percent from philanthropy of which two-thirds derives from foundations and United Way, and less than 8 percent from earned revenue, including billing for clinical services and training contracts. The large governmental component is understandable both in terms of the general public benefits as well as redistributive benefits associated with receipt of services by low income families and children covered by Medicaid and government contracts which pay for much of the training that CCFH provides for public employees. Nonetheless, the low proportion of revenues derived from fees suggests the potential to enhance this source of support. Possibilities include extending services to families better able to pay for them, more effective (sliding scale) payment schedules for treatment and training services, and extension of training, prevention and treatment services beyond the North Carolina region, given CCFH's special expertise in evidence-based practice. Examination of new and enhanced private revenue sources is especially important for CCFH, given difficulties with Medicaid reimbursement including low rates, slow payments causing cash flow problems, and restrictions on overhead expenses (Spears, 2015).

CONCLUSION

Government is the primary source of support for many social purpose organizations, notably those that provide benefits that impact a broad cross-section of society through the provision of public and redistributive goods. This support overcomes the limitations of marketplace funding when beneficiaries are unable to fully pay for the services they receive and where philanthropic funding is challenged by free riding. However, government support presents its own unique challenges for SPOs, particularly the regulatory and reporting requirements deriving from government's mandate to provide services equitably and reflective of overall societal political preferences. Thus SPOs seeking to develop or maintain government funding must be prepared with the capacity to effectively administer its requirements and live within its constraints. In addition, SPOs working with government must clarify for themselves, and with their government funders, the nature of their mutual relationship. Both the vendor and partner roles are legitimate alternatives so long as the nature of the relationship is mutually understood.

In the three cases considered above, major SPOs highly dependent on government funding developed multifaceted strategies for engaging with government so as to successfully support the public and redistributive benefits deriving from their missions and services. For example, GSS, the Centers and CCFH all built substantial staff capacities to negotiate and administer their ever more complex government funding streams. In the cases of GSS and the Centers, mergers achieved a scale that supported this capacity. In addition, while highly reliant on government funding overall, all three organizations diversified their funding streams within this broad category, providing some protection against the volatility of any particular government program (see Chapter 11) while exploiting synergies among preventative, educational and treatment programs to better serve their beneficiary groups. Finally, the Centers, as a dominant human services provider in its jurisdiction, engages in significant advocacy activity to promote government support of social service, health care and educational programming. These three strategies – increasing scale and staff capacity, diversification of government revenue streams, and investment in advocacy – are of growing strategic relevance in the contemporary context of SPO–government relations and have been documented in various other human services SPOs in the U.S. (Smith, 2016).

It is unclear whether government support is likely to become more or less important in the future. Historically speaking, government support of SPOs has maintained its prominence over a long period of time, even during conservative government administrations in the U.S., U.K., Western Europe and elsewhere. Nonetheless, the political climate is volatile in democratic countries and austerity-related reductions have affected government funding of SPOs periodically in the past, and prospectively could do so over the long term future (Smith, 2012). Such trends do not contradict the basic idea that government funding is a logical, fundamental source of support for SPOs seeking to provide public and redistributive benefits, but they do argue for prudence in cultivating multiple sources of public support as well as supplementation through philanthropy and creative application of tax incentives.

For the SPO committed to initiating, maintaining or expanding government support, it seems clear that investment in, and continuing education of, professional staff is advisable if not mandatory. The special skills required include mastering the nuances of contracting, compliance and reporting systems, navigating complex bureaucracies, analytical capacity to monitor and evaluate program performance, and parsing of markets through which government indirectly provides resources through voucher, insurance and subsidy programs. It is understandable why SPOs such as GSS and the Centers have grown by merger in order both to manage their risks through diversification and as importantly to maintain an administrative capacity commensurate with the challenges of securing and managing government funds. It is equally understandable why smaller SPOs have sought over time to become part of these large and comprehensive organizations. While many SPOs offer programs of general public benefit that logically suggest government funding, the challenges for smaller and less experienced organizations can be daunting. A common strategy worth consideration is to look to larger SPOs or intermediaries organizations to serve as administrative umbrellas and fiscal agents until sufficient administrative capacity can be achieved.

REFERENCES

James Buchanan and Gordon Tullock, 1999. *The Calculus of Consent*, Indianapolis, IN: Liberty Fund.

Center for Child & Family Health, 2016. www.ccfhnc.org.

The Centers for Families and Children, 2016. www.thecentersohio.org/.

Fredrik Deboer, 2015. "Closed Campus: Against the Corporate Taming of the American University", *New York Times Magazine*, pp. 64–68, September 13.

Paul DiMaggio and Walter W. Powell, 1983. "The Iron Cage Revisited: Institutional Isomorphism and Collective Rationality in Organizational Fields", *American Sociological Review*, 48, pp. 147–160.

James Douglas, 1983. *Why Charity?* Beverly Hills, CA: Sage Publications.

Electronic Code of Federal Regulations, 2015. "Uniform Administrative Requirements, Cost Principles, and Audit Requirements for Federal Awards", Title 2, Subtitle A, Part 200. November, retrieved on December 13, 2016 from www.ecfr. gov/cgi-bin/text-idx?SID=94d704978327cf918a40f8a923a29418&node=pt2.1.20 0&rgn=div5.

Saunji D. Fyffe, 2015. "Nonprofit-Government Contracts and Grants: The State Agency Perspective", Research Report, Washington, DC: Center on Nonprofits and Philanthropy, The Urban Institute, October 29.

Good Shepherd Services, 2016. https://goodshepherds.org/.

Kirsten A. Gronbjerg and Lester M. Salamon, 2012. "Devolution, Marketization, and the Changing Shape of Government-Nonprofit Relations", Chapter 15 in Lester M. Salamon (ed.), *The State of Nonprofit America*, Second Edition, Washington, DC: The Brookings Institution, pp. 549–586.

Ralph M. Kramer, 1981. *Voluntary Agencies in the Welfare State*, Berkeley, CA: University of California Press.

Stephen P. Osborne (ed.), 2008. *The Third Sector in Europe: Prospects and Challenges*, London: Routledge.

Michael Rushton and Arthur C. Brooks, 2007. "Government Funding of Nonprofit Organizations", Chapter 4 in Dennis R. Young (ed.), *Financing Nonprofits*, Lanham, MD: AltaMira Press, pp. 69–91.

Steven Rathgeb Smith, 2006. "Government Financing of Nonprofit Activity", Chapter 6 in Elizabeth T. Boris and C. Eugene Steuerle (eds), *Nonprofits & Government*, Second Edition, Washington, DC: The Urban Institute Press, pp. 219–256.

Steven Rathgeb Smith, 2012. "Social Services", Chapter 4 in Lester M. Salamon (ed.), *The State of Nonprofit America*, Second Edition, Washington, DC: The Brookings Institution, pp. 192–228.

Steven Rathgeb Smith, 2016. "Cross-Sector Nonprofit-Government Financing", Chapter 3 in Elizabeth T. Boris and C. Eugene Steuerle (eds), *Nonprofits & Government*, Third Edition, Washington, DC: The Urban Institute Press, pp. 103–132.

Kevin Spears, 2015. "Case Study: Center for Child & Family Health", master's degree, directed study final paper; Atlanta; Georgia State University, January 31.

Dennis R. Young and John Casey, 2016. "Complementary, Supplementary or Adversarial? Nonprofit-Government Relations", Chapter 1 in Elizabeth T. Boris and C. Eugene Steuerle (eds), *Nonprofits & Government*, Third Edition, Washington, DC: The Urban Institute Press, pp. 37–70.

Dennis R. Young and Stephen J. Finch, 1977. *Foster Care and Nonprofit Agencies*, Lexington, MA: Lexington Books, D.C. Heath and Company.

Wikipedia, 2016. "Planned Parenthood", retrieved on December 13, 2016 from https://en.wikipedia.org/wiki/Planned_Parenthood#Funding.

8. Investment income-reliant SPOs

INTRODUCTION

Many SPOs depend on returns from investments for a portion of their incomes though it is relatively rare for such organizations to rely almost entirely on such funds. The principal exceptions are grant-making and operating foundations which are endowed with large corpuses of funds and use the financial returns on those funds to generate income for grant-making or operations. Many other SPOs have endowments of course, as well as other special purpose funds that generate financial returns. Overall, investment income is a very small part of SPO operating income though it can be a very strategic component – providing a margin of flexibility when other sources are insufficient. For reporting public charities in the U.S., for example, investment income comprises roughly 3 percent of annual revenue (Roeger et al., 2012).

The connection between benefits theory and investment income is more nuanced than it is for other sources of SPO support because these funds do not derive directly from an exchange relationship with an SPO's beneficiaries. Rather they are enhanced (or diminished) by the acumen of managers and trustees who manage the funds. Still, benefits theory provides insights into the generation and impact of investment funds in several ways. First, the sources of funds constituting the corpus for investment must come from somewhere; thus benefits theory can help address the question of how to raise the capital from which investment returns are generated (see Chapter 10). Second, investment income affects managerial incentives to connect benefits with income. This can be a positive or negative effect – investment income provides a margin for innovation and a possible cushion in difficult times but it may also undermine accountability to beneficiaries and the propensity to exploit prospective sources of support. Finally, investment income does have a beneficiary relationship with future generations because it takes the form of income dispensation over long periods of time. These connections will be addressed below.

As with other sources of funds, investment income also requires special expertise and incurs transactions costs associated with investing funds and budgeting the use of their returns. This too raises interesting questions. In particular, decisions must be made about the longevity of the investment corpus and thus how the funds should be invested, and how much of the return should be spent and how much reinvested to preserve or grow the corpus. This issue is obviously connected to the production of benefits to future generations and to the preferences of donors who contributed the investment capital.

Despite the generally minor role played by investment returns in the operational funding of SPOs overall, there are interesting examples of service institutions that do rely very heavily on such funds. Two such cases are discussed in this chapter – the Cleveland Museum of Art and Cooper Union College. These cases illustrate both the opportunities and pitfalls of relying heavily on investment income.

BENEFITS THEORY AND INVESTMENT INCOME

There are two general sources of funds to establish a corpus for the purpose of generating ongoing investment income: private contributions and the accumulation of operating surpluses (or alternatively, allocations from operating budgets). These sources provide the link between benefits theory and investment income. In the former case, capital funds for endowment must be raised from major individual donors, institutional philanthropy and/or through capital campaigns that draw in contributions from a broad base of donors. In the latter case, SPOs must create streams of earned or contributed income that exceed expenses from year to year, with surpluses allocated to an endowment or investment fund. It is at these levels that the mission of an organization must appeal to gift givers or paying customers of an organization's services. (The reader is referred to Chapters 5 and 6 to review the essential concepts associated with developing income from earnings and fees, and gifts and grants, respectively, and to Chapter 10 for capital funding.) However, philanthropy for the purpose of raising capital funds for investment, or generating profits for capital accumulation, involves some additional nuances.

Surplus Accumulation

In general, significant accumulation of profits by SPOs, especially nonprofit organizations, is challenged by several factors. First, organizational donors commonly insist that their contributions go directly to programs rather than pile up in financial accounts or even used to support administration. This applies broadly to annual givers though perhaps less to donors considering gifts to capital campaigns. Some of the more egregious examples of nonprofit organizations losing public trust are ones that are successful in fund-raising but weak in actual service delivery. *Boys Town*, where contributions poured in as a consequence of a heart-tugging publicity campaign (Martin, 1978), is an iconic example, but modern instances are not rare. Thus, accumulation of surpluses in a contributions-driven SPO can ignite donor dissatisfaction as well as governmental regulatory interest. The concerns of these constituents are two-fold: first, whether contributions are having a direct and immediate impact on mission, and second, whether the creation of an investment fund undermines managerial performance incentives. In addition, government is concerned both with inordinate profit margins and with the potential misuse of such funds as they accumulate. Moreover, watchdog agencies such as the Better Business Bureau/ Wise Giving Alliance promulgate standards such as program expense ratios that highlight nonprofit organizations that do not spend most of their funds directly on services (BBB/Wise Giving Alliance, 2013).

In general, controversy over generation of substantial surpluses by SPOs, especially nonprofits, centers on the effectiveness of an organization to address its social mission. Some argue that emphasis on profits diverts managerial attention from social goals and people in need, so-called "mission drift." Others argue, however, that limitation of surpluses constricts the pool of potential resources that can be devoted to promulgating the mission and expanding services over the long term (Pallotta, 2008). The point here is that running large profit margins and accumulating funds for investment often runs counter to the cultural and political pressures to which SPOs are subject. Thus, accumulating surpluses for the purpose of building corpuses for investment income generation is likely to be a difficult challenge in most cases. Indeed, for nonprofit organizations, there is even reluctance to maintain adequate reserve funds to hedge against short-run risk and unforeseen circumstances (Calabrese, 2013).

Nor is it simply the concerns of donors or government that dampen the possibilities for building investment funds through surplus accumulation. As discussed in Chapter 5 the setting of pricing policies for earned income generation is contingent on organizational objectives. One sets prices of services differently to maximize profit versus maximize service. Thus, at the very least, surplus accumulation via maximizing profits from the pricing of services may entail trade-offs between how many and how well clients are served in the present versus generating the investments to serve organizational constituents in the future.

Capital Contributions

Given the difficulties SPOs face in accumulating profits for purposes of creating investment funds, the more common and effective strategy is to solicit capital gifts. These gifts can be unrestricted in nature, allowing for the building of general purpose endowment funds, or they can be specific, designating funds for particular purposes such as scholarships, building maintenance or lecture series. Here is where benefits theory applies directly. The building of a corpus for the long-term generation of investment funds to support the mission of an SPO is a form of collective good which requires that donors with sympathetic interests be identified and strategies applied to overcome free riding (see Chapter 6).

This also raises the interesting question of who speaks for future generations of beneficiaries, since those beneficiaries cannot speak for themselves or provide commensurate resource support. In some instances, the answer may be transparent. Alumni of universities may support endowments because they want to preserve the legacy of their alma maters into the future and give succeeding generations of students the same opportunities that they had. Survivors of serious diseases may have similar inclinations for supporting the health care and research institutions responsible for extending or improving their lives. A counter argument is that as the economy grows, future generations will be better off than the current one, allowing the former to take care of themselves. Proponents of this argument favor spending down endowments sooner rather than later and using donations to directly support current operations or shorter term projects (Weisbrod and Asch, 2010)

TRANSACTIONS COSTS

For investment income, the cost of doing business entails wise decisions on how to invest funds and oversee their growth and disbursement. This requires SPOs to formulate their approach to growth and to risk, and also to the longevity of particular funds and their disbursement over time. The actual investment of funds in a portfolio of assets and the mechanics of disbursement of investment returns can be outsourced to experts, but only after the leadership of an SPO formulates its risk and payout preferences and policies.

This is not a text on investment strategy so only some general principles, attendant to generating income from different types of funds under an SPO's management, are outlined here. In particular, an SPO may generate investment returns in five general circumstances:

1. Operating accounts for the purpose of paying current expenses. Here, low risk and liquidity are very important. Funds may generate a low return via interest in a bank account but are unlikely to make a major contribution to total operating income.
2. Reserve and contingency accounts held to ensure the availability of resources for unanticipated or unpredictable expenses. Such funds could be invested in certificates of deposit or other such safe instruments, with rolling maturity dates to ensure availability of sufficient funds at any one time.
3. Special purpose funds for projects whose expenses are predictable over time. Here funds may be invested in a variety of financial instruments with a range of maturity dates corresponding to when they are needed. Longer terms investments are likely to yield higher returns. For example, if funds are collected (or borrowed) to erect a building, they should be invested in a way that allows payment of construction costs and loan payments as they come due.
4. Special endowments dedicated to particular purposes such as scholarships, endowed professional positions, or maintenance of particular facilities or collections. Typically these funds would be invested in long-term funds of stocks and bonds of sufficient return to produce the necessary (annual) payout plus an additional margin for reinvestment to ensure maintenance of the real (inflation adjusted) value of this asset over time. A risk level commensurate with this objective must be accommodated.
5. General endowments, either so specified by donors or designated as such by the organization's board of directors. As noted above, such endowments provide a level of flexibility for the organization. If general investment returns are not a major proportion of organizational funding, the organization may be willing to take greater risk with these funds in order to achieve a larger long-run return. However, if the organization is highly dependent on investment revenue then it may wish to be more conservative in its investment strategy to ensure its stability over time, at least until it can diversify its funding.

Needless to say, administration of invested funds requires both expertise and discipline. Engaging proven professional investment management and advice is advisable, and careful segregation of funds with different purposes is good practice. Especially important is the discipline of avoiding the spending of the corpus of an endowment or allowing its real value to wither by failing to reinvest a sufficient proportion of its returns. Unfortunately endowments are too commonly seen as reservoirs of last resort to rescue failing organizations. (See Guthrie's account of the New-York Historical Society as one famous and instructive example; Guthrie, 1996.) However, the question of spending the corpus is more nuanced than this.

In particular, while endowments are usually established to generate investment income into the indefinite future, this is not a principle set in stone. In fact, such practice can lead to serious problems when the intent of the original donor is no longer viable or relevant. As in the famous case of the Buck Trust, the legal principle of *cy pres* may be invoked to alter the purpose of the endowment so that it provides greater social benefits when changes in circumstances unanticipated by the (deceased) donor occur (Brody, 2006). In some situations, the stipulations associated with permanent endowments can inhibit the development of other income streams. For example, the terms of the endowment associated with Cooper Union (see below) seemed to preclude the charging of tuition. And in the case of the Cleveland Museum of Art (see below) the original endowment required that the general art collection be open and free to the general public, requiring the museum to look for other options to diversify its sources of income.

In relation to benefits theory, it makes sense to pay attention to donor intent and preferences in establishing the terms of an endowment. Many donors see the wisdom of sunset provisions for their major (named) gifts, for at least two possible reasons. First, they may indeed realize that the goals addressed by their gifts may someday no longer be relevant or they may be achieved. Hence donors may wish not to tie the hands of future managers in such circumstances. Setting a reasonable sunset term (for example, twenty years) allows an organization to minimize this possibility, as in the case of the Markey Trust (Dickason and Neuhauser, 2000). Second, specifying the distribution of an endowment corpus over some finite time period allows more funds to be directed to the goal in the immediate future. In some cases, this may be a more effective use of funds, or may offer the donor a greater chance to witness goal achievement within his or her lifetime. For example, if the goal is to eliminate a disease and research suggests that such an achievement is possible within a decade or two, concentrated funding may make more sense than indefinite maintenance of an endowment corpus. Alternatively, endowments to support live classical music performance or maintain a designated nature preserve presumably have no expiration dates, though even here one can imagine circumstances that would question these objectives (for example, the development of holographic recordings or the trading of particular undeveloped sites to accommodate economic growth as well as environmental conservation). In sum, preferences of donors may be an important component of a strategy to solicit particular kinds of capital gifts and to shape their specifications. Where the donors are especially interested in long-term impacts favoring future generations, permanent endowments will be attractive. If they are interested in shorter term social impacts, if only to maximize the chances of witnessing them within their lifetimes, capital gifts with sunset provisions and a plan to divest over time may be more compelling.

Another way in which donor preferences can influence the management of endowed funds is the choice of investments made to generate investment income. As noted in Chapter 2, foundations are putting new emphasis on "impact investing" and "mission-based investing" wherein investments are evaluated not only for their risk and financial return but also their social and environmental impacts or their role in promoting selected social or mission-related goals. The same issue applies, conceptually at least, to the management of endowments by operating SPOs. For example, capital donors to universities may or may not be supportive of university investment policies that avoid or give preference to securities of companies based on their social and environmental footprints.

More generally, donors may even be critical of the investment expertise or strategies of SPOs to which they are asked to contribute. That is, the efficacy with which it invests donated funds may influence an SPO's ability to attract endowment capital in the first place. An interesting related notion here is the idea of "evergreen grants" pioneered by the Mandel Associated Foundations. An evergreen grant is one for which year by year renewal is pledged by the donor over an indefinite period of time, with the corpus for such payments remaining under control of the donor or the donor's institution. Evergreen grants blur the boundary of philanthropy and investment income and are really not the same thing even if the income stream is equivalent. In particular, the continuation of evergreen grants is not legally binding. And in the case of recipient SPOs like universities or major arts institutions, the lack of a corpus undermines public perception of the economic and social significance of the institution, and perhaps its credit rating and ability to borrow.

Finally, there is an aspect of investment income that is confounding, largely because of the way it is often accounted for in tax reports (U.S. 990 tax forms) and financial statements. When organizations take net losses on their investments in a given year, that is, the value of their investments incurs a negative change when all interest and dividend returns as well as changes in the value of the invested assets are accounted for, SPOs may report negative investment income. This results from the sensible practice of evaluating investments in terms of their "total return" which consists of interest and dividends plus capital gains (or losses). However, this is qualitatively different from the way other sources of income are reported by SPOs. For example, contributions are usually not reported net of fund-raising costs and earned revenue from sales is not usually reported net of production costs. In these latter cases, revenues are reported on one side of the ledger and expenses on the other. Exceptions can occur where commercial income from activities solely intended for profit generation rather than support of a mission-related service is reported only in net terms, or similarly where contributions income from a special event is reported after costs of the event are deducted. For consistency here in comparing across sources of income, capital losses should be considered as expenses and capital gains used for supporting operations or capital projects as revenues. As such, potential loss in the value of invested capital may be considered a transaction cost (or at least an expense) associated with generating income from investments. In years when interest and dividends are outweighed by capital losses, (gross) investment income would still be seen as positive, but costly just as a money-losing commercial activity or a special event that fails to cover its costs would have revenues that failed to exceed expenses. (See the case of the American Museum of Natural History in Chapter 9.)

SOME INTERESTING CASES

The Cleveland Museum of Art (CMA) and Cooper Union College in New York City are both institutions that have been highly dependent historically on investment income. While CMA has managed successfully over time to leverage its considerable endowment to achieve and maintain its effectiveness as a world class museum, Cooper Union has struggled to live within the constraints of its investment income and to diversify its income to include more robust annual giving as well as earned income (tuition).

The Cleveland Museum of Art

> The mission of the Cleveland Museum of Art is to fulfill its dual roles as one of the world's most distinguished comprehensive art museums and one of northeastern Ohio's principal civic and cultural institutions. The museum . . . seeks to bring the pleasure and meaning of art to the broadest possible audience in accordance with the highest aesthetic, intellectual, and professional standards. (Cleveland Museum of Art, 2016)

The museum opened on June 6, 1916, its creation made possible by Cleveland industrialists who bequeathed money and the Wade Park property for the site. The endowments established by these founders continue to support the museum. Over the course of the 20th and early 21st centuries the museum has grown impressively in terms of programming, collections, buildings and financial resources. Between 1913 and 1930, CMA established its education department and a wide variety of programs for children and adults. During the 1940s and 1950s, a series of large bequests allowed the purchase of significant works that established the museum's international reputation. In 1958, the museum received a sizable bequest from Leonard Hanna Jr., which provided funds for national and international art collecting, including the development of the museum's Asian collection, which ranks as one of the finest in the country.

CMA's original neoclassic building of white Georgian marble was constructed at a cost of $1.25 million. In 1958, the museum opened its first major addition, doubling the size of the museum. Another wing opened in 1971, containing special exhibition galleries, classroom, lecture halls, the Gartner auditorium and the headquarters of the education department. In the 1980s, a further addition containing the museum's extensive library, as well as nine new galleries, was opened. In the early 2000s, a major renovation of the entire museum complex was undertaken with a capital campaign of $335 million dollars.

CMA's core programming centers on maintenance, growth and display of its permanent collections. In accord with its history and core mission, viewing of the permanent collection is free, but admission fees are charged for other activities including special exhibitions. The museum's offerings also include periodic special exhibitions, as well as regular musical performances, films and public lectures on art-related topics. CMA also offers classes for members of the community, school tours and outreach programs for children including a day camp program in which children learn about the cultural institutions in University Circle where CMA is located. These institutions include the Cleveland Orchestra, the Cleveland Museum of Natural History, the Cleveland Institute of Art, the Cleveland Institute of Music, the Cleveland Botanical Garden, the Western Reserve Historical Society, and Case Western Reserve University. CMA's proximity to these organizations provides opportunities for collaboration, like the museum's joint program in art history and museum studies with Case Western Reserve University. Research is another major arena of CMA activity. The museum maintains an important archive pertaining to the history of the museum, a library of 450,000 volumes available to researchers and scholars, and a publications program. Finally, CMA's services include commercial initiatives, such as its Museum Store that is accessible on-site, in off-site locations, and online; dining facilities; and museum space rentals.

CMA's broad mission, wide array of services, and considerable physical assets allow it to serve large and diverse segments of the population, locally, nationally and across the globe. Its core mission is focused on the enjoyment and learning about art by the general public. Specific segments of the population are given special attention, including school children, art students, local artists, researchers and scholars, adults interested in continuing arts education, arts educators, and residents of the Cleveland community. Future generations could be classified as beneficiaries of CMA's efforts to conserve, protect and expand valuable collections, to promote interest in art and to educate about the importance of art in society. CMA's physical assets, including its impressive physical plant, allow it to benefit additional groups as well. Its auditorium hosts music concerts and lectures, its buildings and grounds can host receptions and parties for private or community groups, and its rooms can provide space for educational programs sponsored by other institutions. Given its role as a lead institution in University Circle, and the assets it can make available, it is natural for CMA to partner with other cultural and educational institutions within the Circle and outside.

CMA's history strongly reflects the generosity of leading philanthropists of the early 20th century, who provided substantial endowments so that the institution could benefit the general public without the barriers implicit in charging fees. This legacy still drives the programs and operations of the museum and is both an enabling and constraining force. While the museum has built on its legacy in recent years with strong development efforts, and the charging of fees where this does not conflict with its mandate to benefit the public at large, CMA is still extraordinarily dependent on returns from endowment to support its operations and maintain its facilities and collections. Indeed, not until the 1980s, when operating expenses began to exceed investment income, did CMA begin to seek charitable contributions (Litt, 2014). Since 2011, CMA has relied on investment returns for roughly half of its $40 to $50 million operating income. In 2014, investment returns accounted for 49 percent of operating revenues, followed by contributions (34 percent including memberships) and earned (fee) revenue (15 percent).

Investment revenue deriving from its endowments is obviously a tremendous advantage to CMA, providing it with freedom and flexibility. For example, CMA with permission of the courts, has used investment income from endowment in two instances since 1955 to help pay for new construction costs (Litt, 2014). However, even with this advantage, the museum faces financial challenges as it seeks to maintain and expand its services and collections, and its status as an internationally renowned arts institution.

CMA is also substantially reliant on charitable contributions, but much less dependent on fee revenue than other museums. In the future, however, fee revenue probably holds the greatest potential for growth. While the Cleveland area has a long history of philanthropy and still retains considerable wealth, it is a rustbelt city that has lost substantial population in recent decades. As CMA builds its audiences through education, visitation and membership services, it seeks to maintain and expand its donor base over the long term. It seems likely, however, that philanthropic support will remain local, given the multiplicity of arts and cultural institutions in other cities, nationally and worldwide. However, the Internet may offer opportunities for expanding CMA's audiences beyond Cleveland, and possibly expanding its donor base worldwide as well, by highlighting its vast and unique collections.

Expansion of fee income is constrained by CMA's mission to serve the general public without the constraining factor of fees that would deter participation by citizens of modest means. Other art museums in Cleveland and elsewhere do charge substantial admissions fees and offer various membership plans that cover museum visitation. CMA must search more intensively for fee opportunities that do not infringe on its mission. It already does so with special exhibits of visiting collections, with educational programs for adults and children, commercial sales through its gift shops, rentals of its facilities for external events and other strategies. In the future, it could consider expanding its fee-based strategies to include more frequent use of its magnificent new buildings, atrium and conference rooms and halls for private events, expansion of fee-based educational programming, reexamination of its membership plans to include a wider array of special benefits and pricing options, leasing of some of its inventory to corporations and other parties for private display, and leasing of images from its collections for which it maintains copyright. More fundamentally, CMA could revisit its overall approach to visitation of its collections, considering plans that would allow sliding scales to account for ability to pay or providing free visitation on certain days of the week and not others (see Chapter 5 for a discussion of congestion pricing). The latter would be a radical departure from CMA's customs and culture but may ultimately be necessary to maintain its fiscal health. Short of this, the museum could be more aggressive in suggesting to visitors that they contribute what they can when they enter or leave the museum, or even as they view the collections. Provision of guidelines to visitors on levels of appropriate contribution might stimulate the payment of "voluntary fees." A more radical approach would be to require ticketing, and to ask each visitor if he or she is able to contribute something toward the ticket.

Cooper Union College

The Cooper Union for the Advancement of Science and Art in New York City was established by industrialist and philanthropist Peter Cooper in 1859, based on his belief that top quality education should be universally accessible to all who qualify, regardless of economic or social status. From the beginning, all undergraduates were granted full tuition scholarships, a policy later extended to graduate students as well. Cooper Union is highly selective in its admissions and consistently rated as one of the best colleges in the U.S. It is also an institution of great historical significance, its Great Hall the venue for landmark speeches by seven U.S. presidents including Abraham Lincoln and Barack Obama, progressive social leaders including Frederick Douglas and Susan B. Anthony, and intellectuals including Henry James and Mark Twain (Cooper Union, 2016).

Cooper Union was endowed by Peter Cooper with its six-story building, two floors of which were intended for generating rental income. Andrew Carnegie later contributed $600,000 to the school, and Peter Cooper's family also donated land to the school, on which the Chrysler Building was later built (Kaminer, 2013). The latter became a major portion of the school's endowment generating significant rental income, roughly $7million per year in 2009. The endowment has enabled Cooper Union to maintain its free tuition policy for over a century and a half. Nonetheless, the college has run an operating deficit for the last decade, in the range of $10 to $18 million per year between 2009 and 2013.

A number of factors conspired to put Cooper Union in financial jeopardy around the time of the financial crisis and recession of 2008–2009 and thereafter. In 2009 it opened its new signature $177 million building at 41 Cooper Square, and took out a $175 million loan to help amortize the cost, requiring annual interest payments of approximately $10 million (Kaminer, 2013). The economic crisis itself no doubt contributed to the school's financial pressures, with lower stock market returns and dampened philanthropic support. The problem was longer term, however, with costs rising faster than general inflation, as has been typical of institutions of higher education in the U.S. for decades. Tensions escalated in 2011 when a series of forums was held with students, faculty and alumni to address the looming crisis. In 2012 the college announced that various fee-based strategies would be pursued including expanded continuing education, and tuition charges for some graduate programs. In 2013, the college announced that it would begin charging undergraduate tuition in 2014. Amidst virulent protests and a lawsuit by the Committee to Save Cooper Union (CSCU), a consent decree was reached with Cooper Union, the New York State Attorney General and CSCU that included provisions for returning to a sustainable tuition free policy (Wikipedia, 2016). Meanwhile, the current tuition policy provides for half-tuition scholarships for all undergraduates, supplemented by financial aid to students according to need. Similar tuition policies apply to graduate students.

Undergraduate students who enrolled prior to Fall of 2014 continue to receive full scholarships.

The income portfolio of Cooper Union is changing as a result of the crisis and likely to evolve as the college works out a plan to sustain itself over the long term. Clearly investment income dominates the portfolio. In 2013 68 percent of the total revenues of $56 million derived from this source, compared to 6 percent from fees and tuitions, and 15 percent from charitable contributions. Government grants and contracts amounted only to slightly more than 1 percent. In 2014 the pattern began to change: of total revenues of $60 million, investment revenues dipped to 57 percent while charitable contributions accounted for 28 percent, almost doubling its prominence. Fees at 5 percent and government funding at less than 1 percent both lost ground. Meanwhile, the operating deficit increased from just under $12 million to almost $14 million from 2013 to 2014.

The increase in charitable contributions no doubt reflects response to the school's financial crisis and the jeopardy of its free tuition policy. In particular, alumni have stepped up to preserve the college's special mission and traditions as they see them. The fee component is likely to grow over time, even if an arrangement is found to preserve full scholarships at the undergraduate level. The low level of government funding is puzzling in view of the faculty's high levels of technical competence, but this probably reflects the teaching mission and undergraduate emphasis of the college as compared with funded research. An interesting and hidden component of government support, however, is the unusual arrangement under which property taxes on the Chrysler building are paid to Cooper Union rather than to New York City in the form of payments made by Tishman Speyer, the lessee of the building. This benefit would be lost if Cooper Union ever sold the building.

A variety of considerations have played into the deliberations on changing the tuition policy. The school may have taken on too much debt and was too ambitious in its building plans. Like many other nonprofits, Cooper Union did not anticipate the great recession; and perhaps its endowment gave it a false sense of security or propensity to take risks. Still, scheduled increases in rental income from the Chrysler building will help to reduce the red ink at least temporarily. Projections by a board committee indicate that with various savings and projected rental increases the budget could be balanced in 2019 when the next rental increase for the Chrysler building will occur. In the interim, a bridge loan is underwriting deficits prior to that date. However, deficits are anticipated to grow after 2019 if there is no substantial change in policy (Cooper Union, 2014)

There are interesting issues raised in this case from the viewpoint of benefits theory. Clearly the institution confers substantial private benefits on its students, many of whom can afford to pay some level of tuition. Thus, the administration proposed a policy that would impose tuition while accommodating economic hardship through financial aid, which is typical of institutions of higher education in the United States. However, critics of this policy argue that something would be lost in the culture of Cooper Union and a slippery slope would be entered once tuition became an important income stream. The fact that alumni have stepped up with contributions reflects this sense of special group benefit. However, others argue that it will never be feasible to support the institution solely on the basis of endowment and philanthropy, in part because it is hard to make the case to philanthropists or foundations that gifts should support free tuition for students from families that are well off.

In summary, investment income from endowment has carried Cooper Union College a long way with its free tuition policy. Restoring this policy (for undergraduates in particular) will require finding other sources of funds. Charitable contributions, which have not been robust until recently, are one such source if present and future alumni value the continuance of this tradition sufficiently. The college can also continue to search for other sources of earned income including greater emphasis on tuitions at the graduate level, research contracts and continuing and executive education programming, so long as such initiatives do not threaten the mission of the organization as an excellent undergraduate teaching institution. Finally, it is unclear whether having the luxury of a large endowment may have led the leaders of Cooper Union astray over time. A booming stock and real estate market in the early 2000s encouraged building a lavish new facility and assuming serious levels of debt. Persistent deficits over many years and inexorable increases in the costs of higher education were tolerated until the crisis came. In hindsight it may have made sense to diversify the income base more substantially over time and to examine alternative strategies for supporting the benefits conferred to students, alumni and others.

CONCLUSION

Aside from grant-making foundations, investment-reliant social purpose organizations are relatively rare. Like the CMA and Cooper Union, many derive from the wishes of philanthropists to offer a set of services free of charge to deserving or needy populations into the indefinite future. In these cases, substantial private benefits may be subsidized in order to maintain a culture of inclusiveness unthreatened by economic barriers. While benefits theory suggests that pricing schemes can be devised to reflect individual benefits without seriously reducing access (see Chapter 5), some argue that a collective benefit would be lost in the process. Thus CMA works hard to maintain open, free access to its collections for all members of the community, while the student, faculty and alumni communities of Cooper Union share a special group benefit deriving from its equal opportunity, merit-focused culture that they feel would be threatened by imposing a tuition system.

In both these cases, it is incumbent on the organization to identify alternative streams of income or to reduce costs so that it can live within its means of (sometimes uncertain) returns on investment. Alternatives include other non-threatening sources of fees and grants, as well as mobilizing the contributions of the groups that share the collective benefits (the community in the case of CMA, alumni and students for Cooper Union). For example, another such interesting case is that of the Shriners Hospitals which recently retreated from its policy of completely free care, including its erstwhile rejection of health insurance and Medicaid payments. Presumably Shriners preferred to avoid bureaucratic entanglement with insurance companies and government programming; nonetheless, they were providing legitimate redistributive and public benefits to needy populations. Fiscal distress ultimately led to a change in this policy as the fiscal crisis and stock market plunge of 2008–2009 cut its endowment almost in half and also reduced charitable contributions (Epps, 2010).

Investment-reliant SPOs like CMA and Cooper Union signal the dangers of investment income unmoored directly from beneficiary groups. Both institutions rely on the returns on endowments provided by philanthropists long gone. Accountability is thus one step removed from the sources of funds, leaving leaders in the position of great flexibility and sometimes grandiose plans based on optimistic projections of investment returns. Resulting financial crises can bring such institutions down to earth, and more in touch and ultimately more reliant on the beneficiary groups that heretofore have benefitted from the largesse of previous generations of donors.

Finally it is worth noting that endowments and investment income can also prove to be an embarrassment of riches. Through the looking glass from Cooper Union and Shriners Hospitals one can find Harvard, Yale and other Ivy League institutions whose endowments are enormous and growing and whose appetite for accelerated endowment growth seems insatiable. In these instances critics have called for the elimination of tuition and the selection of students purely on merit (*Economist*, 2016). In part, this reflects the preferences of alumni-donors who continue to give, as if in an arms race with rival universities; it also reflects extraordinary investment acumen and fund-raising prowess of large sophisticated institutions. How can we assess such situations in the context of benefits theory?

First, it is well to note that few SPOs can afford the kinds of investment expertise marshalled by Ivy League institutions (although even these institutions suffered large capital losses in the 2008–2009 recession). Rather, SPOs with substantial funds to invest are wise to engage competent, objective investment advisors and to pursue conservative investment and disbursement strategies so as to preserve the real (inflation-adjusted) value of their corpuses, unless donor preferences dictate otherwise.

Second, benefits theory is most helpful in contexts where social purpose organizations struggle to amass the resources they require to survive and promote their social missions. In the cases of Harvard or Stanford the theory still argues that students receive substantial private benefits and that tuition is a legitimate source of funding to offset at least part of the cost of their education. However, if donors feel that such education is also a redistributive good then certainly scholarship subvention from investment revenues (and direct giving) is reasonable policy reflecting donor preferences. Moreover, if donors feel that there is a public or group good associated with a free-tuition environment that might justify complete elimination of tuition despite the ability of many qualified students and families to pay a share, then they are free to support that policy with their contributions. Perhaps the basic problem associated with runaway endowments is that institutions are not sufficiently accountable to their beneficiaries. A program of donor education that documents the public, collective and private value of alternative uses of investment revenues could help such institutions decide on the degree to which these revenues should substitute for fee revenue or direct contributions.

REFERENCES

BBB/Wise Giving Alliance, 2013. *Donor Handbook*: *Wise Giving Guide*, Washington, DC: BBB/Wise Giving Alliance, Winter, retrieved on December 14, 2016 from www.give.org/globalassets/wga/wise-giving-guides/winter-2013-guide-article.pdf.

Evelyn Brody, 2006 "The Legal Framework for Nonprofit Organizations", Chapter 11 in Walter W. Powell and Richard Steinberg (eds), *The Nonprofit Sector: A Research Handbook*, Second Edition, New Haven, CT: Yale University Press, pp. 243–266.

Thad Calabrese, 2013. "Running on Empty: The Operating Reserves of U.S. Nonprofit Organizations", *Nonprofit Management and Leadership*, 23(3), pp. 281–302.

Cleveland Museum of Art, 2016. www.clevelandart.org/.

Cooper Union, 2014. "September 2014 Board Report", retrieved on December 14, 2016 from http://cooper.edu/about/trustees/reports/september-2014-board-report.

Cooper Union, 2016. "About Cooper Union", retrieved on December 14, 2016 from www.cooper.edu/about.

John Dickason and Duncan Neuhauser, 2000. *Closing a Foundation: The Lucille P. Markey Charitable Trust*, Washington, DC: The Council on Foundations.

Howard R. Epps, 2010. "Shriners Changes Billing Policy", *AAOS Now*, May, retrieved on December 14, 2016 from www.aos.org/AAOSNOW/2010/May/man aging/managing1/.

The Economist, 2016. "College Endowments: Yard Sale", *The Economist*, March 26 to April 1, pp. 32–34.

Kevin M. Guthrie, 1996. *The New-York Historical Society: Lessons from One Nonprofit's Long Struggle for Survival*, San Francisco, CA: Jossey-Bass Publishers.

Ariel Kaminer, 2013. "Free Tuition at Cooper Union May Be Near End", *New York Times*, February 15.

Steven Litt, 2014. "The Cleveland Museum of Art's Transformation Required the Biggest Cash Infusion since 1958 Hanna Bequest: CMA 2014", *Cleveland Plain Dealer*, March 27, retrieved on December 14, 2016 from .www.cleveland.com/arts/index.ssf/2014/03/from_leonard_hanna_to_a_cast_o.html.

Frank W. Martin, 1978. "Father Robert Hupp Shines Up Boys Town's Tarnished Image – and Even Makes Room for Girls", *People*, 10(2), July 10, retrieved on December 14, 2016 from www.people.com/people/archive/article/0,,20071238,00.html.

Dan Pallotta, 2008. *Uncharitable*, Hanover, MA: University Press of New England.

Katie L. Roeger, Amy S. Blackwood and Sarah L. Pettijohn, 2012. *The Nonprofit Almanac 2012*, Washington, DC: The Urban Institute Press.

Burton A. Weisbrod and Evelyn D. Asch, 2010. "Endowment for a Rainy Day", *Stanford Social Innovation Review*, Winter, retrieved on December 14, 2016 from http://ssir.org/articles/entry/endowment_for_a_rainy_day.

Wikipedia, 2016. "Cooper Union", retrieved on December 14, 2016 from https://en.wikipedia.org/wiki/Cooper_Union.

9. Mixed income strategies

INTRODUCTION

Previous chapters have explored, within the framework of benefits theory, why SPOs often pursue one of several different varieties of income as their primary source of sustenance. As such, organizations have been cited that depend on fee or earned income, contributed income, governmental support or investment returns for a large proportion if not most of their revenue. These primary source-reliant SPOs pursue essentially different logics in building their business models. Nonetheless, in most cases, such SPOs also supplement their support from other sources. Moreover, as this chapter emphasizes, many SPOs are even more diversified, relying primarily on no one source and dividing their dependence among alternative sources more evenly.

There are several factors that may lead to this pattern of finance. As organizations grow, they become more capable of administering more than one type of income. For example, in the aggregate, smaller organizations are much more contributions-dependent while larger ones are more fee dependent (Boris and Roeger, 2010) suggesting that many SPOs that begin with a contributions base ultimately find markets for their services as well. Moreover, as SPOs inventory their assets and capabilities they may find some of them underutilized and potentially capable of generating income in one manner or another. For example, attractive physical assets of arts or cultural institutions allow them to generate rental income, or intellectual resources of educational institutions permit them to generate new income streams through public lectures, training programs or consultation services. A desire to manage risk through diversification may also motivate these strategies, a subject discussed in Chapter 11.

Fundamentally, however, it is the mission and the nature of benefits provided by many SPOs that underwrite their pursuit of mixed income strategies. In these cases, benefits consist of mixed packages of compatible private, group, public or exchange benefits, leading naturally to income portfolios that are not dominated by any one source. This may manifest itself in different ways. First, some SPO missions are multifaceted, naturally appealing to different constituencies with various mixes of public and private goods. For example, museums offer entertainment and education to visitors and support research to expand public knowledge. Botanical gardens do the same. Universities educate students and expand knowledge through research and so on. Such institutions naturally oversee multiple programs with potentials to cultivate both fee income and governmental and philanthropic support. Alternatively, SPOs whose missions yield primarily public benefits that are difficult to fully fund through government or philanthropic support may have assets capable of generating net profits from fees through programming that can subsidize the public mission (James and Young, 2007). In this instance too, multiple programs in support of a common mission lead to a mix of earned, contributed and governmental income.

This chapter probes further into the benefits theory rationale for non-dominant income strategies. The costs of such strategies are also considered, including administrative capacity and transactions costs. In addition, certain legal forms may be best suited to administer different income sources; thus mixed income SPOs may require certain combinations of organizational units thus adding another dimension to transactions costs. Finally, two interesting cases of SPOs that have gravitated to non-dominant mixed income portfolios are explored, the American Museum of Natural History in New York and the Lake View Cemetery in Cleveland.

BENEFITS THEORY AND MIXED INCOME PORTFOLIOS

As suggested in Chapter 4, numerous one source-reliant and multi-source non-dominant SPO income portfolios are possible. Here some generic examples are considered where multiple sources of income appears to be the best way of providing robust support for an SPO's operations. Although the borderlines are fuzzy, attention is divided among three types of SPOs in relation to the nature of benefits they generate: re-distributive SPOs, externality-laden SPOs and multi-stakeholder SPOs.

Redistributive SPOs are those which provide essentially private goods to economically challenged populations whose members cannot afford to pay market prices. Examples include affordable housing, education and training services, food services, and youth services such as recreation centers and summer camps. In these cases, targeted recipients may be able to afford part of the cost (market price), such as 30 percent of their income for housing as in the case of Famicos Foundation discussed in Chapter 5. In addition, such SPOs can mix their customer base to include financially well off as well as less wealthy consumers. For example, in pre-school programming it is often desirable to foster such diversity for the benefit of children of all participating families. The fact that fees can be charged through some suitable schedule means that earned income can be an important income stream. However, if mission requires that all qualified participants be included regardless of economic circumstances then operations may not be sustainable on fee income alone. In addition, the charitable social purpose of assisting the less fortunate may be seen as a public benefit, attractive to donors and possibly qualifying for government funding as well. Thus, many re-distributive SPOs can be expected to pursue mix income portfolios consisting of earned, contributed and governmental funding, in various forms and combinations, without any of these sources necessarily dominating.

Externality-laden SPOs are those whose services confer benefits on groups outside their direct recipients and where both direct recipients and external beneficiaries can be engaged in income support. For example, an SPO that offers help to home owners to install solar panels to reduce their electricity bills also limits air pollution from burning fossil fuels. An SPO that helps ex-offenders find employment makes them less likely to reengage in crime, rendering their communities safer. An SPO that supports prenatal care for low income families reduces health and social services costs for their communities at large. Again, the recipients of such services may be able to pay reduced fees, thus generating an earned income stream. In addition, prospective donors drawn to these causes may be willing to contribute gift income or volunteer hours. Moreover, governmental support may be possible through programs intended to amplify the level of the external benefits. These cases can involve a healthy mix of private, redistributive, group and public benefits, thus suggesting mixed income portfolios which are not necessarily dominated by any one source of support.

Multi-stakeholder SPOs are those which simultaneously serve multiple constituencies with different types of benefits. The above examples of redistributive and externality-laden SPOs most often entail more than one beneficiary group, where there is a distinct primary beneficiary group and other constituencies that receive important, although indirect benefits. In other cases, multiple constituencies are intrinsic to mission. For example, a natural history museum is charged not only with entertaining and educating the public about the natural world, but also increasing the knowledge base through preservation and cataloguing specimens and carrying out research on biological, geological and cosmological phenomena. Each of these parts of its integrated mission provides different kinds of benefits – private benefits for visitors, re-distributive benefits to school groups and others from low income communities, general knowledge (group) benefits for science students and their institutions, and society-wide public benefits related to issues such as climate change, species endangerment, food production, and general scientific advancement.

Another good example is universities whose missions involve education, research and community service. Educating students provides private benefits to the students themselves as well as society-wide benefits taking the form of greater economic productivity, and informed citizens capable of more effective participation in democratic governance. Research advances general knowledge, leading to society-wide public benefits in the guise of better technologies, smarter public policies, and new opportunities for businesses and entrepreneurs. Community service programs improve town-gown relationships (exchange benefits between communities and colleges), provide (private benefit) learning opportunities for local citizens, and help community residents in various private and public benefit forms such as health care (for example, dental clinics), legal assistance (law clinics) and volunteering or internship work in social services or arts organizations. Beneficiary groups for the university thus include students, local community residents, society at large, and importantly, alumni who benefit as a group from the enhanced reputations of their alma maters and may serve as proxies for future generations. Thus it is not surprising that universities commonly draw on a wide variety of income streams including earned income (tuitions and fees), contributions (alumni gifts, research grants) and government support (tuition subsidies, research and service grants and contracts). In addition, alumni gifts sometimes take the form of endowments for buildings, scholarships, programs and general institutional support, which often generate substantial streams of investment income. The proportion of income from alternative sources varies with institutional context. In the U.S., for example, private universities are more reliant on fees and contributions than public universities which receive more funding from government. This in part reflects more of a re-distributive emphasis of public universities and a general societal consensus that all students should have access to higher education. In Canada, universities depend primarily on student fees and government support, similar to public universities in the U.S.

The distinctions between re-distributive, externality-laden and multi-stakeholder SPOs are fuzzy. The basic point is that such SPOs are numerous and the diverse beneficiaries and types of benefits they entail commonly lead to multiple income sources where no one source necessarily prevails. These categories also illuminate where SPOs can look for additional income – from beneficiaries or supporters of the various re-distributive benefits and externalities, and from diverse stakeholders.

TRANSACTIONS COSTS

As noted in Chapters 3 and 4, each type of income involves different institutional skills and capacities for effective administration and development. Thus, the challenge for mixed income portfolio SPOs is especially acute. They must master multiple technologies of resource generation and incur the costs of their implementation and operation. For example, in order to diversify, a fee-dependent organization must learn how to manage a contributions program, apply for grants, administer government reporting requirements, and/or manage investments. Thus, all of the transactions costs-related issues discussed in earlier chapters must be addressed simultaneously by a mixed income driven SPO.

In addition, it is sometimes the case that different organizational and legal forms are needed to engage additional sources of income. For example, a contributions-dependent SPO that wishes to generate fee income may find it advisable to establish a wholly owned for-profit subsidiary, or to contract with a profitmaking business, so as to avoid clashes of culture within the organization, or having to minimize the risk of mission drift, administering differential management and reward systems for its profit generation and mission-focused operations, or conform with tax requirements for unrelated business. The Girl Scouts, for example, does not bake its own cookies but contracts with for-profit bakeries. Similarly, performing arts organizations contract with for-profit corporations for their ticket sales, and universities contract with travel agencies to administer travel programs for alumni and they may establish their own dormitory and food services corporations to run those parts of their operations. And organizations with sizeable endowments but without sophisticated investment expertise will commonly contract with financial services firms to manage their investments.

It is not unusual for nonprofit organizations to establish corporations with different tax designations to carry out their advocacy or fund-raising work. For example, an advocacy-focused organization such as the AARP in the U.S. has a 501(c)(4) tax designation as an advocacy organization for older Americans, but also administers a 501(c)(3) foundation to accept charitable contributions for its nonpolitical work. The case of the Lake View Cemetery considered below is similar to this; it has established a 501(c)(3) foundation to raise funds for supporting the general public benefits it provides to the community. The essential point here is that contracting with, or overseeing, separate corporate entities is sometimes another cost of doing business for an SPO with a mixed income portfolio.

In summary, mixed income SPOs must master the transactions and incur the costs associated with each type of income it chooses to include in its portfolio. Moreover, it may also be required to oversee the transactions associated with contractual or multifaceted governance arrangements for separate corporate entities associated with particular forms of income such as earned, gift or investment income. Just as benefits theory explains the diversity of income sources by identifying the various kinds of benefits generated by a given SPO, it also implies trade-offs between pursuing sources of income tied to particular kinds of benefits and the costs of administering each of those sources of income. This issue will be examined further in Chapter 11.

SOME INTERESTING CASES

The American Museum of Natural History in New York City is an example of a mature organization that has developed a robust mix of income sources reflecting its various beneficiary groups. The Lake View Cemetery in Cleveland, while not fully diversified, illustrates the logic of income diversification as driven by benefits theory.

Lake View Cemetery Foundation and Association

The Lake View Cemetery Association is a 501(c)(13) nonprofit organization, a special IRS tax category for cemeteries. It is organized as a private, nonprofit association of lot owners. In addition to the traditional services it provides to families whose loved ones are interred there, Lake View Cemetery benefits the general public through cultural, horticultural, historic and educational programming. This is reflected in the work of the Lake View Cemetery Foundation, established in 1986 to raise funds to restore the President James A. Garfield monument in the cemetery. Since then, the foundation has broadened its funding goals to provide support for the array of services that the cemetery offers to the general public. The foundation is organized as a 501(c)(3) charitable organization and works closely with the Association, although it is separately governed and administered. The mission of the foundation is "maintaining, preserving and enhancing, for the benefit of the general public, the historically and architecturally significant buildings, monuments and areas located within, and the horticulture, botanical gardens, and landscape of Lake View Cemetery and provide education outreach programs" (Lake View Cemetery, 2016). The corresponding vision of the Association is:

> [A] provider of interment services to all races and religions. It is committed to preserving the cemetery, a nationally recognized landmark, as an historic burial

ground that creates a welcoming environment to bereaved families and provides education programs in its historic setting. In pursuing this vision, The Lake View Cemetery Association preserves and honors the heritage of past generations, serves and respects the needs of the present generation, and provides a legacy for future generations. (Lake View Cemetery, 2016)

Correspondingly, according to a combined 2007 Annual Report: "The Lake View Cemetery Foundation provides financial support to The Lake View Cemetery Association to assist in retaining its status as one of the most beautiful garden cemeteries in the nation. This financial assistance helps to provide for community awareness through educational programming, horticultural care and maintenance of historic markers and structures" (Lake View Cemetery, 2016).

The services and programs of Lake View Cemetery can basically be divided into private and public categories, reflecting the organizational specializations of the Association and the Foundation, respectively. The Association primarily serves its customers, those families who have loved ones interred in the cemetery or who have purchased, or are interested in purchasing, space for the future. The expenses associated with this private side of the organization involve maintenance of grounds, interment sites and monuments, and mausoleums. More than half of the operating expenses of the cemetery are devoted to such maintenance, with the rest spent on support staff and office operations. In 1990, the Cemetery opened its community mausoleum, reflecting an increasing trend toward cremation. This, along with its substantial remaining acreage, helps assure the Cemetery's capacity to serve the needs of families, far into the future.

The Foundation's financial support to the Cemetery helps it provide activities targeted to the general public. These activities include maintaining historically or architecturally significant facilities and property, horticultural programs, tourism, and education. Particular community-related projects and events include the Garfield Hike, the Holiday Lights Program, Parade the Circle (a holiday festival in nearby University Circle in which many local, cultural nonprofits participate), Arbor Day, and Nature Walks. Educational initiatives include visits and tours by students from local elementary and secondary schools, and colleges. On a clear day the Cemetery provides a spectacular view of Lake Erie, adding to its tourist appeal. In 2006, the Cemetery Foundation developed a strategic plan that stressed tourism and education. Over the decade from 2001 to 2010, tour visitors increased from 3,000 to 10,000 while the number of educational programs grew from 10 to 19. More broadly still, the Cemetery is a relatively large natural preserve that offers ecological benefits to the City and region, while contributing positively to the overall image of Cleveland as an important city in American history. It also accommodates part of Cleveland's physical infrastructure, containing the largest dam in Cuyahoga County within its boundaries, which helps control the local water flow.

The dual nature of the Lake View Cemetery Foundation and Association also reflects the multifaceted character of its beneficiaries. Families that use the interment services of the cemetery are its customers who receive the benefits of its maintenance and support services. Many of these same families may also see the cemetery as a public good, enjoying its natural amenities, peaceful ambience and historical and cultural attractions, over and above the personal solace it may offer. However, the beneficiaries of this public side of the Cemetery include a much broader group, including tourists, students, horticultural and environmental enthusiasts, and people with special interests in history and architecture. Further, the Cemetery is an integral part of the infrastructure, history and natural environment of Cleveland, thus benefitting the citizenry of the Cleveland region as a whole and indeed the nation.

Although administered separately, the finances of the Lake View Cemetery Association and Foundation can only be properly understood in tandem. The Foundation does not simply make unrestricted grants or revenue transfers to the Association; rather, it provides targeted support for activities and expenses of the Association which relate to the public side of the Cemetery's mission. Indeed, that is the only function of the Foundation.

In terms of expenses, the Association overshadows the Foundation by roughly a ten to one ratio. In 2012, the expenses of the Association totaled $6.1 million compared to $567,000 for the Foundation and this approximate relationship has held steady at least since 2001. The revenue composition of the Association, reflecting the private nature of its services, consists primarily of fee income from its various sales and services to families using the cemetery. The reliance on fees rose steadily from approximately 60 percent of revenues in 2001 to almost 80 percent in 2012. It is notable here that the Association has paid substantial attention to its marketing and pricing policies for interment services. It offers a variety of burial and cremation options and ancillary services with corresponding differentiated fee structures. The Association also receives substantial income from charitable contributions, paid to it from the Foundation. This component of income rose from 6 percent in 2001 to 13 percent in 2013, reaching 16 percent in 2010 and 2011. In contrast, income from investments has declined sharply in relative terms, from 32 percent in 2001 to 8 percent in 2012.

The revenue composition of the Foundation reflects the more public nature of its mission and services. In 2001 just more than half of the

Foundation's revenue came from private contributions and, with some volatility, rose to 65 percent in 2013. The Foundation also collects fee income for some of its services, though this component of income has been quite small, in the range of 2 percent of total revenue in 2012 and 2013. Investment income for the Foundation is important but unsteady, averaging roughly 30 percent over the 2002–2012 period (35 percent in 2013).

The financial condition of the Foundation varies over time, contingent on economic conditions that heavily influence giving and investment returns. So it is not surprising for the Foundation to exhibit wide swings in surplus or deficit, ranging from a surplus of 27 percent of revenues over expenses in 2001 to a deficit of 65 percent in 2010. Of much greater concern is the chronic deficit of the Association which, while showing a modestly declining trend, ranged from 30 percent in 2005 to under 6 percent in 2011, with surplus regained in 2012 and a return to deficit in 2013. Since these deficit figures already account for investment income, it appears that deficits may have been covered by dipping into reserve or endowment funds.

Overall, Lake View Cemetery's income portfolios mirror the mixed private, public mission of its Association and Foundation. While the Association relies primarily on fee income for the private services it provides, the Foundation relies primarily on contributions for the cemetery's services aimed at the general public. The Foundation and the Association seem to work well in tandem to support Cemetery's operations from a combination of appropriate sources. However, while the Cemetery has grown impressively over the past decade, it also appears to be under constant financial stress. This stress has revealed itself in terms of operating deficits and occasionally by substantial reductions in expenditures of the Association.

Addressing the deficit issue will likely require attention to both expenses and revenues. A clear payout policy from investments and reserve funds should help discipline the budgeting process so that deficits can be predicted and better controlled. On the revenue side, the question is whether some sources of income can be enhanced from their current levels. A re-examination of pricing policies, both for the private services and for services to the public, such as tours and educational programs, seems appropriate. The same holds true for contributions income, on two tracks. Families already associated with the Cemetery certainly have an interest in maintaining it as a place of beauty and solace, and their support can continue to be cultivated, both for current giving and bequests. The Foundation, however, can also focus on the various segments of the general public that receive, or could take advantage, of its cultural, historical, horticultural, environmental, architectural, educational and even recreational benefits. This may be an unusual "sell" for a cemetery but Lake View is extraordinary in these areas of activity.

Perhaps the most glaring lacuna in the revenue structure of Lake View Foundation is the absence of government support. As a tourist attraction, and an important historical site containing the remains (and a monument) of a U.S. president among other notables, the Cemetery benefits the general citizenry, locally and nationally. While government funding is problematic at all levels in the current political environment, various avenues might be explored to secure public support over the long term. The City of Cleveland and Cuyahoga County have interests in the Cemetery's environmental impact and its contribution to local economic development through tourism and education. The State of Ohio has an interest in preserving Ohio's historical legacy. And the federal government (for example, the National Park Service) has an interest in presidential history, given the connection with President Garfield, with members of President Abraham Lincoln's cabinet, and other legacies. A possible strategy for the Lake View Cemetery Foundation would be to pursue such avenues of support in partnership with other key local organizations with similar goals, including nearby University Circle, Inc., the Western Reserve Historical Society and Case Western Reserve University.

American Museum of Natural History

According to its website (American Museum of Natural History, 2016), the mission of the AMNH is: "To discover, interpret, and disseminate – through scientific research and education – knowledge about human cultures, the natural world, and the universe."

AMNH was established in 1869 by an elite group of New Yorkers. In 1874 it secured its current site adjacent to Central Park and built the core of its present building, which opened in 1877. Its cornerstone and building dedications were attended by U.S. presidents Ulysses S. Grant and Rutherford B. Hayes, respectively. Over the period from 1880 to 1930 AMNH was instrumental in a series of path breaking expeditions to remote corners of the earth including the North Pole, Siberia, Outer Mongolia, the Gobi Desert, Congo and the North Pacific. Its most famous scientist was Margaret Mead who worked in its Anthropology department between 1926 and 1978.

The history of the AMNH from the early 20th century to the present is replete with expansion, addition of new exhibition halls, and unique facilities and attractions including the 5-story Branosaurus cast, the tallest free standing dinosaur display in the world, and the National Center for Science Literacy, Education and Technology, created in partnership with the National Aeronautics and Space Administration (NASA), a federal government agency. Major renovation of its buildings was undertaken in 1996 and completed in 2009.

AMNH offers a wide variety of activities reflecting its broad mission. This includes various programs and exhibitions for visitors, as well as research and educational programming. Permanent exhibitions focus on biodiversity; the environment; birds, reptiles and amphibians; earth and planetary science, fossils, human origins; mammals; and space. Facilities include a Discovery Room with hands-on activities for visitors; the Haydn Planetarium and Big Bang Theater, and a hall housing the New York State Memorial to President Theodore Roosevelt, known for his dedication to conservation. Recent current thematic exhibitions include those on Gold, the Horse, Darwin, Climate Change, Dinosaurs, Spiders, the Brain, and Einstein. In 2006 the museum initiated its popular Night at the Museum Sleepover program for families and groups of children ages 6 through 13.

The AMNH is also an active research institution with divisions and centers devoted to anthropology, zoology, paleontology, astrophysics, earth and planetary sciences, biodiversity, genomics, and computational sciences. It houses important research resources including a research library and the scientific papers of Charles Darwin. In addition, in 2006 the museum established the Richard Gilder Graduate School which offers a master's degree (M. Phil) program and a Ph.D. in comparative biology within the museum. The overall operating (expense) budget in 2015 was approximately $162 million. As of 2015, AMNH enjoyed an endowment of approximately $657 million of which $170 million was restricted to special purposes.

The AMNH's revenue portfolio reflects the various kinds of benefits it offers and the beneficiary groups that it serves. Contributions account for 26 percent of total operating income compared with 10 percent from government, 15 percent from investments, and 33 percent from fee income. The fee income includes memberships and admissions payments, part of which may be considered contributions; the remainder derives from auxiliary activities some of which may be considered fee income. Still, the AMNH's operating income portfolio is reasonably balanced with no one source dominating. On the other hand, capital expenses (roughly $109 million in 2015) were financed by contributions (80 percent), government support from New York City (3 percent) and transfers from investment funds (17 percent).

A long history, strong connections with local government, support from higher income citizens, and prudent management has allowed the AMNH to develop an income portfolio substantially reflective of its beneficiary base, as well as accumulation of endowment assets that complement the direct income streams from donors, users and government. Volunteers also constitute an important source of support for the museum although the value of their contributions is not reflected in its financial statements. On its website the museum claims more than 1000 volunteers who contribute 130,000 hours of their time to the museum annually.

AMNH's balanced income portfolio can be understood in four parts. First, visitors and participants in AMNH programs pay fees in exchange for the private benefits they receive. These include occasional visitors and tourists as well as regular visitors who often join as members. Some of these participants, including students, lower income families and seniors receive re-distributive benefits, and hence discounted fees or the option to pay less. Second, AMNH produces substantial educational benefits for the general public (societal benefits in the form of a better informed and more productive citizenry), and research benefits in the form of new knowledge about the natural world. Some of this public benefit is supported by local government funding, mostly reflecting the particular benefits to New York City and its residents. To a greater extent, however, these benefits are more widely supported by contributions of donors and volunteers, including members who contribute over and above the value of private, individual benefits they perceive for themselves. Third, donors are encouraged to contribute to the public good by additional private goods incentives that accompany contributions or memberships at various levels. These incentives range from discounts on gift shop purchases to naming rights for various exhibit halls or facilities in the museum. Fourth, AMNH offers a corporate giving program that provides exchange benefits to companies in return for publicity and brand recognition and opportunities to host corporate events in the museum.

Diverse mechanisms are used to convert benefits into financing, especially within the context of membership. General admission fees allow access to permanent exhibitions ($22 in 2015) with additional charges for special exhibits and shows such as IMAX, the Space Show and the Titanosaur (dinosaur) exhibit. Visitors are asked if they would prefer to pay less, to accommodate their economic circumstances. Students, seniors and children are offered discounts. Members receive free admission to all exhibits, and tourists can purchase passes which allow them to visit several New York City attractions within a certain limited period of time (up to 30 days depending on the particular pass).

Membership packages are offered at a variety of levels and on different tracks including Family, Adult and Digital, the latter designed to accommodate members living more than 150 miles from New York City. Basic Adult and Family memberships start at $105 per year and higher levels within these tracks offer additional benefits such as guest tickets, invitations to receptions, parking privileges and discounts in the gift shop and restaurant. Significantly, memberships are largely deductible as contributions for income tax purposes. At the highest levels of giving, donors in AMH's Patron Circle are honored with recognition as members of the President's Society ($50,000) and the Chairman's Circle ($75,000). The AMNH offers many such designation levels between basic memberships and these top categories, so as to appeal to donors along a spectrum of giving capacity and willingness to contribute. Naming opportunities reflect larger gifts; these include naming parts of the museum, such as the Bernard Family Hall of North American Mammals, naming seats in one of the museum's theaters, and a "Name a Fossil" program. AMNH also offers a planned giving program including options for bequests, annuities and trusts. Those donors with interests in the long-term sustainability of the museum can contribute to endowment funds.

In summary, AMNH's balanced income portfolio has allowed it to sustain itself and grow significantly for almost a century and a half, though not without challenges. From 2001 to 2013 expenses outpaced revenues in half of those years, sometimes very substantially. In three of those years, investment losses contributed significantly to the problem, demonstrating that investment income is not necessarily a bulwark against the vicissitudes of the service and donation markets. While total expenses have stayed within a relatively narrow range in these thirteen years, between $164 million in 2002 to less than $200 million in 2013, revenues have been substantially more volatile.

With its relatively heavier reliance on charitable contributions, and manifold strategies for cultivating and encouraging donations for both operating and capital purposes already in place, the museum likely needs to consider other mechanisms to capture both private and public benefits. Given the many and substantial private benefits its offers to visitors, students and families, it may need to reassess its level of reliance on fee income, which now provides only a fifth of its total income. Revisiting of fee structures, as well as further utilization of its ample and attractive physical plant and its knowledgeable staff for private events, may be worth considering. New services to expand the museum's market beyond its essential base in New York City, through the Internet and social media, also seems worth exploring given its world class collections and research infrastructure. Similarly, AMNH produces very significant general public benefits to society at large, relatively modestly supported by New York City government in the context of its contribution to the city as a tourist destination and local educational resource. Scientific knowledge benefits go well beyond this, however. Additional government support, from state and federal sources seems justified though likely a hard sell in the current conservative political environment.

CONCLUSION

While Lake View Cemetery and the American Museum of Natural History are both relatively old nonprofit institutions, the diversification of income streams and balancing of sources to reflect benefits is much better developed in the latter case than the former. From the start, AMNH engaged with donors, government, visitors and volunteers and over the long term, through contributions, built endowments and investment income as well. Lake View Cemetery by contrast was initially focused on private and group benefits to participating families, and only later began to support its public benefits through the incorporation of a charitable foundation. Interestingly, in both cases, however, general public benefits do not appear to be sufficiently recognized through government support. Hence both institutions rely relatively heavily on private contributions to carry the burden and expand support for redistributive and public benefits.

Both Lake View Cemetery and the American Museum of Natural History may be understood as externality-laden and multi-stakeholder SPOs whose missions also encompass redistributive benefits. The Cemetery's stakeholders divide clearly between users of its interment services, the educational benefits to other visitors, and the general environmental and civic benefits to society at large. These distinctions underwrite the separate organizational structures of the Association and the Foundation, each with its specializations in generating different forms of income reflecting their alternative distributions of private versus public benefits. The AMNH, given its multi-part mission is intrinsically a multi-stakeholder SPO whose beneficiaries include local and global visitors who reap its private benefits, students who benefit individually and contribute to society's productivity, and society-at-large which gains the benefits of a more educated citizenry and gains from research on the natural world. Both institutions generate important redistributive benefits which are accommodated by differential fee schedules and free programming for income-challenged users.

In general, SPOs whose missions reflect a strongly diverse combination of private, re-distributive and public benefits and externalities, are natural candidates for diversified and balanced income portfolios combining earned, contributed and governmental income. Their success in achieving such balance, and the wisdom of pursuing it, will depend on their capacities to manage the different technologies of resource development associated with these alternative sources including the possible necessity of segmenting different parts of their mission foci into separate but coordinated organizational units.

REFERENCES

American Museum of Natural History, 2016. www.amnh.org.

Elizabeth T. Boris and Katie L. Roeger, 2010. "Grassroots Civil Society: The Scope and Dimensions of Small Public Charities", *Charting Civil Society*, Washington, DC: The Urban Institute, No. 24, February.

Estelle James and Dennis R. Young, 2007. "Fee Income and Commercial Ventures", Chapter 5 in Dennis R. Young (ed.), *Financing Nonprofits*, Lanham, MD: AltaMira Press, pp. 93–119.

Lake View Cemetery, 2016. www.lakeviewcemetery.com.

10. Capital financing

INTRODUCTION

Benefits theory applies to both capital and operating income; however, capital income involves a number of nuances requiring special attention. First, it is important to note the connection between capital funding and investment income; the latter derives from returns on financial capital accumulated as endowment or other invested funds. As a result, as discussed in Chapter 8, investment income is only indirectly connected with benefits and beneficiaries. However, the investment capital from which investment income is generated is more directly linked to benefits and beneficiaries. An arguable exception is accumulation of capital through retained net earnings, an internal strategy not linked directly to benefits and beneficiaries. Although even here there is an indirect link to beneficiaries through the operating revenues, such as fees or gifts, from which surpluses may be generated.

Second, investment capital for endowments is just one of several forms of capital used by SPOs. In particular, while virtually all SPOs produce services as opposed to physical goods, thus requiring significant allocations of labor, they also require capital assets such as buildings or equipment. Indeed, SPOs in some fields of service are relatively capital intensive – requiring significant funding for physical plant. Third, different legal forms of SPO, for example, nonprofits versus social businesses, are more adept than others at attracting alternative forms of capital financing – for example sale of equity versus receipt of capital grants. Fourth, recent innovations such as social impact bonds, program-related investments, community bonds, community investment notes, crowd-funding, social investment funds, and new hybrid legal forms of SPO such as L3Cs, benefit corporations and community interest companies have been devised to bridge the barriers that reduce access of SPOs to various sources of capital.

This chapter starts with an overview of different forms of SPO capital and capital requirements. Next, consideration is given to the different sources from which capital needs can be financed. A discussion follows on how the particular missions of SPOs, hence their services, benefits and beneficiaries, affect both their capital requirements and their capacities to secure capital investment from those beneficiaries. Consideration is then given to how alternate legal forms of SPO affect their abilities to attract different forms of capital financing (for example, loans versus sale of equity). This discussion extends to new forms of SPOs and modes of capital financing that are, in part, intended to overcome the restraints associated with classical forms of enterprise and resource allocation. Finally, three interesting case studies – the Rock and Roll Hall of Fame, the Evergreen Cooperatives in Cleveland and Park Pride in Atlanta – help illustrate some of the issues surrounding capital financing of SPOs in the context of benefits theory.

FORMS OF CAPITAL AND SPO CAPITAL NEEDS

Salamon (2006) defines capital (financing) as "the revenue [resources] needed to finance items intended to last more than a year." (The substitution of "resources" for "revenues" is suggested here because capital financing can also take the form of borrowing, which technically would not count as revenue.) Within this definition, Salamon identifies both "hard" and "soft" capital. *Hard investment capital* refers to buildings, equipment and other tangible property. *Soft investment capital* refers to funds required to develop new programs, prepare strategic plans and improve the capacity of human resources (staff). In his study of "complete capital" Levine (2013) more broadly identifies four categories of capital required to address complex social challenges of the kind embraced in the missions of SPOs. These are financial capital, intellectual capital, human capital and social capital. There are obvious cross-overs between Salamon's and Levine's categories, with financial capital correlating closely with hard capital and intellectual, human and social capital more easily thought of as soft capital. By and large, SPOs seek external financing for hard capital, especially those SPOs that would be considered "capital intensive" because they require substantial physical plants and equipment. Salamon's (2006) survey cited technology, acquisition of land and buildings, and vehicles and equipment as major categories of capital needs for nonprofit organizations, although program development, staff training and strategic planning were also identified as important.

The nature of capital needs varies considerably by SPO mission and by stage in the life cycle of organizational development. In particular, fields such as higher education, the performing arts, hospitals and nursing facilities rely on buildings and equipment more than counseling agencies or environmental advocacy organizations. But these broad distinctions mask many variations and indeed choices that SPOs in a given field of activity can make. For example, performing arts organizations can choose to invest in their own performing spaces or they can move among different venues, and they can employ full time salaried ensembles or use part-time players. Thus the Cleveland Orchestra must ensure the viability of its magnificent concert hall, Severance Hall, and employs a largely full time salaried group of professional musicians while the early music ensemble Apollo's Fire performs in a variety of church and other venues and frequently engages itinerant specialists in early music. Both organizations are highly successful but have very different business models. The orchestra is much more capital intensive, especially with respect to hard capital, while Apollo's Fire enjoys both the flexibility and the limitations of not having its own performance space or a permanent full contingent of musicians. Similarly social service organizations such as Meals on Wheels or the Food Bank in Atlanta, Georgia have greater capital requirements than other local social service organizations such as the Georgia Justice Project or Families First, because of the technologies required to carry out their particular missions. These examples also illustrate that capital requirements can vary by organizational life stage. The Atlanta Food Bank started in a church basement and now occupies a massive physical storage and distribution plant and vehicle fleet. Similarly, Apollo's Fire may grow to a point where scheduling in local venues becomes prohibitively difficult and a permanent performance space becomes important. The history of Chicago's Steppenwolf Theater is instructive here (Proscio and Miller, 2003). Steppenwolf started in cheap rental space and outgrew this model as its popularity rose. Moreover, Steppenwolf ultimately became owners of significant real estate and theater capacity that required upkeep and occupancy to be economically sustainable.

In general, SPOs with significant "fixed costs" require a different pattern of capital financing than those whose costs are mainly variable and hence easily reduced when output-related revenues flag. Indeed, the issue of fixed costs in the performing arts helps explain the emergence of performing arts centers such as the Kennedy Center in Washington, DC, the Lincoln Center in New York, the Woodruff Arts Center in Atlanta, the Boch Center in Boston, and Play House Square in Cleveland. These nonprofits specialize in filling the seats of performing arts venues by serving multiple local and visiting performing arts organizations and relieving individual performing arts SPOs of the need to directly raise capital funds for facilities or ticketing and marketing systems.

Similar examples exist in the youth services area. In particular, organizations like Boys & Girls Clubs have been built around the concept of physical clubs located in local communities where youth can congregate for programs and activities. Other organizations such as Big Brothers/Big

Sisters follow a different model, preferring to offer their services within schools and community centers and in partnerships with other youth-serving organizations, minimizing requirements for maintaining physical facilities of their own.

An SPO's business model influences the possible sources of capital because it partly determines the nature of benefits it can generate. In particular, SPOs with significant physical facilities have greater opportunity to generate private or exchange benefits in the form of naming rights that can attract major donors or business sponsorships. Moreover, a physical building implies commitment to the community where it is located, increasing the likelihood that local community residents will support their perceived group benefits through donations or governmental allocations.

SOURCES OF CAPITAL

Benefits theory helps illuminate where SPOs can productively seek sources of capital because it poses the question – what benefits are received by providers of capital in return for their capital investments? Sources of capital may be broadly divided between *internal* and *external* sources. Internal sources include retained earnings (accumulating financial surpluses into funds for capital purposes), specific budgeting of operating funds for depreciation, repairs and capital enhancements, and so-called sweat equity consisting of volunteer effort by entrepreneurs and their associates in the process of building their organizations. External sources include individual and institutional gifts and grants, government grants and indirect costs charged to government contracts, borrowing from banks and other financial institutions, and sale of equity or ownership rights. Each of these sources is associated with different groups of capital providers and beneficiaries. Borrowing is of special interest because leveraging of assets with debt can put an SPO at risk of financial failure if the organization exceeds its ability to repay loans.

Research on the capital structure of organizations suggests some intrinsic preferences between internal and external sources of capital finance. Much of this research focuses on so-called "pecking order theory" (Calabrese, 2011; Yetman, 2007). Specifically, pecking order theory posits that business corporations generally prefer financing capital needs through internal sources such as retained earnings, followed by external financing – with a preference toward borrowing over sale of equity. In the nonprofit sector, pecking order theory has been reformulated to suggest that nonprofits also prefer internal to external sources of capital finance. Specifically, Calabrese has offered a modified pecking order theory for nonprofits that recognizes constrictions against sale of equity and managerial preferences to maintain minimal levels of internal funds rather than completely exhaust such funds before seeking external support for capital needs. In this version, nonprofits prefer internal sources of finance (retained earnings) to borrowing, but within limits. (Note that in accounting terms, profits or net earnings for nonprofits are referred to as changes in net assets.) As discussed below, however, various beneficiary groups and suppliers of capital, such as donors and lenders, influence the desirability and availability of both internal and external sources, thus nuancing SPO decisions to pursue alternative sources of capital funding in different circumstances. For example, hospitals in the U.S. generate surpluses which they are reluctant to use for capital purposes because retaining high levels of cash helps maintain high bond ratings. On the other hand, many nonprofits are reluctant to generate surpluses or retain cash so as not to appear too commercial or less needy to their donors.

Internal Sources

Capital financing through retained earnings presumes that an SPO can generate ongoing and substantial operating surpluses and have the discipline to put some of this surplus into funds for specific capital purposes. On paper this seems like a reasonable thing for any organization to do. It is good financial management practice to designate each of the following types of capital funds:

- *Working capital funds* to smooth out predictable cash flow variations over an annual cycle. For example, contributions-reliant SPOs often receive a disproportionate amount of their gifts toward the end of a tax year, when donors are reminded to take advantage of charitable deductions before the deadline. Since expenses are more likely to follow a more uniform pattern over time, working capital funds can help fill in the cash flow gaps when expenses exceed revenues.
- *Operating reserve funds* protect SPOs from unanticipated downturns. These are "rainy day" funds that help SPOs get through rough patches when revenues suddenly drop, such as the termination of a grant whose renewal was expected or an unanticipated expense such as purchases of new furniture after a building fire or weather disaster. Nonprofits are commonly advised to keep two to six months of operating expenses on hand in such funds, although there is no standard practice. Indeed, researchers have found that nonprofit organizations often fail to maintain operating reserves at all (Calabrese, 2013).

- *Capital replacement reserves* for maintaining and providing for long-term replacement of physical facilities. These commonly take the form of depreciation funds to which operating funds can be regularly budgeted. They can also take the form of sinking funds specifically designated for the construction of new facilities.
- *Endowments* for generating investment income for general operations or for special purposes such as scholarships, curatorships, or professorships, special programs or the maintenance of particular buildings or other assets. Endowments create opportunities for naming rights associated with assets in perpetuity or over some designated period of time.
- *Risk capital funds* for discretionary use to experiment with new ideas, ventures, or new strategic initiatives. Such funds may offer SPO executives flexibility to pursue innovations outside the normal programming of the organization.

In theory, allocating expenses within an SPO's operating budget toward each of these types of funds can be accommodated by internal sources of capital funding. However, each source of internal capital funding also imposes its own constraints deriving from its beneficiary group. Benefits theory suggests that each of these forms of internal capital financing will be subject to limitations associated with the beneficiary groups that directly or indirectly supply these resources or have a more general stake in the SPO's work. In particular:

Retained earnings are restrained by the organization's capacity to generate substantial operating surpluses. As discussed in Chapter 5, even if the organization produces private benefits for which it can charge fees, there may be mission-related reasons to avoid profit-enhancing pricing, especially if benefits are redistributive in nature. And even where private goods are offered on a commercial basis for the explicit purpose of raising net funds, SPOs will often face pressures from their various constituents to limit their profit-generating success so as not to appear overly commercial or to avoid tax problems. Moreover, where substantial profits are generated there may be considerable pressure to allocate them to support ongoing services and programs rather than to longer term capital needs. For SPOs that are contributions-reliant such pressures will be most intense, with donors often preferring to have their contributions put directly to work in service provision rather than saved for capital expenses. The practice of incorporating capital needs into current annual budgets faces similar pressures. For many SPOs, especially nonprofits, it may be difficult to maintain the discipline of regular contributions to capital funds (even working capital and operating reserves) through current budget allocations because mission-related needs and wants reflected in the preferences of beneficiary groups of consumers and donors will almost always exceed an SPO's fiscal capacity, so the tendency is to allocate all available funds directly to current service provision. In some cases, however, nonprofits may be tempted to disguise profits through accounting practices or even by changing their operations so as to avoid the political costs of appearing too profitable. In that circumstance, redirecting financial surpluses to a capital improvement fund may be more desirable.

Cooperative enterprises or membership-driven associations may be exceptions to the notion that retained earnings are a difficult way of raising investment capital. In these cases there is a confluence between service beneficiaries and providers of financial support, and generation of profits and/ or regular budget allocations may be viewed as easier ways to accumulate funds for capital purposes than separate appeals to members or to outside sources. Indeed, external funding is unlikely unless public benefits that fall outside the membership group can be cited, while internal sources are more likely because membership is similar to ownership in its incentives to maintain benefits of direct impact to members or shareholders who may view themselves as investors. Thus housing cooperatives or condominiums commonly finance their capital needs internally, for example through increases in fees that can be set aside for this purpose.

Finally, *sweat equity* is mostly likely to take the form of early efforts of social entrepreneurs to build their organizations and programs. As the term implies, this is most often manifested as unpaid labor. Frequently, however, organizational founders will also allocate their own material and financial assets, using personal bank accounts and credit cards, and leveraging physical assets such as their houses and vehicles. Sweat equity is rarely a sustainable form of capital financing and it applies mostly to soft capital such as planning and building of long-run human resource capacity. This is because founders see sweat equity as an investment, both in their personal future income and in the social benefits they seek to produce for their mission-related community of beneficiaries. Thus, in the long-run, sweat equity will not sustain an SPO's capital requirements. Social entrepreneurs such as Bill Bolling, the founder of the Atlanta Community Food Bank, or Jeannette Sorrell, founder of Apollo's Fire, the early music ensemble in Cleveland, put substantial amounts of uncompensated sweat equity into the early development of their organizations but eventually became paid executives.

External Sources

Pecking order theory notwithstanding, SPO's are generally likely to look to external sources for a substantial portion of their capital needs, especially as they mature beyond their initial stages of development. These sources include charitable contributions from individuals and foundations, government grants and contracts, borrowing from financial institutions, and sale of equity. As noted above, not all of these sources will be available to a particular type of SPO. For example, conventional nonprofits cannot sell equity shares and social purpose businesses in the form of for-profit firms will have difficulty attracting charitable contributions. However, as discussed below, various hybrid forms have been developed in order to expand SPO's access to external capital. Each external source of capital funding may be examined through the lens of benefits theory to assess its potential in particular circumstances, by focusing on the proclivities of beneficiary groups behind these sources.

Individual donors may be important sources of SPO capital in several ways. Major donors may be attracted by the private benefits that SPOs can confer in tandem with their contributions, especially various forms of recognition including inclusion in ascending levels of donor circles such as described in Chapter 9 in the case of the American Museum of Natural History, and naming rights on buildings, scholarship funds and other capital assets. Donors will of course also be motivated by the group, public and redistributive benefits that their gifts enable.

Capital campaigns are often an important strategy for raising individual (and institutional) donations for capital purposes. The idea of a capital campaign is to specify a menu of capital projects and needs and to set a target for campaign success and completion. Major individual and institutional donors are usually sought for lead gifts to give the campaign a head start before it goes public. This provides private benefits to major donors in the form of special recognition and it creates incentives for smaller individual donors to contribute to the collective good by participating in a joint effort to raise the mercury in the iconic campaign thermometer often employed to graphically demonstrate progress toward the target. As the target is approached, social pressure increases on those individuals in a donor community who have not yet contributed. This is a way of overcoming the tendency of beneficiaries of a public or group good to free ride on the generosity of their peers.

Institutional donors such as charitable foundations can be an important source of SPO capital in the form of capital grants. Indeed, many foundations confine their grant-making to capital projects, often because this is how they can leverage their relatively scarce resources to provide group or public benefits over a long period of time. Capital grants tend to be precisely targeted and confined within a discrete time frame, allowing foundations to claim social impact without having to subsidize SPO expenses over an extended period. While many charitable foundations now recognize the value of providing operating funds as well, this is generally not their forte. Foundations usually seek to fund SPOs that can demonstrate other means of sustaining themselves from year to year. Relatedly, an important innovation is the Program-related Investment (PRI), which usually takes the form of a low cost loan (Motter, 2013). Foundations can make such allocations for capital purposes to SPOs with the expectation that funds will be repaid over time. This in turn increases the leverage that foundations have for generating public benefits with their limited resources.

Corporate foundations or giving programs may also contribute to the capital funding of SPOs, for somewhat different reasons. Corporations often want to be seen as good corporate citizens that contribute to community-based capital campaigns. They may also seek exchange benefits in the form of brand recognition by having their names attached to new facilities or programs. For example, Home Depot, Southwest Airlines, Georgia Pacific, Southern Company, SunTrust and AT&T each have a major exhibition section named for them in Atlanta's Georgia Aquarium. This practice is especially true of corporations in industries related to the SPO's mission. Thus pharmaceutical companies may wish to endow labs or research programs in universities and health care institutions, and entertainment companies may offer capital gifts to museums or performing arts centers devoted to their industry. Thus, the Rock and Roll Hall of Fame was established through the formation of a foundation by music industry company executives; the foundation eventually helped fund the establishment of the museum itself (see below). Various music companies provide major gifts to the museum. Similarly, corporate health care and recreational firms contribute to Park Pride which addresses the capital needs of neighborhood parks (see below). Finally, the Ronald McDonald houses provide an interesting case in point, especially in terms of the potential hazards of corporate sponsorship. These houses offer residential accommodations for families of ill children in local hospitals. The national McDonalds corporation initiated the concept and provides some operational funding but local houses must raise their own capital (and operating) funds, sometimes with help from local franchisees. However, bearing the McDonalds name can prove to be a burden in seeking funds from other sources because McDonalds is perceived as the benefactor.

Government can also be an important source of capital funding for SPOs in various ways. Again, the Rock and Roll Hall provides a good illustration, as it was conceived as an important driver of economic development in Cleveland. As a consequence, the City of Cleveland, Cuyahoga County and the State of Ohio are all major contributors to the museum. Government capital support can manifest itself in ways other than capital grants as well. These include purchase of service contracts that include provisions for funding overhead that may accommodate borrowing costs for new construction or reimbursement for the depreciation of capital assets, borrowing through the issuance of tax exempt bonds, and tax credits provided to for-profit companies that can build and own buildings which can then be rented to nonprofits requiring these facilities. Government as a source of capital for SPOs reflects the general public benefits that SPOs may offer, such as economic development in the case of the Rock and Roll Hall or Evergreen Cooperatives (see below), or support for affordable housing as in the case of the Famicos Foundation (see Chapter 5).

Borrowing from banks and other financial institutions, or through government in the case of tax exempt bonds, can be an important source of capital financing for SPOs. Indeed, more than half of all nonprofits in the U.S. carry some kind of debt (Yetman, 2007). In addition, the securing of tax-exempt debt has been increasing, especially for larger U.S. nonprofits such as hospitals and universities, reaching an aggregate of almost $400 billion in 2011(Brody and Cordes, 2016). Large nonprofits have greater access to cheaper debt via tax exempt bonds, while contributions-reliant nonprofits make less use of debt than those more dependent on earned revenue. In particular, tax exempt bonds not only require the capacity for significant staff work and expertise, more likely available to larger organizations, but also the ability to generate a substantial and predictable earned income stream in order to secure a desirable bond rating.

These facts provide clues about the interests of issuers of debt. Consider that donors may be wary of supporting SPOs that are highly leveraged and possibly at risk of failure. In addition, donors may feel that their contributions are likely to pay for (past) debt rather than for the future mission-related benefits they prefer to support. This consideration does not arise in the case of earned revenue, where private benefits are provided in exchange for fees. Issuers of debt financing are concerned about the ability of borrowing SPOs to pay back the loans. The presence of a predictable revenue stream in the form of earned income may offer more assurance for banks and other profit-oriented lending institutions than other forms of future revenue such as contributions or government grants which may be considered less reliable or sustainable over the longer term. For nonprofit organizations in particular, the lack of ownership rights may also inhibit the designation of collateral to secure debts. In particular, assets such as endowments cannot be easily collateralized (Calabrese, 2011). Thus the ability to project a reliable future income stream becomes all the more important for the purpose of borrowing for capital needs. Add to this the fact that most lending institutions are generally more experienced and comfortable with loans to businesses and individuals than to SPOs and one can understand the caution with which they may approach SPO lending. Moreover, simply from a public relations point of view, it can seem rather cold-hearted for a bank or mortgage company to foreclose on a home-less shelter, church or community center. Important public relations costs may be incurred that can translate into losses of business patronage and profits. In part, this is why Yetman (2007) recommends that SPOs establish a credit record by borrowing and paying back so-called "reputation loans" so that the risk concerns of lenders can be eased. The ability to borrow is an additional reason for an SPO to establish reserve funds as well. Such cash reserves can serve as collateral as well as sources of emergency cash.

Finally, it is worth noting that borrowing can be helpful in conjunc-tion with other forms of capital financing. For example, nonprofits will often borrow with "bridge financing" to complement a capital campaign in order to move forward with construction projects while they collect on multi-year pledges. It is good practice, however, to avoid borrowing first and then initiating a campaign to pay the loan. Donors may then balk at contributing to debt relief rather than additions to mission impact. Indeed, many foundations have policies prohibiting such gifts. However, some foundations now show increasing interest in Program-related Investments (PRIs) which commonly take the form of low cost loans, sometimes with modest or flexible expectations for pay back (Motter, 2013).

The *sale of equity* or ownership shares can be an important source of capital for certain kinds of SPOs including social purpose businesses and standard cooperatives. Conventional nonprofits have no owners per se and are prohibited from selling stock, and most social cooperatives are organ-ized as nonprofit organizations. However, there are various indirect ways for nonprofits to sell equity in aspects of their operations. For example, nonprofits can have ownership of for-profit enterprises which then sell equity to other shareholders for the purpose of raising funds for capital facilities that the nonprofits require for their mission-related work. An interesting example is Pioneer Human Services, a nonprofit which assists high risk individuals to build work histories in order to help them secure gainful employment (Cordes, Poletz and Steuerle, 2009). In order to expand the opportunities for its clients Pioneer created a for-profit invest-ment fund Pioneer Social Ventures LLC to attract private equity from investors interested in investing in local communities while receiving a reasonable financial return. Alternatively, as noted previously, nonprofits can earn tax credits from projects involving affordable housing, historical preservation or other qualifying activities, which they can sell to for-profit firms. In turn, those incentives may induce for-profit providers to raise other (equity) capital in order to engage in projects of interest to the nonprofit (such as affordable housing).

Still, the nonprofit form of organization is fundamentally constrained in its capacity to attract equity capital. Thus, various new, hybrid types of SPOs such as Low Profit Limited Liability Companies (L3Cs), Community Interest Companies (CICs) and Benefit Corporations that combine characteristics of the nonprofit and for-profit forms may be understood in part as new vehicles for SPOs to access capital through equity markets. As described by Brewer (2016) and Steinberg (2015), alternative legal forms of SPO attract and manage equity investors in different ways:

- Conventional nonprofits have no owners and cannot access equity capital, except indirectly through partnering arrangements with for-profit firms as noted above.
- L3C, Benefit and Flexible Benefit Corporations of various types (in many U.S. states) make clear in their incorporation documents that they intend to pursue social as well as financial goals. This protects management from liability to shareholders insisting on maximum financial returns, and it signals to socially minded investors their intent to pursue social goals and possibly limit profits.
- Community Interest Companies (in the U.K.) give priority to social goals and, if they choose to incorporate as companies "limited by shares," can pay dividends to equity investors subject to restrictions of a partial "asset lock" that controls the price of shares and to whom they may be sold (or distributed in the case of dissolution) (Steinberg, 2015).
- B Corporations (in the U.S.) are for-profit companies that adhere to the social and environmental standards of B Lab, a nonprofit certifying organization. B Lab certification signals to investors both the practices and values of the company, with implicit consequences for its financial prospects and social impacts.
- Cooperatives (in the U.K., Europe, U.S. and elsewhere) provide membership shares which may in some cases (for example, housing cooperatives in the U.S.) be seen as a form of equity that can appreciate or depreciate in value and which may be sold within the context of specific rules and regulations consistent with the organization's mission (Michie, 2015).

The cooperative form deserves further attention here. First, as noted, so-called social cooperatives are commonly incorporated as nonprofit organizations, in Canada, the U.S., Italy and elsewhere. Such cooperatives do not finance capital needs by selling equity or shares. Cooperatives in some areas such as housing and farm marketing do sell equity shares, however, and some of these are large corporations such as CHS, a Fortune 100 company owned by farmers, ranchers and other stockholders, that sells energy and agriculture related products and supports agricultural business through various services including insurance and advisory services (CHS, 2016). However, other cooperatives, in such fields as credit unions, child care, home health care and low income housing do not have share capital, while still others have partial asset locks under which selling of shares is heavily restricted. Cooperatives in such fields as credit unions often rely on retained earnings to finance capital needs since they have restricted access to other sources (Mook, Maiorano and Quarter, 2015).

The securing of capital funds through the sale of equity is literally a frontier in the field of social finance in which there is currently much experimentation, innovation and debate (Nicholls, Paton and Emerson, 2015). However, the underlying premise is that prospective equity investors (as well as lenders) vary widely in their motivations and the degrees to which they insist on maximum financial returns and/or particular levels of risk for their capital investments. Thus, scholars and designers of social finance schema propose different possible layers of investment in SPOs, according to the different types of investors they may attract. Thus, Oleksiak, Nicholls and Emerson (2015, p. 230) describe the Deutsche Bank-sponsored Eye Fund's structure which "attracted many (mostly institutional) investors with different objectives" including socially motivated commercial investors, development finance institutions and PRI/social investors who accepted different rates of financial return and were willing to accept different levels of risk. Similarly, as reported by Steinberg (2015, p. 84), Brakman Reiser describes "a tranched membership structure proposed by advocates of the L3C, designed to promote access to equity capital and incentivize efficiency while pursuing a sustainable social mission."

In the context of benefits theory, the various types of SPO are able to appeal to the interests of socially-minded investors in different ways and degrees. Some investors must be offered strictly private benefits in the form of competitive market returns while others may require a combination of private financial benefit and personal satisfaction deriving from the knowledge that they are helping to support provision of a public good. Still other institutional investors, such as charitable foundations and corporations seeking to be socially and environmentally responsible, invest in a manner consistent with their particular organizational missions.

Conventional business corporations may also decide of their own volition to address social goals. This is a relatively straightforward strategy for closely held businesses where owners can do what they want. It gets more complicated with publicly owned corporations or partnerships with widely distributed shares where the preferences of other shareholders (or potential predator/takeover investors) must be accommodated or resisted. The cases of Newman's Own which donates all of its profits to charity, or Ben & Jerry's whose social and environmental goals were subjugated to profit-making pressures when it was taken over by Unilever, are classic examples. The case of WCLV (WCLV, 2016) is one in which for-profit owners of a classical radio station chose to engineer a conversion into nonprofit form rather than have it ultimately absorbed into the commercial marketplace where its focus would inevitably change. (For additional examples see Legorreta and Young, 1986.) Indeed, the latter scenario is an interesting one with respect to the role of equity capital in building a social purpose organization. One clear scenario for owner/entrepreneurs motivated to grow such an organization is to build it as a for-profit with their own equity capital and that of similarly minded investors and later convert it or sell it to a nonprofit organization willing to carry on the mission in perpetuity. Such a scenario is possible in various fields such as hospitals where for-profit to nonprofit conversions have occurred and journalism where social missions of for-profit entities have been threatened by commercial pressures. (Note, the reverse case is also of interest; for example many nonprofit hospitals have been sold to for-profit corporations, with the proceeds going into a foundation or other nonprofit entity as a source of fresh capital for social initiatives.)

SOCIAL IMPACT BONDS: A HYBRID INNOVATION

The Social Impact Bond is a recent innovation that, despite its name, is not so much a bond as a contract relationship between government and private investors who agree to take on risk in the financing of an innovative social program in return for financial reward (and social recognition) contingent on program success. In the words of Nicholls and Tomkinson (2015, p. 336): "a SIB involves a set of contracts, the basis of which is an agreement by government to pay investors for an improvement in a special social outcome once it has been achieved." Callanan, Law and Mendonca (2012) further elaborate that SIBs are more like multi-year, multi-stakeholder partnerships bound by a series of contracts, rather than bonds or debt instruments per se; hence they carry more risk than traditional government bonds. As such, SIBs provide a combination of risk capital and working capital for a nonprofit, government or other SPO provider to carry out a new approach to addressing a social goal. Although SIB schemes vary in their details, essentially investors front the money for a designated program. If the program succeeds by preset benchmarks, the government (and possibly other sponsors) pays investors for the cost of the program plus a risk premium. If benchmarks are not achieved, no payment is made.

The purpose of SIBs is to increase the infusion of capital funds into the social sector (SPOs) and to minimize government spending on unsuccessful programs. SIBs require both reliable and valid metrics that effectively capture the social goals that are sought, and they must provide sufficiently high potential financial returns to attract investors willing to bear the risk. Here too, however, the potential pool of investors may include both profit-seekers and social investors willing to accept risk and more modest returns. And given the central role of metrics, it is not surprising that SIBs have targeted social problems that are easily translatable into quantitative indicators such as recidivism, educational achievement, drop-out rates, and homelessness.

According to Nicholls and Tomkinson (2015), SIBs are underway in at least a half dozen countries including the U.K., U.S., Australia, Belgium, the Netherlands and Canada. Two of the best known are the Peterborough project in the U.K. and the Rikers Island initiative in the U.S., both centered on reducing recidivism in correctional systems. In the Peterborough case, a special organizational entity called the Social Impact Partnership (SIP) was created as an intermediary body between investors and a government fund under the Ministry of Justice. Contracts between the Ministry and the SIP stipulated that payments would be made "in the event that reoffending is reduced for male, short-sentenced prisoners released from HMP [Her Majesty's Prison] Peterborough" (Nicholls and Tomkinson, 2015, p. 345). A total investment pool of 5 million pounds sterling was created from 17 investors including 10 charitable foundations and trusts. Funds were invested in several integrated social support strategies addressing the needs of prisoners and their families, during and after incarceration. As of 2014, the project appeared to be moderately successful with the rate of reconvictions approaching the target levels required to trigger payments back to investors (Nicholls and Tomkinson, 2015).

Similarly, the Rikers Island SIB in New York City focused on reduced recidivism for juvenile offenders. In this case, the major investor was the security firm Goldman Sachs (GS) which invested $9.6 million in the project with the potential payback from zero up to $20.5 million if the program were completely successful by achieving a recidivism rate reduction of more than 20 percent (Rudd et al., 2013). However, GS did not bear all of the risk. In particular, the bond was underwritten by Bloomberg

Philanthropies, guaranteeing at least a $7.2 million return of capital. Thus GS essentially risked $2.4 million if the project failed to at least return its capital investment. In the end, the Rikers Island initiative did not lead to significant recidivism reduction, hence no payments were made to Goldman Sachs aside from the Bloomberg philanthropy guarantee (Vera Institute of Justice, 2015).

Of interest from the viewpoint of benefits theory is the nature of investors drawn into the SIB arrangements. In both the Peterborough and Rikers Island cases, very significant participation was required by investors with social rather than financial goals, principally charitable foundations. Nonetheless, SIBs allowed the provision of both private benefits to financially driven investors, as well as social benefits favored by charitable donors and government deriving from prospective successful programming to reduce recidivism and government expenses.

CROWD-FUNDING AND OTHER NEW FORMS OF CAPITAL FUNDING

Crowd-funding, through hundreds of Internet and social media sites, is rapidly becoming an important source of capital funding for social purpose organizations. These include platforms to raise donations (for example, Indiegogo.com), provide loans (for example, Kiva.org), make equity investments (for example, Equitynet.com) or offer other rewards in exchange for project start-up funding (for example, Kickstarter.com) (Mook, Whitman, Quarter and Armstrong., 2015). In the U.S., the Securities and Exchange Commission now approves crowd-funding portals to raise equity, by-passing traditional securities brokers, and providing an expanded channel for social enterprises to raise capital funds by amassing investments from many small investors. Crowd-funding appears to be especially attractive for raising start-up capital for new projects by smaller organizations and less well-known social entrepreneurs, given its ability to reach large numbers of Internet-savvy, socially conscious potential donors, lenders and investors (Lehner, 2015). But even better known organizations are taking advantage of this mechanism. For example, the nonprofit Big Apple Circus in New York City recently embarked on an online campaign to raise capital for staging its upcoming season (Bellafante, 2016).

The role of platforms as fiscal intermediaries is critical to crowd-funding in its various manifestations, given the diffuse population of prospective donors, lenders and investors involved. They provide in one place, detailed information on alternative investment, lending and giving opportunities, so that prospective capital providers can make more informed decisions, whether they value social impact, personal reward or a combination of thereof. The platforms also collect and report on investment totals and document testimonials on alternative projects, offering feedback in the form of the "wisdom of crowds" (Surowiecki, 2005). And they monitor and screen potential fraud and abuse by fund seekers, helping to side step the "lemons problem" that can undercut participation (Ackerlof, 1970). All of these are important to potential resource providers, whether they are gift givers, lenders or investors. As such, platforms are instrumental in building trust between potential funders and recipient SPOs and entrepreneurs. In particular, the platforms' provision of reliable data helps overcome the "information asymmetry" problems intrinsic to evaluating multiple alternative opportunities at a distance (Economist magazine, 2016). In addition, the platforms can offer incentives to ensure that funds are properly used and not wasted. One common option is to return funds to the provider if the target level of funding sought for a given project is not reached, the so-called "provision point mechanism" or "assurance contract" in fund-raising. Such strategies can help overcome free riding in the voluntary support of collective goods (as discussed in Chapter 6), and they are useful as well in raising equity and loan capital where there is a risk of fraud or abuse. In short, crowd-funding platforms perform the function of reducing the transactions costs to large groups of prospective beneficiaries/investors who value what SPOs are offering and seek reliable avenues to invest, lend or donate to them. These investors offer individually modest but collectively substantial resources.

Another important innovation is the mobilization of investment capital for social impact through new funds and financial instruments accessible to socially motivated small investors. An important example is the Calvert Foundation established in 1988 as a nonprofit offshoot of Calvert Investments. Calvert Foundation pioneered the Community Investment Note (Calvert Foundation, 2016) which allows interested parties to invest as little as $20 in a fixed income security based on returns of a diversified portfolio consisting of investments in nonprofit organizations, microfinance institutions, social enterprises and loan funds that focus on vulnerable communities in the U.S. and worldwide. These investments consist largely of loans as well as stocks and other securities that support affordable housing, community development international microfinance, fair trade and social enterprise, with two-thirds allocated in the U.S. and one-third internationally. While the Community Investment Note is not without risk, Calvert claims a more than 99 percent investor repayment rate. The notes are offered on terms of 1 to 15 years with a financial return of 0 percent to 4 percent. In addition, investors are provided with annual social impact reports and quarterly updates. As a charitable nonprofit, the Calvert Foundation also receives foundation grants itself to support its operations. The Community Investment Note has enabled the foundation to maintain an investment portfolio of more than $180 million in 200 enterprises in 80 different countries. This mechanism is clearly designed to appeal to many small, socially minded investors who benefit from a mix of modest, secure financial returns and the satisfaction that investments are having a positive social impact in distressed communities. It does so by minimizing the transactions costs associated with such investments, reducing risk through diversification, and by offering notes in manageable denominations and maturities.

While Community Investment Notes allow socially minded investors to invest in a portfolio of SPOs, Community Bonds permit individual nonprofit organizations to issue their own bonds to such investors (Di Verdi, 2012). In Canada, the Centre for Social Innovation (CSI) has pioneered the use of such bonds to finance the purchase and restoration of buildings in Toronto for its own use and to provide workspace for other "social mission organizations" (Centre for Social Innovation, 2016). In particular, in 2010 CSI raised $2 million by selling $10,000 (taxable) bonds with a 4 percent return, maturing in five years. In 2016 CSI had on offer another Community Bond to purchase and renovate an additional building, for its own use and to house such SPOs as the Toronto Fringe Festival, Toronto Tool Library and TechSoup Canada, with three options requiring $10,000, $50,000 or $1,000 investments at interest rates of 4 percent, 4.5 percent and 3 percent respectively. The bonds are neither guaranteed nor tax exempt, but they are backed by mortgages to which investors have claim after other lien holders. Thus the bonds involve risk and they are not rated by bond rating agencies but they appeal to socially minded investors with particular interests in the work of the issuing SPO and who can accept the risk while receiving a reasonable rate of financial return. In the case of CSI, there is a good track record of payments upon which its recent offering is based. As with other types of borrowing, CSI also counts on its earned revenue streams to assure its borrowers that interest payments will be made and principal repaid.

INTERESTING CASES

The Rock and Roll Hall of Fame (R&R Hall) and Evergreen Cooperatives in Cleveland and Park Pride in Atlanta illustrate three different approaches to the capital funding of SPOs. In the case of the R&R Hall, industry and other contributors, government, and museum visitors are key beneficiary groups responsible for generating income used for capital formation. Park

Pride, a charitable nonprofit organization dedicated to the preservation and development of neighborhood parks, serves to mobilize capital from corporate and individual donors in order to support the capital needs of local parks and greenspaces in Atlanta neighborhoods. Evergreen Cooperatives brings together government, foundations and several major "anchor" institutions in one distressed area in Cleveland to finance new cooperative green, worker owned businesses employing local residents, through an innovative cooperative development fund.

The Rock and Roll Hall of Fame and Museum

The Rock and Roll Hall of Fame and Museum located in Cleveland, Ohio grew out of the work of the Rock and Roll Hall of Fame Foundation in New York, which was instrumental in its founding and continues to support its work. Efforts leading to creation of the Rock and Roll Hall began in 1983 when a group of music industry leaders formed a nonprofit organization to recognize the creators and performers of rock and roll music. That organization became the Rock and Roll Foundation, established in 1985 in New York. The foundation was subsequently approached by officials from Cleveland and the state of Ohio with the idea of the museum, given Cleveland's seminal history in developing and promoting rock and roll. The foundation eventually sanctioned the project and selected Cleveland as the site in 1986. The museum is organized as a 501(c)(3) nonprofit organization, distinct from but symbiotic with the foundation. The museum opened in 1995 with a series of celebratory events including an all-star concert to help with initial capitalization. In 2008 the foundation provided an $8 million gift to the museum's capital campaign, which it used to build its library and archive center and later redesign its interior space. In 2009, the foundation staged a 25th anniversary concert in New York to help fund the museum's initial endowment. The foundation continues to provide funding for the museum's capital projects and remains the largest single contributor to the Museum (Rock and Roll Hall of Fame, 2016).

The mission statement of the Rock and Roll Hall of Fame and Museum is:

> [T]o educate visitors, fans and scholars from around the world about the history and continuing significance of rock and roll music. It carries out this mission through its operation of a world-class museum that collects, preserves, exhibits and interprets this art form and through its library and archives as well as its educational programs. (Rock and Roll Hall of Fame, 2016)

Given its mission to educate visitors, fans and scholars from around the world about the history and continuing significance of rock and roll music, the museum collects, preserves, exhibits and interprets this art form and promotes and preserves it through its library, archives and educational and community programs. The museum's programs can be broadly divided into four areas: Exhibitions of resident and visiting collections; targeted educational programming; community programs and special events; and archival development and research. Its collections attract museum visitors from all parts of the nation and the world (some 90 percent from outside the Cleveland area). The educational programs are targeted to (mostly local) children and teachers, carried out largely in partnership with schools and other local institutions such as University Hospitals, the Beck Center for the Arts, and Case Western Reserve and Cleveland State universities. The R&R Hall also offers a variety of more general programs for the local community. These include celebration of Black history month, an American Music Masters series of lectures by artists and professionals, and a series of special (fund-raising) events including community festivals, the Fortune Battle of Corporate Bands – an amateur band competition sponsored by corporations, and a Rock and Roll Hall Annual Benefit Concert.

Archiving and research constitute a critical facet of the R&R Hall's programming. In 2012 the museum opened a 23,000 square foot Library and Archive facility on the campus of nearby Cuyahoga Community College, which houses a comprehensive collection of materials on the history of rock and roll. Finally, the museum collaborates with other local nonprofit institutions in community benefit activities, such as the *Guitarmania* public art project in 2002 which placed artistically unique guitar sculptures on display outside prominent Cleveland organizations, and community partnerships with United Way, Make-a-Wish Foundation and other charities, to help those charities raise funds for their own causes.

As a world-class institution with a universal mission, the R&R Hall serves a global community with its archival, exhibition and educational programming. This community of beneficiaries includes fans of rock and roll from all parts of the world, multinational corporations with a connection to the music industry or to brands that gain from association with music celebrities and the rock and roll music genre, scholars of music and popular culture, educators who use the resources of the museum to inform their students, and those who perform or are otherwise employed in the production and distribution of popular music itself. Thus, independent of its location, the R&R Hall serves the interests of all who benefit from the popular music industry since it showcases the industry and preserves, displays and educates about its contributions to society.

The R&R Hall was also conceived as an engine of economic development and renewal for the City of Cleveland and its surrounding region. To the extent that the museum draws tourism and other forms of commerce to

Cleveland, it benefits the region's citizenry whether or not they are specifically interested in music per se. It is noteworthy that rock and roll is integral to the identity and history of the City of Cleveland and a major reason why Cleveland was chosen as the site for the museum. As such it confers a general community benefit to the citizens of Cleveland in the form of public image and reputation, effects that are somewhat intangible but no doubt contribute to the city's competitive position as a tourist destination and place to live and work.

Additionally, many of the programs of the museum are specifically targeted to Cleveland-based beneficiary groups. These include a significant proportion of the audience that visits the museum annually, students and teachers in local school districts who take advantage of the museum's educational programming, local companies and ordinary citizens who participate in the museum's various community-oriented events, and local fans, musicians and researchers who use its resources for their own purposes.

The benefits of the museum can be appreciated as stemming from a mixture of public and private type goods. Visitors, students, teachers, gift store customers and scholars benefit from the private goods or services they individually consume – ranging from classes to exhibitions to access to historical materials. Companies also benefit individually from their associations with the museum through public relations benefits that help them promote their particular commercial interests, while school districts and universities enhance their educational and research offerings by partnering with the museum. These private and exchange type benefits suggest multiple roles for fee income and sponsorships to support the museum's operations and capital needs.

Alternatively, the public and collective benefits of the museum are shared widely by various constituencies. The business community in Cleveland and the music industry broadly benefit from the visibility and positive image that the museum brings to these segments of the business economy, benefitting all companies in these categories. Communities of artists, scholars and music lovers benefit from the presence of the museum, over and above their individual use of museum services, suggesting a role that philanthropy can play in the financing of the museum. Finally, as a critical element in the economic welfare of the city and region, the museum offers general public benefits accruing to all local citizens in the form of civic pride and prosperity, suggesting a role for local and state government to invest in the museum through tax-based resources.

The Rock and Roll Hall depends on a diverse mix of financial sources to support its operations as reflected in its various beneficiary groups. However, this mix is heavily weighted toward fee income, although the relative level of contributions seems gradually to be increasing while government support is modest and sporadic. A $35 million capital campaign approved in 2006, although targeted to the building of a permanent library and archive, may have stimulated the growth of contributions and established the basis for future investment income. Indeed the campaign included provisions to support general museum renovation as well as the start of a board-designated endowment fund to generate income for operations.

Given the close association between the museum and the industry it represents, it is perhaps surprising that corporate support is not more strongly represented in the museum's income portfolio. At roughly 15 percent of contributions, or less than 5 percent of operating revenues overall, corporate interests appear to disproportionately benefit from the museum, compared to the support they provide to it. Corporate names are prominent in the displays of the museum itself, and the star power of rock and roll is compatible with the promotion of many marketed products. Corporate memberships or sponsorships therefore seem relatively undeveloped as a resource strategy for the long-term health and growth of the museum, despite business's omnipresence in its programming. However, corporate support seems better reflected in the grant-making of the Rock and Roll Foundation in New York which raises its funds mostly through fund-raising events to which corporations subscribe.

The collective (public and group) benefits offered by the museum are also considerable and probably underfinanced. Local government strongly supported the effort to bring the annual awards ceremony (previously held in New York) to Cleveland in 2009 and continues to make a steady investment in the organization. As a key element in Cleveland's economic development, the museum seems likely to stay on government's radar but at roughly 5 percent of the museum's operating revenue, it seems unlikely that general government can do more for this specialized institution. More likely is increased support from educational institutions and school districts which already recognize and support the benefits of music education, and the value of preserving cultural artifacts for research. The museum has made considerable efforts to develop these partnerships as a way to enhance the public side of the museum's programming.

More specifically, the capital needs of the R&R Hall have been supported in several ways – through capital campaigns, the building of endowments including board-designated funds deriving from operating income and infusions of grant funding by the Rock and Roll Hall of Fame Foundation which accumulates and disburses funds to the museum from its own endowment and fund-raising events. Corporate beneficiaries provide essential capital through contributions and sponsorships of special events. The Foundation also generates capital through investment income on its endowment which it passes along to the museum in the form of grants. In this way, the Foundation serves as an effective fund-raising intermediary for the museum, building its own capital by mobilizing the support of disparate corporate and other beneficiaries and then disbursing grant funds to the museum as needed for both capital and operating purposes.

Park Pride

Park Pride is a 501(c)(3) nonprofit organization in Atlanta whose mission is "to provide programs, services, funding and leadership to engage communities in developing and improving parks and greenspaces" (Park Pride, 2016). While its own capital requirements are modest, Park Pride is essentially in the business of building and maintaining the capital infrastructure of parks and greenspace of Atlanta's neighborhoods. Park Pride offers various programs including: partnerships with groups in more than 80 neighborhoods to improve local greenspace through its Friends of the Park program; coordinating volunteers to work in local parks through its Volunteer Program; helping communities articulate visions for their parks through its Park Visioning Program; and stimulating involvement in the Atlanta BeltLine, a major public/private partnership project that is converting old railroad right of way into walking and bicycle paths around the city, through its Adopt-the-Beltline program; and sponsoring a series of events for local park advocates and enthusiasts including conferences, picnics, workshops and park tours. All of the forgoing initiatives can be viewed as mobilizing the "soft capital" needed by neighborhood groups to build and maintain their green spaces. Park Pride's main initiative, however, to which it devotes more than half of its annual budget, is a re-granting program that provides funds to some 15 community groups in the City of Atlanta and unincorporated areas of neighboring DeKalb County to finance capital improvements in parks, helping communities to bring their park "visions" to fruition. These grants are funded by gifts from local foundations including the Robert W. Woodruff Foundation, Home Depot Foundation and Cecil B. Day Foundation (Park Pride, 2016).

Park Pride's own financing is largely contributions-based, with approximately 82 percent of its roughly $1.5 million in revenues deriving from gifts and grants, compared to 17 percent from earned income and less than 1 percent from investment income. Major contributors include locally based corporations such as Home Depot, Cox Enterprises, Georgia Power and Georgia Pacific; major local nonprofit contributors including Kaiser Permanente, the Atlanta Botanical Garden, Piedmont Healthcare, the Conservation Fund and the Trust for Public Land, as well as several dozen individual donors.

In essence, Park Pride functions as a capital accumulation and distribution mechanism. Rather than serving its mission directly with a capital improvement program of its own, it mobilizes the resources of multiple local institutional and individual donors toward the common purpose of servicing the capital needs of Atlanta's local parks. Indeed, most of its institutional donors have affinities to Park Pride's mission, including corporate donors with interests in local construction and infrastructure, health care institutions addressing public health, and nonprofits concerned with environmental conservation and nature. None of these donors would themselves have a sufficiently strong interest in local parks, but together through Park Pride, a significant if not critical mass of capital funding is mobilized. Park Pride thus serves to overcome both free-rider effects of numerous beneficiaries, as well as the transactions cost that would be associated with multiple fund development efforts by neighborhood level groups.

Evergreen Cooperatives

The Evergreen Cooperative Initiative is a complex and ambitious project to stabilize and revitalize the local economy in Cleveland through the development of worker-owned cooperative businesses that create new, sustainable jobs in low income neighborhoods. The effort, begun in 2008, is led by the Cleveland Foundation and works with local government and other major founding "anchor" institutions – Case Western Reserve University, University Hospitals, and the Cleveland Clinic – in the Greater University Circle area of the city where these institutions are located. The effort was capitalized by a $3million grant from the Cleveland Foundation and funding from the other anchor institutions, as well as local and federal government funds, through the newly created Evergreen Cooperative Development Fund LLC (called The Fund). The vision is to have this fund grow to more than $50 million in assets, through investments by the anchor institutions, local and national foundations, all levels of government, and individuals, in the form of gifts and grants, program-related and "socially responsible investments" as well as tax credits and low interest loans. The Fund, managed by the economic development nonprofit organization Enterprise Cleveland, provides low interest, long-term financing to start-up cooperative enterprises that provide services to the anchor institutions and employ local residents (Evergreen Toolkit, 2016; Evergreen Cooperatives, 2016; Brodwin, 2016).

Evergreen is notable for its role in generating and allocating capital funding for SPOs at two levels. At the municipal level it creates a pool of investment capital for start-up worker-owned cooperative businesses.

This pool then helps capitalize the businesses themselves. To date, these businesses include:

- The Evergreen Cooperative Laundry (ECL), an industrial scale laundry which services the needs of University Hospitals and the Cleveland Clinic. ECL was capitalized with investments by The Fund, as well as loans from the federal and city governments, loans from local banks and tax credits under the federal New Market Tax Credit program.
- The Ohio Solar Cooperative (OCS), a clean energy business that owns, installs and maintains solar panels on rooftops of the anchor institutions. It is also capitalized by the Fund, other loans and grants, as well as federal New Market and Solar tax credits.
- Green City Growers (GCG), a large scale hydroponic food production greenhouse located in the heart of the city. The area's hospitals and health care facilities, as well as local supermarkets, are its customer base. GCG is capitalized by the City of Cleveland which secured the land, by state grants and loans, a loan from the Fund, and New Market tax credits.

While early in its development the Evergreen Cooperatives initiative is interesting from a benefits theory point of view in several ways. First, it is an effort to engage beneficiary groups and institutions in a comprehensive manner, focusing on the particular (exchange) benefits to major local institutions, the general public good stemming from an improved local economy, and the redistributive benefits to local residents and neighborhoods, the latter two embodied by government and philanthropic interests such as the Cleveland Foundation. Second, these beneficiaries are cultivated in multiple ways to yield capital resources for social enterprises, including loans, grants and tax credits. Third, the initiative exemplifies how various forms of SPO can be engaged in socially significant projects, including nonprofits, cooperative for-profit businesses, public/private partnerships and major nonprofit institutions. Based loosely on the model of the Mondragon Cooperative Corporation in Spain (Whyte and Whyte, 1991), the Evergreen Cooperative initiative has generated great interest on the part of several other U.S. cities seeking to solve their issues of urban redevelopment and poverty alleviation.

OVERVIEW

As with operating income, the sources of capital financing generally reflect the nature of benefits that SPOs provide. SPOs that offer private benefits financed by earned income can accumulate surpluses for capital purposes through retained earnings. SPOs that provide public or group benefits can solicit charitable gifts for capital acquisition or the accumulation of capital assets into endowment funds, enhanced by private incentives such as naming rights, to overcome free riding. Capital campaigns also mobilize incentives for capital financing of public and group goods by setting goals and exerting social pressure on community beneficiaries. SPOs offering public or re-distributive benefits funded by government may recover indirect costs for overhead expenses, including depreciation of capital assets, and may also take advantage of governmental grant and tax incentive programs.

Borrowing and sale of equity are especially important mechanisms for capital financing of SPOs, and both of these mechanisms are more easily available to SPOs that offer private benefits that can be financed through earned income. In particular, future earned income streams offer some assurance of ability to repay loans, against which lenders can judge risk. Similarly, sale of equity is essentially based on the capitalized value of future income streams, most easily gauged by ongoing sources of fee income deriving from the provision of private benefits, rather than more episodic and uncertain grant income or government funding underwriting group, public and redistributive benefits. Moreover, individual or institutional donors may resist giving to indebted SPOs for fear that their gifts will be used to pay for past obligations rather than future benefits.

Despite differences in mission and the nature of benefits provided, all SPOs have capital financing needs, especially those with more capital intensive operations such as universities, museums, and hospitals. As a result, SPOs must be creative and flexible in their capital financing strategies, pushing against constraints imposed by the nature of benefits they offer and the particular legal forms through which they operate. Creative strategies take two basic forms – special mechanisms to enhance the ability to raise capital through the sources of income naturally suited to their circumstances, and innovative approaches to access sources of capital not easily accessible to them. For nonprofits, the first category includes capital campaigns, naming strategies and other incentivizing means of boosting capital giving, as well as specialized institutional units explicitly constructed to mobilize charitable capital. In the case of the Rock and Roll Hall of Fame, the Rock and Roll Foundation specializes in mobilizing gifts from industry and philanthropic institutions for the purpose of making capital as well as operating grants to the museum.

Similarly, Park Pride defines its mission as one of providing support to local neighborhood organizations, largely through accumulation of funds to support the capital grants it makes to build or improve local parks and greenspaces. Evergreen Cooperatives takes advantage of governmental tax credit programs and engages anchor institutions in the capital financing of cooperative businesses specifically designed to service some of their needs.

The second category includes efforts to draw equity capital into the social sector through new legal forms and financing mechanisms. Thus, new kinds of social businesses seek to attract a wider spectrum of investors whose motivations may include both personal financial gain and support of social benefits. Similarly, social impact bonds are designed to attract major private investors willing to bear considerable risk for both their own financial benefit and the chance to contribute to a public good, while new socially-focused finance funds such as the Calvert Foundation and the Evergreen Cooperative Development Fund lower the transactions costs for multiple parties, small and large, to invest in socially impactful projects and organizations. Other innovative mechanisms as well, such as crowd-funding, community investment notes, and community bonds can be understood as strategies to extend the borrowing and equity financing possibilities of social purpose organizations (especially smaller and newer ones) by accessing a broader population of potential donors and investors interested in both private gain and social impacts including the provision of valued public goods.

One lesson of these new approaches is that the fundamental work of social purpose organizations can often be appealing to a wider array of sources of capital financing than is conventionally associated with any particular organizational form. At the root of this lesson is the fact that most SPOs, in whatever form they exist, offer (actually and potentially) a mix of private, group, public, redistributive and exchange benefits. Often these benefits can be translated into capital support without radical transformations or wholly new finance mechanisms. Nonprofit organizations in particular have been creative in providing private incentives to support charitable giving for public and group goods, and in overcoming free rider effects. Moreover, they have obtained broader access to equity investments through indirect ownership arrangements and partnerships, and to borrowing by being transparent in their finances and establishing good credit records over time. Similarly, cooperatives, whose benefits are traditionally focused on and financed by their members, can leverage charitable gifts by promoting the public benefits encompassed by their missions, and they can extend equity financing and borrowing by engaging in earned income ventures and selling shares to the public at large. As well, socially-minded businesses may obtain access to government funds and to program-related investments of charitable foundations by highlighting the public benefits associated with their ventures. These various strategies help account for the blurring of the boundaries between government, business, cooperative and nonprofit organizations over time (Billis, 2010; Mook et al., 2015b). Similarly, the experimentation with new legal forms such as social businesses and social cooperatives reflect efforts of SPOs to access the capital that they need to fully exploit the array of public and private benefits they are capable of addressing within the context of their missions.

REFERENCES

George A. Ackerlof, 1970. "The Market for 'Lemons'", *The Quarterly Journal of Economics*, 84(3), pp. 488–500.

Gina Bellafante, 2016. "Big Apple Circus Tries to Keep Its Tent Upright", *New York Times*, June 5, pp. 24–25.

David Billis, 2010. *Hybrid Organizations and the Third Sector*, New York: Palgrave Macmillan.

Cassady V. Brewer, 2016. "The Ongoing Evolution in Social Enterprise Legal Forms", Chapter 3 in Dennis R. Young, Elizabeth A. Searing and Cassady V. Brewer (eds), *The Social Enterprise Zoo*, Cheltenham, UK and Northampton, MA, USA: Edward Elgar Publishing, pp. 33–64.

David Brodwin, 2016. "A New Economy Grows in the Shadows of the Republican National Convention", *U.S. News & World Report*, July 21, retrieved on December 14, 2016 from .www.evgoh.com/2016/08/10/a-cleveland-success-story-u-s-news-world-report/.

Evelyn Brody and Joseph J. Cordes, 2016. "Tax Treatment of Nonprofit Organizations: A Two-Edged Sword?", Chapter 4 in Elizabeth T. Boris and C. Eugene Steuerle (eds), *Nonprofits and Government: Collaboration and Conflict*, Third Edition, Lanham, MD: Rowman & Littlefield, pp. 133–161.

Thad Calabrese, 2011. "Testing Competing Capital Structure Theories of Nonprofit Organizations", *Public Budgeting & Finance*, 31(3), pp. 119–143.

Thad Calabrese, 2013, "Running on Empty: The Operating Reserves of U.S. Nonprofit Organizations", *Nonprofit Management and Leadership*, 23(3), pp. 281–302.

Laura Callanan, Jonathan Law and Lenny Mendonca, 2012. "From Potential to Action: Bringing Social Impact Bonds to the U.S.", New York: McKinsey and Company, May.

Calvert Foundation, 2016. www.calvertfoundation.org.

Centre for Social Innovation, 2016. http://socialinnovation.ca/communitybond.

CHS, 2016. www.chsinc.com.

Joseph J. Cordes, Zina Poletz and C. Eugene Steuerle, 2009. "Examples of Nonprofit-For Profit Hybrid Business Models", Appendix 3.1 in Joseph J. Cordes and C. Eugene Steuerle (eds), *Nonprofits & Business*, Washington, DC: The Urban Institute Press, pp. 69–82.

Stefanie Di Verdi, 2012. "Community Bonds Explained", *MoneySense*, retrieved on December 14, 2016 from www.moneysense.ca/columns/communitybonds-explained/.

The Economist, 2016. "Secrets and agents: information asymmetry", July 23, pp. 55–56.

Evergreen Cooperatives, 2016. http://www.evgoh.com.

EvergreenToolkit, 2016. www.EvergreenToolkit.org.

Judith Manfredo Legorreta and Dennis R. Young, 1986. "Why Organizations Turn Nonprofit: Lessons from Case Studies", Chapter 11 in Susan R. Rose-Ackerman (ed.), *The Economics of Nonprofit Institutions*, New York: Oxford University Press, pp. 196–204.

Othmar M. Lehner, 2015. "Crowdfunding in Social Finance", Chapter 16 in Alex Nicholls, Rob Paton and Jed Emerson (eds), 2015. *Social Finance*, Oxford: Oxford University Press, pp. 521–542.

Antony-Bugg Levine, 2013. "Complete Capital", *Stanford Social Innovation Review*, Winter, pp. 17–18.

Jonathan Michie, 2015. "Co-operative and Mutual Finance", Chapter 5 in Alex Nicholls, Rob Paton and Jed Emerson (eds), 2015. *Social Finance*, Oxford: Oxford University Press, pp. 133–55.

Laurie Mook, John Maiorano and Jack Quarter, 2015. "Credit Unions: Market Niche or Market Accommodation?", *Nonprofit and Voluntary Sector Quarterly*, 44(4), pp. 814–831.

Laurie Mook, John R. Whitman, Jack Quarter and Ann Armstrong, 2015. *Understanding the Social Economy of the United States*, Toronto: University of Toronto Press.

Nicole Motter, 2013. "Why Program-Related Investments are Not Risky Business", retrieved on December 14, 2016 from www.forbes.com/sites/ashoka/2013/02/21/why-program-related-investments-are-not-risky-business/#58ec42eb1f8e.

Alex Nicholls and Emma Tomkinson, 2015. "The Peterborough Pilot Social Impact Bond", Chapter 12 in Alex Nicholls, Rob Paton and Jed Emerson (eds), *Social Finance*, Oxford: Oxford University Press, pp. 335–80.

Alex Nicholls, Rob Paton and Jed Emerson (eds.), 2015. *Social Finance*, Oxford: Oxford University Press.

Anna Oleksiak, Alex Nicholls and Jed Emerson, 2015. "Impact Investing: A Market in Evolution", Chapter 8 in Alex Nicholls, Rob Paton and Jed Emerson (eds), *Social Finance*, Oxford: Oxford University Press, pp. 207–49.

Park Pride, 2016. www.parkpride.org.

Tony Proscio and Clara Miller, with Alice Fisher, Jason Kuschner and Wells Chen, 2003. "Rising in Stages: How Steppenwolf Excelled First on the Boards, Then in the Board Room, and Ultimately on the Balance Sheet", New York: Nonprofit Finance Fund.

Rock and Roll Hall of Fame, 2016. www.rockhall.com; also, interview with Brian Kenyon (April 2014).

Timothy Rudd, Elisa Nicoletti, Kristin Misner. and Janae Bonsu, 2013. "Financing Promising Evidence-Based Programs: Early Lessons from the New York City Social Impact Bond", New York: MDRC.

Lester M. Salamon with the assistance of Stephanie L. Geller, 2006. "Investment Capital: The New Challenge for American Nonprofits", Communique No. 5, Listening Post Project, Center for Civil Society Studies, Johns Hopkins University.

Richard Steinberg, 2015. "What Should Social Finance Invest In and with Whom?", Chapter 2 in Alex Nicholls, Rob Paton and Jed Emerson (eds), 2015. *Social Finance*, Oxford: Oxford University Press, pp. 64–95.

James Surowiecki, 2005. *The Wisdom of Crowds*, New York: Anchor Books.

Vera Institute of Justice, 2015. "Impact Evaluation of the Adolescent Behavioral Learning Experience (ABLE) Program at Rikers Island: Summary of Findings", New York: Vera Institute of Justice.

WCLV, 2016. www.wclv.org.

William F. Whyte and Kathleen K. Whyte, 1991. *Making Mondragon: The Growth and Dynamics of the Worker Industrial Complex*, Second Edition, Ithaca, NY: Cornell University Press.

Robert J. Yetman, 2007. "Borrowing and Debt", Chapter 11 in Dennis R. Young (ed.), *Financing Nonprofits*, Lanham, MD: AltaMira Press, pp. 243–268.

11. Income portfolios

INTRODUCTION

As suggested in Chapter 3 the income support of SPOs is naturally conceived in terms of "portfolios," for three reasons. First, it is the rare SPO that produces just one type of benefit. Second, as benefits theory articulates, different types of benefits are associated with different sources of income. Third, SPOs span a very wide variety of missions, services and hence benefits; thus, the particular mix of income sources is not formulaic, that is, no one size fits all. Rather, the key question for any SPO is – what specific combination of earned income, contributions, government support, and investment income best supports the particular mission and circumstances of the organization?

More generally, it is sensible for SPOs to think in terms of portfolio mixes in multiple ways. SPOs manage portfolios of programs, assets, and investments as well as income sources. These portfolios of course are interrelated. Investment portfolios, for example, consisting of cash, stocks, bonds, and real estate holdings, determine the level of investment income, as well as its volatility or risk, a potentially important component of an SPO's income mix, as considered in Chapter 8. There can be a fine line as well between investment portfolios and earned income. For instance, an SPO might own a mission-related business (for example, a museum's off-site gift stores) whose net sales can be seen as either earned income or returns on investment. Asset portfolios, which may include real estate, equipment, financial assets, intellectual capital and social capital, also influence the ability of an SPO to generate different forms of income. For example, financial assets generate investment income, physical assets such as attractive buildings and grounds can generate earned (rental) income, intellectual capital can lead to earned income opportunities through licensing of patents or marketing of expert knowledge, and social capital in the form of community relationships can translate into capacity for charitable fund-raising. (It is also important to recognize that some assets can be a net drain on revenue, for example, depreciating equipment or buildings, or art collections in storage.)

SPO program portfolios have received particular attention in the

Table 11.1   SPO program portfolio

	High mission impact	Low mission impact
Profitable	Stars	Cash cows
Not Profitable	Saints	Dogs

Source: Adapted from Oster (1995).

nonprofit literature. For example, the seminal work of Estelle James (1983) led to the understanding that nonprofits could subsidize mission-focused or "preferred" services with less preferred but profitable services to facilitate maximum mission impact (or management satisfaction) within feasible resource limitations. This thinking undergirds the popular program portfolio matrix pioneered by Sharon Oster (1995) and others (see Table 11.1). In this construction, nonprofits are guided toward eliminating programs that contribute neither to mission impact nor net financial support (so-called Dogs), maximizing the net income potential of programs that are profitable but peripheral to mission (Cash Cows), investing in programs that are both financially self-sustaining and mission impactful (Stars) and balancing programs that are essential to mission but require subsidy (Saints). In this framework, the goal of SPO program portfolio management is to achieve a mix of programs that produces a desired combination of mission impact and financial surplus.

Income portfolios clearly derive from program portfolios as each program component will imply reliance on particular sources and levels of income. However, the analysis of SPO income portfolios involves other considerations as well, as discussed next.

PORTFOLIO THEORY AND THE MIX OF SPO INCOME

In general, portfolio theory is most fully developed in the finance literature where the focus is on the best mix of alternative financial investments to meet an investor's preferences for financial return and level of risk (Markowitz, 1952). This perspective has been applied to the financing of nonprofit organizations and offers substantial insights. However, there are also important differences between managing financial assets and managing SPO income portfolios. As discussed below, the classical portfolio theory approach is complementary to benefits theory, although it cannot be applied naively without regard to the idiosyncratic nature of

SPO missions and circumstances, and the mechanics and administrative capacity for generating income from alternative sources.

Bruce Kingma (1993) was one of the first to recognize nonprofit organization income as a portfolio issue and to apply classical portfolio theory. His analysis is based on the proposition that a nonprofit manager seeks to minimize risk associated with achieving a given level of total revenue derived from different sources. As such, the application of financial portfolio theory is straightforward:

> The problem of choosing a risk-revenue package for a nonprofit organization is identical to the classic finance problem of choosing a risk-return package. For the portfolio manager, the expected return of a portfolio is the weighted sum of the expected returns of the portfolio assets. The risk of a financial portfolio is the weighted sum of the variance and covariance of the individual assets in the portfolio. For a nonprofit manager, the expected revenue for a nonprofit organization is a weighted sum of the expected revenues from each of the organization's revenue sources. The predictability of a nonprofit organization's revenues is a weighted sum of the variance and covariance of its individual revenue streams. (Kingma, 1993, p. 109)

In layman's terms, Kingma argued that if the intrinsic volatility of each revenue source (for example, earned revenue or contributions) can be specified (that is, their variances), and if the correlation in volatility of any two income streams can be assessed (that is, covariances, or how much they vary in tandem versus independently) then portfolio theory can inform the nonprofit manager as to how much risk will be associated with any desired level of total income. Portfolio theory can be applied to calculate the portfolio composition that achieves the maximum value of expected return for any given level of risk, or that achieves the minimum risk associated with any given level of expected return. Hence, the theory asks the nonprofit manager to make a choice of desired revenue and select an income portfolio to minimize risk, or to specify a level of acceptable risk and select an income portfolio to maximize revenue.

In his study of nonprofit foster care agencies in New York State Kingma found, contrary to common beliefs about maximum diversification as a panacea to minimize risk, that these organizations could reduce risk by increasing their dependence on government funding – an apparently more stable source of funds (at that time) than charitable contributions or other sources. This particular finding seemed to confirm Gronbjerg's (1990) earlier conjecture that social service nonprofits could achieve greater funding stability through increased reliance on government. However, Kingma's conclusion is more nuanced than that:

neither complete dependence on one funding source nor complete diversity of funding will minimize the variability of income. Instead, each nonprofit organization manager, in order to choose the correct level of revenue diversity, must consider the variance of all streams of revenue, the covariance between these streams, and the expected level of growth of each stream. (Kingma, 1993, p. 118)

A similar conclusion was reached by Grasse, Whaley and Ihrke (2016) in their application of portfolio theory to nonprofit U.S. arts organizations and history museums. In particular, these authors calculated efficient alternative revenue portfolios of generally increasing concentration (decreased diversification) as higher levels of expected revenue growth were sought.

Application of portfolio theory to nonprofit income portfolios is consistent with benefit theory's stipulation that each SPO must make its own determination of the appropriate mix of sources, rather than follow some arbitrary formula. It is also complementary to benefits theory in the sense that it depends on separate determination by SPO managers of the potential sources of funding that can support the organization's mission. Moreover, it puts an additional burden on management to assess not only the potential level of prospective income from different sources but also the volatility of each source. This is a relevant concern to SPOs reliant on any potential source of income. For example, what is the risk that a government contract will be paid on time or in full (a concern discussed in Chapter 7)? To what extent will donors' gift pledges be fulfilled? Will projected demand for fee-based services meet or fall below expectations? Will stocks and bonds yield the anticipated return of investment revenues? These are all realistic concerns for present day SPOs which must be factored into income portfolio decisions.

Finally, portfolio analysis also requires, as discussed in prior chapters, an assessment of the transactions costs associated with each source of revenue, since each income stream should be viewed in net terms. That is – how much funding can be expected from a given source, net of the transactions costs required to cultivate that source? Fundamentally, however, portfolio theory tells us nothing about how to achieve the prospective returns from each source of income. This requires an understanding of the benefits, beneficiaries, and mechanics of income development and management for each prospective income source.

Essentially, Kingma and Grasse, Whaley and Ihrke, and other scholars concerned with the financial vulnerability of nonprofit organizations, focus on the management of risk. Indeed, there is now a substantial literature on measures of financial vulnerability of nonprofit organizations (for example, see Chang and Tuckman, 1991; Greenlee and Tuckman, 2007; Carroll and Stater, 2009). Much of this literature is concerned with the role of diversification in reducing revenue volatility. Interestingly, findings from this literature tend to reinforce the perspective underlying portfolio theory. In particular, portfolio theory postulates that if efficiently managed, nonprofits can increase their revenues only by assuming additional risk. For example, Chikoto and Neely (2014) found that revenue concentration can foster growth but at the expense of increased risk (see also, Frumkin and Keating, 2011). The key assumption here is efficiency, however. Benefits theory complements portfolio theory by suggesting that SPO leaders may not always fully assess the potential for income from their organizations' current and prospective beneficiaries. As such, SPOs are not efficient until all such possibilities are explored; hence, increases in income without increased risk may be possible until efficiency is achieved through a full exploration of all sources of prospective income. Portfolio theory is consistent with this idea as it essentially calculates an "efficiency frontier," recognizing that actual organizations may not be on the frontier. It asks that managers adjust and expand their income mix so that they reach this frontier. This is how benefits theory plays a complementary role to portfolio theory.

Another aspect of portfolio theory complementary to benefits theory is that alternative sources of income may be correlated with one another. In particular, research suggests that one source of income may, perhaps with some delay, "crowd-out" or "crowd-in" another source (Thornton, 2014). For example, if a nonprofit receives an increase in income from government, charitable contributions may decrease, either because donors feel less compelled to contribute or because management decides to spend less on fund-raising (Steinberg, 1993). While management can control what it spends on fund-raising, thus avoiding the latter effect, it may have only limited influence on the behavior of donors. Nonetheless, as Thornton (2014) demonstrates, the structure of government grants, for example matching requirements, can affect whether donors increase or decrease their contributions. This complicates the application of portfolio theory which relies on historical statistical data on inter-source variation that may not apply to new ways of structuring financial arrangements.

More generally, portfolio theory requires SPO leaders to draw on existing data and historical experience to assess the volatility as well as correlation of potential sources of income. While SPO leaders may have no choice but to estimate risks in this manner, this approach does not protect them from unanticipated sources of future risk. This is the so-called "black swan" problem discussed by Taleb (2010). The "perfect storms" associated with events such as the great recession of 2008–2009 in the United States, for example, may systematically undermine all sources of income simultaneously. Or, consider changes in political administrations that reverse expectations about the reliability of government support. Kingma's and Gronbjerg's findings that increased reliance on government helps to stabilize funding of social service organizations ring less true now than they have historically; since the time of their analyses government retrenchment has become more common in a volatile economy and government spending is not necessarily invoked as a countercyclical strategy for economic stability or a primary solution to social ills.

In the perfect storm case, where government cuts back even as charitable giving and investment and earned income decline, the strategy of income diversification does not help because diversification is premised on alternative income sources varying relatively independently of one another. This is why other strategies of risk management are required and why the composition of nonprofit income portfolios cannot be entirely determined by ordinary considerations of risk. In short, diversification applies as a protection from "unsystemic risk" associated with normal patterns of volatility that are understood and anticipated. Other approaches are required to protect against "systemic risk." In particular, the prudent set aside of reserve funds (see Calabrese, 2013), responsible borrowing policies, as well as maintaining other forms of "organizational slack," including endowments, excess staff capacity that can be furloughed or space that can be rented out under fiscal stress, and greater reliance on variable rather than fixed costs (for example, rental rather than ownership of real estate) should be considered in an SPO's overall approach to risk management, to protect against unanticipated and catastrophic events.

Further, it may be observed that the strategy of diversification applies within as well as among broad categories of nonprofit income. Thus SPOs can diversify their sources of grants and contributions, their streams of government funding, and their sources of earned income, just as they can diversify the financial portfolios that generate investment income, applying the concepts of risk and return from portfolio theory. Here too, benefits theory offers a complementary perspective by identifying the benefits and beneficiaries around which additional streams of income of a given type may be cultivated. Issues of crowd-in and crowd-out and systemic effects also apply at this level. For example, donors may resist supporting multiple programs of a given organization or they may divert their support from operating support to a capital campaign, and fee-paying customers will make substitutions among service offerings if their budgets and time are limited. Alternatively, if donors are properly cultivated then a gift of one type (for example, volunteering) may lead to others (for example, annual donations) over time, and customers exposed to one fee-based service may find others of later interest. Government contracts with one agency may lead to contracts with other agencies. And so on. Such crowd-out and crowd-in effects will influence the degree to which diversification effectively protects against risk. More research needs to be done at this intra-source level of income portfolio analysis.

Finally, it is important to note that the desirability of diversification is related to an SPO's stage of organizational development. As noted throughout this book, every source of income requires its own expertise and administrative capacity. This applies most strongly to diversification across sources but also within sources. For example, different government agencies have their own rules and procedures, and grant-making foundations vary considerably from one another in their perspectives and requirements. Newer and smaller organizations are necessarily more limited in their capacities to manage multiple sources and indeed may be harmed by pursuing diversification too quickly or prematurely. Thus newer organizations are likely to begin with one or two sources and to diversify over time as they gain experience, acquire additional resources and expertise, and adapt their organizational structures to accommodate diverse ways of developing resources. Larger, more differentiated organizations may be better able to achieve the diversification required to take full advantage of the prospective beneficiary groups connected to their missions. At every stage of development, the engagement of governing boards, staff, potential beneficiaries and resource providers, in strategic thinking and planning, can underwrite incremental pursuit of suitable levels of diversification to enable maximum mission effectiveness within acceptable levels of risk taking.

SOME INTERESTING CASES

As noted in Chapter 1, there is certainly no shortage of vulnerable SPOs succumbing to financial disaster or in danger of doing so, even longstanding established organizations such as Hull House in Chicago or the New York City Opera. It is instructive to examine the latter cases from the perspective of their income portfolios, to illustrate risk factors and to ask whether an income development strategy based on benefits theory could have helped avoid catastrophe. More broadly, it is useful to examine a class of similar organizations for their program and income portfolio choices, in order to assess whether adjustments in income portfolios driven by benefits theory can identify opportunities for enhanced income support. The study of Jewish Community Centers by Wilsker and Young (2010) offers such an assessment as discussed below. Finally, the case of *Ecoliving*, an Italian social cooperative illustrates how portfolio diversification can evolve over time in a start-up organization.

The New York City Opera (NYCO)

The NYCO was established in 1943 with the mission of making opera accessible to a wide audience at affordable prices, to offer innovative choices of repertory and to provide opportunities for American singers and composers (Wikipedia, 2016). NYCO operated with much success but also some financial volatility, until the early years of the 21st century when serious financial difficulties that had been brewing for a decade, forced it to close its doors in 2013 when it filed for bankruptcy. (It re-emerged in 2016 under new management with a new 2016–2017 season.) Over the years, the opera broke much new ground including the incubation of new stars such as Beverly Sills and Plácido Domingo, presentation of new American repertory, as well as musicals and operettas, and technical innovations such as running English subtitles for foreign language offerings.

It is instructive here to focus on developments leading to financial failure in 2013. NYCO's mission is grounded in making opera accessible to general audiences. As a result, from the outset, prices were kept low, limiting earned income. At the same time, the desire to innovate, stage new works, and attract star performers, put upward pressure on expenses. All this created significant financial strains and required greater emphasis on charitable funding and the development of endowments. For example, when Beverly Sills became General Director of the opera in 1979, the company faced a $3 million operating deficit. Ms. Sills, however, turned out to be a prodigious fund-raiser, lifting the opera from deficit to surplus over her ten year tenure, while tripling its budget and reducing ticket prices by 20 percent in a quest for expanded audiences (Wikipedia, 2016).

With the onset of the great recession in 2008–2009, NYCO's situation began to unravel. The economic collapse undermined expected charitable contributions, and displacement from its venue at Lincoln Center due to renovations increased its expenses. NYCO reported an $11 million deficit for the fiscal year ending in June 2008 after a long series of deficit years dating back to 2002. Large deficits continued through 2011 when they were temporarily staunched by new management, with heroic measures including renegotiation of union contracts and leaving the venue at Lincoln Center to reduce rental costs. However, substantial deficits continued to be incurred thereafter. An analysis by Stewart (2013) suggests that mismanagement of NYCO's endowment contributed to the organization's demise. In particular, endowment assets were sold for cash as the market plunged in 2008 and were not reinvested as the market recovered. Ominously, a substantial part of the liquidation was used to pay off the large accumulated debt. In all, Stewart reports that the opera's endowment declined from approximately $50 million in 2001 to $5 million in

2013. Prior to its filing for bankruptcy, the opera had hoped for a large bailout gift from a major philanthropist such as Michael Bloomberg who had been an opera supporter over the years. However, this did not materialize.

From a portfolio and benefits theory viewpoint, the NYCO experience raises several red flags. Was the company historically over-reliant on charitable gifts and contributions and less inclined to exploit sources of earned income? And was the company made inordinately complacent by having built a substantial endowment that its board perceived as a backstop? Historically, earned income appears to have varied widely as a proportion of revenues, from as much as 80 percent of gifts and grants in 2007 to only 44 percent in 2010; the latter excludes 2008 when NYCO had to vacate its premises at Lincoln Center due to renovations and earned income dipped to 14 percent of contributions, and after 2011 when the organization hit the skids, left Lincoln Center to become an itinerant company and saw its earned revenues drop to roughly 30 percent or less of its (also declining) contributions base. In its more robust years prior to 2008 NYCO appears to have succeeded in achieving a rough balance of contributions and earned income fairly typical of performing arts organizations. By comparison the world famous Metropolitan Opera, located in New York City, derived approximately 48 percent of its operating income from contributions and 44 percent from earned income in fiscal year 2015 (Metropolitan Opera Company, 2015). The decline of earned revenue because of the disruptive circumstances surrounding its venue, combined with the volatility of contributions (from donors likely influenced by both the decline of box office success and financial instability) proved to be a critical factor for NYCO. The loss of endowment itself had a more indirect effect. Investment income only constituted a modest portion of total revenue over the years (less than 5 percent) but exploitation of the endowment's corpus as a backstop measure to relieve debt significantly undermined the organization's long-run fiscal integrity.

In 2009, a White Paper prepared by Lincoln Center recommended several ways in which the finances of NYCO could have been improved to recover from its difficulties following the recession (Levy, 2015, Appendix C). These included a capital campaign to rebuild the endowment, exploiting opportunities for naming rights of internal spaces in the David H. Koch theater, pursuit of additional rental revenues for that theater, and obtaining a foundation challenge grant to help launch the 2009/10 season. These recommendations recognized untapped potentials for support by major individual donors and foundations that value the importance of the opera as a cultural institution, additional earned (rental) revenues from valuable underutilized assets, the need to restore regular box office revenues to historical levels, and the importance of both investment revenues and a diversified income portfolio for the financial stabilization of NYCO.

Hull House

Hull House was a venerable institution co-founded in Chicago by the legendary social reformer Jane Addams in 1889. Addams remained head of the institution until her death in 1935. Hull House helped pioneer the concept of a neighborhood settlement house and under Addams's leadership came to encompass a wide range of social, cultural, residential services, and advocacy focused activities. Some of the early accomplishments of Hull House were "the first public playground in Chicago, the first swimming pool in Chicago, and the first citizen preparation classes in the United States. . .[as well as]. . .investigations of sanitation, truancy, tuberculosis, infant mortality, and cocaine use in Chicago, prompting changes in laws and public programs" (Cohen, 2012). In the 1960s, Hull House vacated its original house to make way for a new urban campus of the University of Illinois (Flynn and Tian, 2014). Subsequently, it reorganized its multiple sites as the Addams Hull House Association, an umbrella association of community social service centers across the city of Chicago, focusing on the provision of various social services including foster care, domestic violence counseling, child development, and job training for children, families and community groups. Whereas originally the organization was self-funded through volunteer effort, fees, and Addams's own considerable fund-raising capacity, services under the new regime came to be largely funded by government programs (Thayer, 2012). In recent years, the Association struggled financially, and in January 2012 abruptly ceased operations, declared bankruptcy, and closed its doors.

Under Addams, Hull House eschewed government funding, as well as corporate support, viewing itself as a critic of government and a promoter of social justice. In the end, however, Hull House became dependent on government for nearly 90 percent of its income, and subject to the vagaries of the government contracting and reimbursement system in Chicago and the state of Illinois (Cohen, 2012). An analysis by Flynn and Tian (2014) shows that Hull House experienced large drops in total revenue over the period 2001 to 2010, becoming increasingly heavily dependent on government funding, with only 10 percent reliance on charitable contributions, underinvestment in fund-raising, a high debt ratio and a cash flow problem stemming from an extraordinary level of accounts receivable. Moreover, like New York City Opera, Hull House was insufficiently candid about its financial struggles, waiting until it was too late to secure effective emergency assistance.

From the viewpoint of benefits theory and risk management, Hull House's failure provides several insights and also raises some red flags. After Addams's death, the mission of Hull House effectively morphed from social change agent and community builder to one of social service provider. Concurrently, its financial base moved from volunteer effort and charitable contributions to government funding. It's hard to know if the voluntary foundations built by Addams could have been sustained without her. But doing so would have required an explicit effort to maintain community programming and advocacy and continued cultivation of a volunteer and donor base that could support these functions. Changes in the economic environment probably required greater reliance on public service delivery and government support. Other original settlement houses such as Henry Street Settlement in New York and University Settlement in Cleveland have made this transition (Cohen, 2012). In terms of risk management, the change in Hull House's focus brought into play two risk factors. First, its income portfolio flipped from one general source to another rather than become more diversified. Second, the flip was to a source that became more unstable and unreliable (especially in terms of cash flow) in recent years – that of government contracting for social services. Without sufficient reserve funds Hull House was unprepared for shocks that it experienced in its flow of funds from government contract reimbursement.

Jewish Community Centers Association of North America (JCC Association)

The JCC Association, according to its site on LinkedIn, is

> [T]he continental umbrella organization for the Jewish Community Center Movement, which includes more than 350 JCCs, YM-YWHAs, and camp sites in the U.S. and Canada. JCC Association offers a wide range of services and resources to help its affiliates to provide educational, cultural, social, Jewish identity-building, and recreational programs for people of all ages and backgrounds. JCC Association supports the largest network of Jewish early childhood centers and Jewish summer camps in North America, and is also a U.S. government accredited agency for serving the religious and social needs of Jewish military personnel through JWB Jewish Chaplains Council. (Jewish Community Centers Association of North America, 2016)

In 2007 the JCC Association surveyed its affiliates, gathering detailed data on programs, including sources of revenue and expenses by program type. Wilsker and Young (2010) analyzed the data from 87 JCCs responding to the survey. A special feature of this data was that it broke down both revenue and expenses by program, allowing the researchers to use program expenses as a measure of output for different kinds of services reflecting different kinds of benefits. In addition, the dataset demonstrated that different JCC's make different choices about their program portfolios and hence the composition of their income portfolios. This variation permitted statistical analysis of the connection between services and benefits on the one hand, and income streams on the other.

The JCCs, in their roles as multi-purpose centers for recreation, education and community life of the Jewish and other residents in their local communities, offer many different kinds of programs, which could be grouped into four categories: health and fitness, youth services, life and learning, and special services. In turn, each of these categories could be characterized by the public/private nature of the benefits they provide. In particular:

- *Health and fitness* consists of personal physical fitness facilities and programs, recreational activities, and aquatics. These could be characterized as providing private benefits to the individuals (members) who partake of them.
- *Youth services* include pre-school, summer day and overnight camps, and the Maccabi games (akin to Jewish Olympics). These too could be considered as offering private benefits to the individual children (or their families) who chose to participate, perhaps with a group benefit component given the emphasis on cultivating Jewish youth.
- *Life and learning* includes adult cultural and social activities, and Jewish life and learning programs. These were intended to strengthen the local Jewish community as a whole, and as such could be considered as generating group or public benefits.
- *Special services* are a mixed bag of acculturation programs (for example, for Jewish immigrants), social services for families in need, special programming for people with disabilities, and conferences to address topics of community interest. As such, these too could be considered as providing public benefits (or possibly redistributive or group benefits).

Overall, the analysis showed that increases in expenses on services associated with private benefits were significantly related to the generation of earned income while increases in expenses in services generating public benefits were associated with increases in gift or government income. At the same time, no significant effects of changes in expenses on investment income were reported. The latter is consistent with the fact that investment income is not derived directly from program activity but rather from investment management; hence, it should not be affected by changes in the benefits mix (at least not in the short run, although over the long-term capital gifts could be affected). More specifically, the researchers found that:

- Reallocation of expenses from special services (public/group/ redistributive) to health and fitness services (private) were positively and significantly associated with changes in earned income and negatively and significantly associated with changes in both institutional and individual giving.
- Reallocation of expenses from special services (public/group/ redistributive) to youth services (private) were also positively and significantly associated with changes in earned income and negatively and significantly associated with changes in individual and institutional giving.
- Reallocation of expenses from life and learning (public/group) to health and fitness (private) again were positively and significantly associated with changes in earned income and negatively and significantly associated with changes in individual and institutional giving.
- Reallocation of expenses from life and learning (public/group) to youth services (private) once again produced the same significant results.
- Reallocation of expenses from health and fitness (private) to youth services (private/group) produced a negative and significant decrease in earned income. This is possibly explained by a greater degree of publicness (group benefit) to youth services, relative to health and fitness, since activities such as pre-school and Maccabi games have community wide external benefits.

Given these results, the researchers asked whether net increases in revenues would be produced if expenses were increased for the various types of program activities. As expected, a 1 percent increase in special services (public/group) expenses was associated with significant increases in institutional giving and government support, but also (surprisingly) earned income. An increase in health and fitness (private) expenses of 1 percent was, as predicted, associated with a significant increase in earned income, while an increase of 1 percent in youth services (private/group) expenses was associated with a significant and large decrease in government funding. Finally, an increase in spending for life and learning (public/group) was associated with a significant and large increase in government funding. Given the scale of spending in each of these categories, not all projected increases in program expenses associated with increases in various kinds of revenue, seemed advisable, however. Indeed, in all but one case did projected revenue increases exceed the stipulated increase in expenses. Namely, increased spending on special services would cost approximately $922 on average, but was projected to produce an increase in revenues of $3,064, the sum of projected increases in government funding, institutional giving, and earned income.

Such results must of course be accepted with caution. Given the cross-sectional nature of the data, it is tenuous to attribute causality. Moreover, the data are relatively aggregated in character, masking fine grain service content within the four broad categories. Moreover, the nature of benefits associated with each of the categories is a matter of reasoning, not direct measurement. Nonetheless, the results are highly consistent with the predictions of benefits theory and point the way to managing SPO program and income portfolios to achieve more efficient and impactful financial and programmatic results.

Ecoliving (EL)

Ecoliving (EL) is a type B social cooperative in the Emilia-Romagna region of Italy (Bassi, Soh and Young, 2016). Type B social cooperatives are so-called "work integration social enterprises" (WISEs) which engage marginalized or challenged workers in the production of their goods and services in order to integrate them into the economy at large. As such, they are incorporated as nonprofit organizations under Italian law, although they operate in the commercial economy. In this case, EL employs former drug addicts and people with mental illness from the Emilia-Romagna region to work in its food and health-related businesses. EL was founded in 2011 by 20 members, 17 local individuals associated with the cooperative movement in Emilia-Romagna and three other local social cooperatives. All of the founding members had expressed interests in healthy living and work integration of people with special needs.

EL is a small enterprise with an annual operating income of approximately €600,000 euros ($700,000USD) in 2014. Its mission is to promote wellbeing through improvement of food, lifestyle and respect for the environment. The organization provides food services for people with special dietary requirements such as celiac disease and diabetes, including new parents with special needs. It operates in a single, accessible commercial facility called "Apebianca" (white bee) which houses an organic food shop, a bio-vegan bistro, a local producers' (farmers') market, and a variety of retail shops selling clothing, toys, stationery, perfume, furniture, and other products. EL also offers free consultation services, an area for children to play, oversees a local watershed and organizes events for children and adults. Apebianca has become synonymous in the region with "organic," "genuine," "good," and "pure," and has received local government quality certification (called BioAgriCert).

EL operates with a "charter of values" that emphasizes economic well-being, social justice and respect for the environment in the region. Since its founding, membership has doubled and annual revenue has tripled (as of 2014). It has also diversified its revenue base substantially, from 100 percent membership dues in 2011 to two-thirds reliance on sales of goods and services by 2014. Member dues still constitute approximately 14 percent of operating revenues, while in-kind donation of goods and services (by members) and returns on the management of financial assets accumulated since its founding account for the remainder.

The development of EL's revenue portfolio substantially reflects the distribution of its benefits. Its various businesses sell products that provide private benefits to its consumers, for which they pay reasonable if not full market value prices. Moreover, the continued support of members through member dues and in-kind contributions, as well as loans, reflects the group and public benefits associated with EL's work to promote proper nutrition, a clean local environment and amenities and resources for healthful living, particularly for people with special needs. Conspicuous in their absence are support from local government and from philanthropic sources (aside from in-kind member support), given EL's broader environmental, social and health-related efforts. However, EL's trajectory of income diversification is not necessarily complete and it may yet seek to exploit these sources in the future. Indeed it is unusual for Italian social cooperatives not to be supported by government contracts or grants.

CONCLUSION

SPO finance is best understood in terms of portfolios composed of various proportions of income from different sources. However, naïve adoption of portfolio theory from the investment literature provides only partial guidance. Classical portfolio theory centers on minimizing risk for a given financial return or maximizing return for a given level of risk. However, assessing the prospective returns and risk levels of alternative income sources is a matter of judgment for nonprofit leaders. This is where benefits theory can contribute by assessing the prospective income potentials associated with the benefits produced by an SPO and the associated costs and volatility of those sources.

Applying the lens of benefits theory to various cases reviewed here reveals several important themes. First, both risk and income potential are affected by too heavy reliance on one or two income sources. This was the case in Hull House, which swung from reliance entirely on private charitable sources to overwhelming reliance on government. At either stage, the organization both sacrificed potential income from beneficiaries that might have provided additional support from an alternative source and a degree of stability that would have resulted from avoiding the volatility of a single source.

The foregoing ties into a second observation: that SPOs often wear blinders when it comes to exploiting additional sources of income. This may have been the case with Hull House in both stages of its development – perhaps too rigid a position against government funding under Jane Addams, and too little appreciation of community benefits that could support charitable contributions in the later stages of its operation. In a more subdued way, the New York City Opera may have been subject to the same effect – unduly constraining its ticket prices or differentiating its price schedules in order to ensure accessibility. On the other hand, NYCO's substantial success in cultivating charitable contributions proved to be a (short-lived) advantage when it was required to endure a reduced season due to renovations in its regular venue at Lincoln Center. Other cases also suggest that failure to fully exploit additional income sources is not uncommon. The case of Cooper Union, discussed in Chapter 5, could be interpreted this way. The New-York Historical Society turned down government funding in its early days, a decision it lived to regret (Guthrie, 1996). And the Cleveland Botanical Garden, known earlier as the Garden Club, for many years operating as an inward-focused elite group of members with interests in plants mostly supported by memberships and gifts, eventually transformed itself into the multifaceted, community-focused multi-source funded organization that it is today by tapping into hitherto unexploited sources of support for community-based programming. By contrast, Ecoliving seems to have consciously embraced a strategy of diversification of its income portfolio over time, from the start.

A third observation is that endowments present clear dangers to nonprofit leaders and managers in terms of the complacency they may underwrite and the downward spiral they may engender by serving as an inappropriate source of, or collateral for, imprudent borrowing. NYCO is a prime example of this, as was the New-York Historical Society. While some scholars have suggested that endowments be used partially as "rainy day funds," that viewpoint is questionable (Weisbrod and Asch, 2010). It was put forward in the aftermath of the great recession of 2008–2009, in objection to the decisions of some institutions with very large endowments to reduce current expenditures to compensate for losses in investment revenue stemming from reductions in the market values of their endowments, essentially sacrificing present for future benefits. There is a legitimate issue as to how much emphasis an SPO should put on present versus future benefits and beneficiaries and hence what role an endowment should play in overall income and asset portfolios. However, given that such a policy decision has been made, responsible fiscal management would eschew the routine raiding of endowment corpuses and favor explicitly designated reserve funds to be employed for emergency purposes.

Fourth, benefits theory highlights the issue of "crowd-out" or "crowd-in" of one income source with another in an SPO income portfolio, from a more fundamental perspective than is commonly considered. In particular, the analysis of the JCCs suggests that pursuit of certain benefits to the exclusion of the others, by adjustments in underlying programs, results in increases in some sources and reductions of others. Indeed, that goes to the heart of benefits theory and contains a basic lesson for SPO leaders: income portfolio adjustments are less the product of decisions about what sources to pursue than what programs to offer, with the former following from the latter. One implication here is that SPOs should be wary of over-compartmentalizing their resource development and program planning functions. Effective resource developers need to be knowledgeable about their organization's programs, and program managers should be cognizant of the resource implications of the services they provide.

Fifth, the issue of income portfolio management applies at two broad levels: diversification among sources and within sources. Thus, Hull House was subject to substantial risk in its final days because it was extraordinarily reliant on social services funding by particular agencies of government in Chicago. A broader base of government funding as much as a better balance among sources may have been helpful. Similarly, reliance on a more diverse array of private donors might have mitigated NYCO's difficulties. The fact that the JCCs generate earned income in multiple ways probably works to their advantage in stabilizing their finances as well as fully exploiting the private benefits they offer. Some research has highlighted the value of within source diversification, even where income is limited to one or two general sources (Foster and Fine, 2007).

REFERENCES

Andrea Bassi, Jung-In Soh and Dennis R. Young, 2016. "Applying the Benefits Theory of Nonprofit Finance to Social Cooperatives", International Society for Third Sector Research, bi-annual conference, Stockholm, July.

Thad Calabrese, 2013. "Running on Empty", *Nonprofit Management & Leadership*, 23(3), Spring, pp. 281–302.

Deborah A. Carroll and Keely Jones Stater, 2009. "Revenue diversification in nonprofit organizations: Does it lead to financial stability?" *Journal of Public Administration Research and Theory*, 19, 947–966.

Cyril F. Chang and Howard P. Tuckman 1991. "A methodology for measuring the financial vulnerability of charitable nonprofit organizations", *Nonprofit and Voluntary Sector Quarterly*, 20, pp. 445–460.

Grace L. Chikoto and Daniel Gordon Neely, 2014. "Building Nonprofit Financial Capacity The Impact of Revenue Concentration and Overhead Costs", *Nonprofit and Voluntary Sector Quarterly*, June, 43(3), pp. 570–588.

Rick Cohen, 2012. "Death of Hull House: A Nonprofit Coroner's Inquest", *Nonprofit Quarterly*, August 2.

Daniel Flynn and Yuhne (Evelyn) Tian, 2014. "The Death of Hull House", *Nonprofit Quarterly*, Winter, pp. 35–42.

William Foster and Gail Fine, 2007. "How Nonprofits Get Really Big", *Stanford Social Innovation Review*, Spring, retrieved on December 14, 2016 from http://ssir.org/articles/entry/how_nonprofits_get_really_big.

Peter Frumkin and Elizabeth K. Keating, 2011. "Diversification Reconsidered: The Risks and Rewards of Revenue Concentration", *Journal of Social Entrepreneurship*, 2(2), 151–164.

Nathan J. Grasse, Kayla M. Whaley and Douglas M. Ihrke, 2016. "Modern Portfolio Theory and Nonprofit Arts Organizations", *Nonprofit and Voluntary Sector Quarterly*, 45(4), pp. 825–843.

Janet S. Greenlee and Howard Tuckman, 2007. "Financial Health", in Dennis R. Young (ed.), *Financing Nonprofits: Putting Theory into Practice*, Lanham, MD: AltaMira Press, pp. 315–336.

Kirsten A. Gronbjerg, 1990. "Managing Nonprofit Funding Relations: Case Studies of Six Human Service Organizations", New Haven: Yale University, PONPO Working Paper No. 156.

Kevin M. Guthrie, 1996. *The New-York Historical Society: Lessons from One Nonprofit's Long Struggle for Survival*, San Francisco, CA: Jossey-Bass.

Estelle James, 1983. "How Nonprofits Grow: A Model", *Journal of Public Policy Analysis and Management*, 2, 350–365.

Jewish Community Centers Association of North America, 2016. www.linkedin.com/company/jcc-association.

Bruce R. Kingma, 1993. "Portfolio Theory and Nonprofit Financial Stability", *Nonprofit and Voluntary Sector Quarterly*, 22(2), pp. 105–119.

Reynold Levy, 2015. *They Told Me Not to Take That Job*, New York: PublicAffairs Books.

Harry Markowitz, 1952. "Portfolio Selection", *The Journal of Finance*, 7(1), pp. 77–91, March.

Metropolitan Opera Company, 2016. "Annual Report 2014–2015", retrieved on December 14, 2016 from www.metopera.org/metoperafiles/annual_reports/2015-16/FY%2015%20Financial%20Statements%20Final.pdf.

Sharon M. Oster, 1995. *Strategic Management for Nonprofit Organizations*, New York: Oxford University Press.

Richard Steinberg, 1993. "Does Government Spending Crowd Out Donations? Interpreting the Evidence", in Avner Ben-Ner and Benedetto Gui (eds), *The Nonprofit Sector in the Mixed Economy*, Ann Arbor, MI: University of Michigan Press, pp. 99–125.

James B. Stewart, 2013. "A Ransacked Endowment at New York City Opera", *The New York Times*, Business Day Section, October 11.

Nassim Nicholas Taleb, 2010. *The Black Swan*, New York: Random House.

Kate Thayer, 2012. "Hull House Closing Friday", *Chicago Tribune*, January 25.

Jeremy P. Thornton, 2014. "Flypaper Nonprofits: The Impact of Federal Grant Structure on Nonprofit Expenditure Decisions", *Public Finance Review*, 42(2), pp. 176–198.

Burton A. Weisbrod and Evelyn D. Asch, 2010. "Endowment for a Rainy Day", *Stanford Social Innovation Review*, Winter, retrieved on December 14, 2016 from http://ssir.org/articles/entry/endowment_for_a_rainy_day.

Wikipedia, 2016. "New York City Opera" retrieved on December 14, 2016 from https://en.wikipedia.org/wiki/New_York_City_Opera.

Amanda L. Wilsker and Dennis R. Young, 2010. "How Does Program Composition Affect the Revenues of Nonprofit Organizations?: Investigating a Benefits Theory of Nonprofit Finance", *Public Finance Review*, 38(2), 193–216.

12. Benefits thinking: ideas and tools for practice

INTRODUCTION

Conceivably, application of benefits theory to shape and fine-tune the financing of social purpose organizations could become an exact science. This would require development of precise ways of identifying beneficiaries, measuring the benefits they receive, and calibrating the various mechanisms to collect income from those beneficiaries, or their agents, in proportion to received benefits. Indeed, some SPOs do try to measure the benefits they produce and to convince funders of the value of supporting them for providing those benefits. For example, this is the tack taken recently by Lincoln Center in its effort to convince New York City that it should help fund the renovation of one of its concert halls (Cooper, 2016). However, it is early days in the learning trajectory for this approach and such precision is not easily achievable, especially for busy leaders of organizations with modest analytical capacities. Nonetheless, the real value of benefits theory lies in applying its principles to current resource development practice in a conceptual way, even if this just helps to move organizations in the right direction from one year to the next or to identify new sources of support. The purpose of this last chapter is to crystallize the key lessons and ideas and offer some tools to apply benefits theory to practice without having to rely on sophisticated technology or complex data analysis techniques.

KEY LESSONS AND IDEAS

Benefits theory is built on a number of key ideas. First, that the financing of SPOs should be driven by the mission of the organization. Second, that there is a logic that connects the mission of the organization, its programs, the benefits that it produces and the beneficiaries it serves, to its sources of income. This logic is transactional – an exchange of resources for benefits provided. Third, that multiple sources of finance are potentially available to SPOs and that their exploitation depends on the nature of benefits provided. The latter might be understood as alternative possible "business models." Fourth, unless current and potential benefits and beneficiaries are consciously assessed, SPOs may miss important sources of income support. Fifth, alternative sources of income require alternative skill sets and involve different costs of cultivation and administration or "transactions costs" which must be considered before SPOs include or expand them in their income portfolios. Finally, SPOs may sometimes be well advised to fine-tune the cultivation of income sources for which they already have experience but from which additional income or mission impact might be developed.

Mission-Driven

Over time, SPOs will be tempted by various trends and fads suggesting that some approach to funding is a panacea. Commercial ventures, endowments, crowd-funding, cause marketing and the like have all had their days in the sun. The sun still shines for most such options but not as panaceas. Moreover, SPOs should not, and usually do not, blow with the wind. There is no one size fits all funding formula and each SPO is unique. Mission is the anchor from which an appropriate and effective income mix can be developed in each instance. For traditional nonprofit organizations social mission is the explicit bottom line. In this case, economic stability and financial success are important to achieve social mission but mission impact is the ultimate criterion by which success is measured. Financing alternatives follow directly from that. The only exception is when the social mission becomes obsolete in which case the nonprofit organization will have difficulty finding support. It should then shut down (mission accomplished or unachievable) or reformulate its mission as an effective anchor for the future.

However, the world of SPOs is increasingly diverse, containing many forms of organization that seek to balance social mission with market success (profits). In this case, the SPO must first specify the particular balance it seeks to achieve. Often this is done in terms of limits on profitmaking and distribution of profit. Various choices are possible, ranging from strict profit distribution limits of cooperatives or community interest companies to more profit-focused limited liability companies. However it is specified, it is incumbent on organizational leaders to acknowledge and operationalize this balance so that it can properly guide the choices of services, benefits and beneficiaries that will serve as its basis for cultivating alternative sources of income.

Benefits Logic

Figure 3.1 postulates that mission is accomplished by its translation into specific services and programs which in turn produce a particular array of benefits and beneficiaries from which an income strategy can be developed. Missions are usually very general, however, and there may be more than one way to accomplish any given mission. For example, an SPO seeking to integrate marginalized workers into the workforce may do so by employing them directly in an ongoing business to give them experience and on the job training, or by offering specific types of retraining, counseling or placement services to prepare for future employment. The Georgia Justice Project (see Chapter 6) struggled with this question, at first pursuing the former strategy through its New Horizons Landscaping Service and later deciding in favor of a more traditional approach to rehabilitation and support for offenders. The point is not that one way is necessarily better than another but that the alternative approaches work differently, generating potentially different benefit and beneficiary patterns and hence different possible income strategies. Program logics are sometimes called "theories of change." In the GJP case, the first approach counts on participants gaining a track record of employment and a particular skill set while the second approach depends on counseling participants to make career choices best suited to their own abilities and interests. These alternative approaches are likely to generate different patterns of benefits, for the individual participants and their prospective employers, as well as for service consumers and society at large. This in turn will affect prospects for income support from various sources. For example, the first approach generates private benefits to service consumers that can be supported by fees, while the second approach generates more diffuse public benefits requiring grant support. The basic lesson for practice is that the program logic should be clearly specified and understood before an income strategy can be successfully developed.

Multiple Sources

A special quality of social purpose organizations is that they can potentially call on diverse sources of income support. This is crystal clear for traditional nonprofit organizations and is increasingly being recognized for new forms of SPO including social cooperatives and social businesses. A key lesson for practice is that *resource or income development is not the same thing as charitable fund-raising*. This seems obvious in light of the now well-documented financial underpinnings of charitable nonprofit organizations in the U.S. and other countries. The case is perhaps more subtle for new and emerging forms such as social businesses for which documentation currently lags, but here too sources of support are diverse. Indeed the point of some of the new legal forms of enterprise is to enhance the possibilities for attracting new sources of funds, such as equity capital or foundation loans, for social purposes. Perhaps the most important lesson for practice, however, is that SPOs must broaden their capacities for resource development substantially beyond charitable fund-raising, to include possible expertise in earned income development, government contracting and grant seeking, investment income and management of diverse income portfolios. As demonstrated in Chapters 5 through 9 in this book, reliance on any of one the foregoing sources, or diverse mixes thereof, may appropriately characterize any given SPO. Indeed it is the rare SPO that is solely dependent on just one source, or on charitable funding exclusively. This requires that SPOs (especially nonprofit organizations) recast their development departments as more eclectic resource development operations and that the education of SPO managers encompass a much broader appreciation of the skills and possibilities for financing their organizations.

Just as SPOs require logic models to understand how the programs they implement lead to mission impact and benefits, they also need *business models* to clarify how their income streams lead to sufficient support to assure sustainable operations. The various illustrative SPOs cited in Chapters 5 through 10 have different business models, which count on different sources of income to cover the costs of their operations and accommodate future growth. Again, there is no one right way to finance an SPO, but there is a logic to doing so, no matter what sources of income the SPO is counting on. The business logics of each source are sketched in the various chapters of this book. These must be combined in practice with careful analysis of the costs of providing the services deriving from mission, in order to demonstrate financial viability. In short, a business plan describes how the organization intends to generate its income and how it covers its operating expenses and capital costs. Benefits theory helps to specify an effective and viable income strategy, an essential element of the business plan.

Leaving Money on the Table

Another important lesson of benefits theory is that until an inventory of benefits and beneficiaries is made, an SPO is likely to have overlooked or neglected important potential sources of income. For example, the public benefits offered by the Lake View Cemetery and the group benefits conferred on alumni of Cooper Union were not substantially converted to governmental or charitable support, respectively, until in the latter case, financial crisis loomed. The same might be observed for fee income in the case of the Cleveland Museum of Art or Cooper Union. In these cases, institutional constraints may hold back the full exploitation of certain sources of support, especially fees; nonetheless their consideration must be in play if these institutions are to consider the full spectrum of options made possible by the particular kinds of services they offer.

Another aspect of failure to fully explore resource possibilities is under-utilization of assets. It is not unusual for SPOs to have excess capacities that can be used for income generation without compromising mission achievement. Examples include a museum's rental of space for private parties or a school's implementation of a corporate sponsored community lecture series by tapping its own faculty resources. Such possibilities require SPO leaders to scan organizational assets for the *potential benefits* they can generate, in addition to the benefits the organization already delivers from its mission-related programming. Benefits theory stipulates that one should begin with a prospective benefits analysis rather than a direct inquiry into possibilities for additional sources of income.

A third strategy for fully exploring resource potentials derives from the concept of *economies of scope*. Most people are passingly familiar with the idea of "economies of scale" wherein unit costs of production diminish as the scale of production increases. Similarly, it is often the case that it becomes more economical for an organization to produce two or more services in tandem than it would be to produce them separately (Chandler, 1990). Such synergy may derive from the sharing of certain costs such as facilities or office services, from coordination of services to a common clientele, or the sharing of information, expertise or other resources. Thus, having established provision of one service, it can make sense for an organization to consider providing a second one. For example, a provider of meals to home-bound elderly may be well-positioned to offer mobile health or counseling services as well. By the same logic an art museum can offer supplementary educational experiences to local schools. Having identified additional services suggested by potential economies of scope, an SPO can then examine who would benefit from such program diversification, what form those benefits would take and hence what new sources of income can be cultivated.

Most cases offered in this book suggest that economies of scope can be important for SPOs, especially the larger multi-service SPOs such as the Tucson Botanical Garden (Chapter 4), Famicos (Chapter 5), the Atlanta Community Food Bank (Chapter 6), The Center for Child & Family Health (Chapter 7), the Cleveland Museum of Art (Chapter 8), the American Museum of Natural History (Chapter 9) and the Rock and Roll Hall of Fame and Museum (Chapter 10). However, this concept is by no means limited to large comprehensive SPOs. Indeed the latter organizations, having essentially matured, are likely to have already discovered many of the potential synergies associated with providing new kinds of services. Smaller SPOs may be just beginning on that journey and finding ways to grow, not only in scale but in scope as well.

Transactions Costs

As noted throughout the book, each generic source of income, and indeed each specialized source within broad categories, requires special expertise, making diversification of income sources a more idiosyncratic exercise than purchasing a new security in an investment portfolio. In the latter case, portfolios can be diversified by doing the requisite research and paying transactions fees no matter what particular securities are being added to a portfolio. In the case of income sources, however, a major investment must be made in a new part of the business model in order to diversify. However, once a source is added and the requisite expertise and capacity is in place, it becomes easier to expand that source relative to others. The lesson here is that even where additional sources of income have been identified through the analysis of current and prospective benefits and beneficiaries, implementation depends strongly on organizational capacity. Smaller SPOs are necessarily more likely to depend on fewer sources, and diversification naturally accompanies organizational growth, for two reciprocal reasons: growth engenders enhanced capacity to manage additional sources of income, and additional sources of income underwrite organizational capacity expansion. The lesson for practice is that SPO leaders should pursue income sources sequentially and incrementally, specializing at first in the sources associated with the SPO's principal mission related benefits and later diversifying to secondary and tertiary sources. For example, a school can initially build its program around tuition revenues, reflecting the individual benefits it provides to students, perhaps with a pricing scheme accounting for redistributive benefits, before diversifying to capture alumni benefits through a giving program. Alternatively, an environmental conservation program may initially specialize in government grants that reflect its generation of public goods, before branching out to capture charitable giving from wildlife enthusiasts or fees from recreation seekers. Various organizations cited in this book appear poised for diversification. Cooper Union is expanding to include tuition funding, Lake View Cemetery may eventually capture government funding to underwrite the public benefits it offers, and MADI Apparel may ultimately cultivate charitable contributions or government funding to support its international work.

Further Exploiting Current Sources

Given the challenges of diversification, some SPOs may be well advised to make better use of existing sources of income. The most obvious area for improvement is the fine-tuning of pricing strategies associated with the generation of earned income. As discussed in Chapter 5, there are multiple ways to design pricing structures to enhance mission impact and increase net income or both. A number of SPOs described in this book take advantage of differential pricing policies to extend their services to consumers with limited purchasing power while maintaining or increasing their revenues and extending the individual and redistributive benefits they offer. This includes Famicos which ties the rents it charges its residents to a fixed percentage of their personal incomes, the Rock and Roll Hall and the American Museum of Natural History which asks discounted and voluntary payments from school groups and families of limited means, and Cooper Union whose new tuition policy is tied to income-related scholarship allocations. The lessons for practice are two-fold: first that redistributive services need not be free of charge to accommodate mission achievement; second that differential pricing may expand mission impact by accommodating low income consumers while generating additional revenue at the margin to support the SPO overall.

A second important pricing related strategy is package pricing which can enable expanded mission impact and revenue enhancement, as well as transactions cost savings. Membership packages as offered by the Jewish Community Centers considered in Chapter 5 illustrate this strategy. In this case, members have access to multiple services and facilities with a single payment, saving on transactions costs associated with charging separately for individual service components, encouraging members to use mission-enhancing services they might not otherwise use (for example, yoga classes or specialized training equipment), and allowing price level specifications capable of both profit generation and accommodation of low income members.

A third strategy is congestion pricing, which as illustrated in Chapter 5 allows possible saving in capital costs as well as accommodation of additional service demand by spreading usage over different time periods or locations. Organizations such as the Fox Theatre in Atlanta or the Rock and Roll Hall in Cleveland which charge entrance fees can make good use of this strategy to accommodate additional beneficiaries in circumstances of low demand, generate additional revenue where demand is high, and lower costs by easing staff allocation and facility capacity problems.

The general lessons here for practice are that pricing policies deserve careful attention in the SPO context, that they can significantly impact the mission and sustainability goals of the organization, and that they can differ in important ways from conventional business sector pricing practices. Moreover, they are intimately connected with the mission and profit related goals of the organization. Thus, while an SPO primarily reliant on earned income may find it easier to develop additional earned income streams than one that has no such experience, it remains critical that the particular goals of each stream be clear. In particular, pricing for maximum net income differs from pricing to accommodate demand while breaking even, which is again different from pricing at a loss that will be subsidized from other sources in order to increase social benefits.

Other broadly defined sources of SPO income may be viewed in the same light. At the most basic level this is obvious. An SPO that charges for its services in one market may have a fairly easy time expanding into adjacent markets. For example, Famicos (see Chapter 5) could logically extend its affordable housing program to other areas of the city and region without too much difficulty, should it be sanctioned by its government sponsors to do so. Similarly, organizations already conversant with foundation or government grants can more easily diversify to include proposals to additional grant-making organizations, and so on. Moreover, this argument can be extended with modest qualification to variations of sources within broad categories of SPO income. For instance, experience with annual fund-raising may constitute a logical point of departure for generating contributions for a capital campaign or through special events, although building of some additional skills and capacities may be required. Similarly, capacity with government grants may translate relatively well to securing government contracts, and investing in real estate may draw on some of the same skills as investing in financial securities. In each case, diversification within income classes may be easier than diversifying into a new class. However, at each stage a judgment must be made in terms of potential impact and return. Because the beneficiary base is likely to remain substantially the same within classes of income, ultimately it may be worthwhile to diversify by major source, in order to capture new beneficiaries, than to further diversify within a broad income source category. This is again an argument for an incremental approach to expanding an SPO's financial base within categories until it makes sense to make a jump to (and invest in) another category. The lesson from benefits theory is to pay attention to the base of benefits and beneficiaries on which new income streams are premised, as well as to the transactions cost required for adding new sources.

TOOLS

Hopefully SPO leaders will find benefits theory fairly intuitive, allowing them to think through the financial strategies of their organizations in a new and coherent way based on the ideas, principles and examples discussed in the chapters of this book. The Appendix offers some further structure in the form of worksheets and protocols that will help leaders think through the process of income portfolio development. These materials are recommended to management and leadership teams as aids to facilitate discussion and the collection and analysis of available data. The materials follow a sequence of questions that must be addressed in order to translate mission into effective financial strategies and income portfolios: How is mission translated into services, benefits and beneficiaries? What is the public/private character of the benefits? What are the appropriate ways of connecting these benefits to the resources required to support them – through direct or indirect support from beneficiary groups? How well is the structure of benefits matched to current sources of income? What sources of income should be explored or expanded? What are the costs of expanding certain sources versus developing new ones? In the end, how well does the income portfolio reflect the organization's benefit structure, how well does it protect against risk, and how well is the organization positioned for future growth? Finally, a series of worksheets is provided to help SPOs explore additional options within various income source categories. These include more productive pricing policies for earned income; seeking new partnerships and sponsorships; the wisdom of building an endowment; and tactics for overcoming free riding in charitable giving.

CLOSING COMMENT

The arena for addressing the complex social problems of the 21st century is now rich in its variety of organizational forms, social missions, programmatic approaches and financial instruments. The financial support of social purpose organizations must be similarly robust, engaging multiple sources in order to fully engage the resources that can be brought to bear. The purpose of this book is to provide a way of thinking about this robustness in a manner that is both intellectually coherent and powerful in practice. This way of thinking is framed here as the *benefits theory* of finance for nonprofit and other social purpose organizations.

While it draws on several established intellectual foundations including the theory of public goods in economics, organization and management theory, finance theory, and the growing literature on nonprofit organizations and the broader social economy, benefits theory is still in its infancy in terms of full theoretical elaboration, nuanced application to different kinds of social purpose organizations, and the development of precise tools with which to apply the theory in practice to the finance and development of specific organizations. This is an exciting field for future research, analysis and application – with the potential to mobilize societal resources on a scale and with a nuance commensurate with today's social challenges.

REFERENCES

Alfred D. Chandler, Jr., 1990. *Scale and Scope: The Dynamics of Industrial Capitalism*, Cambridge, MA: Harvard University Press.
Michael Cooper, 2016. "Lincoln Center Outlines How It Benefits New York", *New York Times*, June 14, pp. C1-C2.

Appendix: tools for practicing leaders

Below, a series of worksheets is provided, and their use illustrated for a hypothetical SPO – *City Tots* – that provides pre-school programming for children in an urban setting, including enriched day care during the school year, a summer day camp, an advocacy program that promotes expanded pre-school education, and an annual Community Day that offers entertainment and informational services for local community residents. Readers can reproduce and customize these worksheets to fit their own circumstances.

MISSION, SERVICES, BENEFITS AND BENEFICIARIES

Worksheet A.1 asks how the mission of the organization is carried out through its array of services. This requires the leadership team to think through the character of the benefits produced by the organization.

WORKSHEET A.1 MISSION, BENEFITS AND BENEFICIARIES

<u>Mission</u>: *To enhance the lives of pre-school children in urban settings through education*

<u>Benefits/Beneficiaries</u>

Programs	private	redistributive	group	public	exchange
Pre-K school	Children and families (1)	Low income families able to participate (2)	Children learn from each other/ benefit from diversity (3)	Better, more productive citizens; lower crime (4)	PR and marketing value to company sponsors (5)
Summer day camp	Children learn; parents can work (1)	Low income families able to participate (2)	Children learn from diversity (3)	More peaceful communities (5)	PR and marketing value to company sponsors (4)
Advocacy				More productive society (1)	
Community Day	Citizens are entertained (3)		Community bonding (4)	Supports advocacy (1)	PR value to company sponsors (2)
Overall	1	2	3	4	5

Note: A 5-point scale denotes order of importance (1 is most important) in Worksheets A.1–A.4.

As articulated in the worksheet, *City Tots* generates most of its benefits by educating individual pre-school children in its school year and summer camp programs. As part of its mission it accommodates children from low income families, providing redistributive benefits that must be paid for, at least in part, by sources other than the direct fees that these families pay. There is also a group benefit associated with diversity and the fact that children learn from each other, especially from children of different backgrounds. Ultimately public benefits are produced based on evidence that education in the early years leads to better prospects for a productive working life and less risk of crime and other social problems. Finally, company sponsors can benefit by giving exposure to their products, especially companies that offer educational and recreational products for small children, and by touting their support for this good cause.

HOW DO BENEFITS CONNECT WITH POTENTIAL SOURCES OF INCOME SUPPORT?

Worksheet A.2 is intended to flesh out possible sources of support associated with the various types of benefits generated by the SPO's programs. Again, priorities are specified for the most important and likely sources, for each type of benefit and for the organization overall.

WORKSHEET A.2 BENEFITS AND SOURCES OF SUPPORT

Sources of Support

Benefits	*Beneficiaries*	*fees*	*donations*	*volunteers*	*government*	*corporate*
private	Children/ families	1		2		
redistributive	low income children/ families	3	1	4	2	
group	cohorts		1			
public	community/ society				1	
exchange	sponsors			2		1
Overall		1	2	3	4	5

For *City Tots* fees are the most logical source of support for the individual benefits provided to children and their families and since this is the primary benefit this SPO offers, fees are also likely to be the primary source of income. Fees can also help support redistributive benefits if fee schedules are designed to charge more for higher income families in order to help subsidize participation by children from low income families. Gifts or donations are also an important source of income, to support both redistributive and group benefits. The most logical source of gifts is higher income families whose children gain from the diversity of the cohorts to which their children belong. Volunteering is a third important source of potential support. Volunteers from both lower and upper income families may volunteer for their own reasons: the former to compensate in part for their limited ability to pay in monetary form; the latter to enhance the experiences of their own children. Some volunteers may also receive exchange benefits. For example, student teachers may receive valuable experience and some parents may derive satisfaction from spending more time with their children and their classmates. Finally, government has an interest in educating more productive future citizens; if there is a government program for which *City Tots* can qualify, it can make its case for a government grant or subsidy on this basis. Finally, corporate sponsors may be willing to provide support on the basis of exchange benefits if they receive appropriate publicity, if they can expose their products to use within *City Tots* programs or possibly if they can provide corporate volunteers to serve on the board to receive valuable leadership experience.

MATCH OF CURRENT VERSUS POTENTIAL SOURCES OF SUPPORT

Worksheet A.3 compares the logical sources of support stemming from benefits theory analysis to the SPO's current portfolio of support. In this tableau, zeroes are inserted for sources that are not currently cultivated. The worksheet thus helps identify future opportunities as well as possibilities for changing the relative emphasis on alternative sources of support.

WORKSHEET A.3 CURRENT VERSUS LOGICAL SOURCES OF SUPPORT

Source	Logical	Current	Opportunity
fees	1	1	Modify fee structure to accommodate redistributive benefits
donations	2	3	Seek more gifts from higher income families to support group benefits
volunteers	3	2	Cultivate volunteers as a source of monetary giving
government	4	0	Explore eligibility for government programs
corporate	5	4	Explore additional possibilities with producers of children's educational and recreational products

In our example, *City Tots* currently depends primarily on fees for its support, with secondary dependence on volunteers. Its philanthropic support could potentially be increased by emphasizing its group and redistributive benefits and cultivating volunteers (who have already revealed a desire to support the organization). *City Tots* has a nascent corporate sponsors program that could potentially be expanded by recruiting additional producers of child and education-related products. It currently has no government support but could explore possible sources on the basis of the general community and long-term societal benefits it offers.

COSTS OF EXPANDING CERTAIN SOURCES AND DEVELOPING NEW ONES

As discussed throughout the book, each source of revenue involves trans-actions costs, and diversification of sources requires investment in new expertise and administrative capacity. Greater cost is associated with diversifying among sources than within a source category, given an organization's existing administrative capacity and expertise. The decision to diversify requires weighing the new investment costs against the potential returns on that investment. Worksheet A.4 is intended to help SPO leaders work through this decision at any particular juncture in the organization's development. The priority numbers under each source indicate the relative importance of expanding within or diversifying into each source.

WORKSHEET A.4 COSTS AND PRIORITES FOR EXPANSION AND DIVERSIFICATION OF INCOME SOURCES

Source:	fees	donations	volunteering	government	corporations
Diversify to include category				Hire grant writer and grants administrator (2)	
Expand or diversify within category	Staff time to restructure fees; marketing consultant to test impact of new structure (4)	Hire development consultant, install annual giving software and cultivate high income parents (1)			Hire marketing/ corporate relations staff to cultivate and manage additional sponsors (3)

For *City Tots* the most salient opportunity is to develop a gift program to further tap the group benefits received by children of higher income parents. The organization's current efforts have heretofore been ad hoc and not well targeted or administered. Further investment in a giving program could yield significant revenues but would also require substan-tial investment in expertise, software and personal cultivation by staff. Second, the public benefits provided to society by *City Tots* are currently untapped. While seeking and administering government support would be expensive and require special expertise it could also, if successful, provide significant additional income. *City Tot's* corporate support program has also been opportunistic and ad hoc. Further development of this source would require investment in additional marketing, public relations and gift management staff. Finally, *City Tots* already realizes substantial returns on private benefits from fees but may be able to derive additional revenue by instituting a more effective sliding scale policy to supportive redistributive benefits. This could require additional staff or consultant time and is likely to produce modest gains if properly executed. Overall, given the failure of *City Tots* to engage important potential sources of support for the public and prospective exchange benefits it can produce, priority should be given to expanding gift income and exploring possibilities for government funding.

RISK MANAGEMENT AND GROWTH

Issues of risk management and growth are best approached through a series of diagnostic question as specified in Worksheet A.5. These questions build on the data from prior worksheets and ask leaders for their informed judgments about areas of resource growth and volatility, financial management and growth capital. Below, the questions are answered in the worksheet for *City Tots*.

WORKSHEET A.5 RISK AND GROWTH

Diagnostic Questions:

1. Are there benefits currently provided for which appropriate income streams are not cultivated?

    Yes, City Tots produces public goods in the form of improved life chances for children, leading to more productive citizens and lower incidence of crime and other social problems. Government support for these benefits would be appropriate but is not yet cultivated.

2. Does the organization have underutilized resources or can it exploit potential economies of scope which can generate new benefits that may lead to new sources of income?

    Yes, we have our own building with meeting rooms that could be used off-hours by community groups to generate rental income. We also have a summer camp ground that could be used by outdoor groups out of season, also for potential rental income. Our staff has substantial expertise in pre-school programming and with some additional investment could effectively provide consultation services or published materials at market prices to assist similar organizations in other places.

3. Are there promising opportunities to further diversify sources of income?

    Yes, pursuit of government funding is a logical possibility.

4. Would addition of new income sources increase or decrease overall income volatility?

    Addition of government revenue would reduce unsystematic risk through diversification. Once initiated, government funding could be a stable source of income. However, heavy dependence on government could introduce the possibility of systemic risk because of volatile politics on the question of government spending.

5. Are there promising opportunities to expand existing sources of income?

    Yes, currently gift income is not fully exploited. Upper income families could be asked for contributions to support group benefits stemming from diversity.

6. Are reserve funds set aside to cope with unanticipated events?

    Yes, but minimal. City Tots currently holds one month of operating expenses in an emergency reserve fund. This should be increased to at least 3 months.

7. If the organization were to expand its programs, requiring additional space and other resources, how might it fund these capital needs?

    City Tots could mount a capital giving campaign focused on higher income participating families, or it could borrow from a bank based on its steady stream of earned income.

Overall, the worksheet allows leaders of *City Tots* to focus on key areas of income development based on the public and group benefits it already produces, and on assets that it does not fully utilize; and to consider the value of diversification and reserve funds for risk management.

ADDITIONAL NUANCES

The design of resource development strategies entails many variations and possibilities, especially within broad resource categories such as earned income or charitable giving. These variations include alternative pricing strategies, cultivation of sponsorships and partnerships, development of endowments and tactics to overcome free riding to bolster giving. The following series of worksheets is designed to facilitate discussions about these options. Again, *City Tots* is used for illustration.

PRICING

All earned income streams are associated with some kind of fee structure. The determination of pricing policies can be highly technical (see Young and Steinberg, 1995) but all pricing strategies must be based on specification of the goals of the services that are being priced. In particular, pricing depends on the degree to which the service is intended to make profits versus contribute to mission impact. Once this issue is resolved consultants can be used to work out the details. Worksheet A.6 is intended to flesh out the mission/profit goals of an SPO's programs. Note that different pricing policies will apply to different programs, depending on their respective goals. Three general situations are depicted: highly mission-focused programs for which pricing policies may generate financial losses; programs seeking to balance mission impact with financial sustainability by breaking even or limiting losses; and programs intended solely to produce net revenues, requiring profit-generating pricing policies. The worksheet asks SPO leaders to classify each of the organization's programs so as to assess the match between its current pricing practices and its goals.

WORKSHEET A.6 PRICING OF SPO SERVICES

<u>Mission Centrality</u>

Pricing Intent	High	Medium	Low
Maximize mission impact (max output subject to loss constraint)			
Balance mission and income (breakeven)	*Pre-K program*	*Summer day camp*	*Community day*
Maximize profit		*(Consultation and publication services)*	*(Facilities rental)*

Currently *City Tots* prices all of its fee generating programs to breakeven. However, given the centrality of the Pre-K program to its mission impact, the organization could consider developing its pricing policy to allow broader participation, although this would require a source of subsidy. Introduction of a program for rental use of its facilities, which would have low mission impact but substantial profits, could help enable this change. Similarly a fee-based consultation and publications program could prospectively generate limited profits and contribute modestly to mission impact as well. Finally, the Community Day program is viewed primarily as a fund-raiser. As such, it should not simply breakeven but rather should seek to generate net income. Entrance fees and the prices of corporate sponsorships could be reexamined and redesigned with this in mind.

PARTNERSHIPS AND EXCHANGE BENEFITS

Generation of sponsorship income depends on an SPO's proclivity to produce exchange benefits. Worksheet A.7 is intended to flesh out opportunities for increased income from prospective sponsorships through a series of diagnostic questions. Possible answers by *City Tots* are offered for illustration.

WORKSHEET A.7 SPONSORSHIPS

1. What current SPO programs or resources have market value to current and prospective corporate sponsors?

    Community Day offers corporations marketplace visibility and public relations value.
    Association with the Pre-K program offers educational providers and makers of children's products market exposure for corporate products such as learning materials, play equipment and nutritional items.
    Summer Day Camp offers market exposure for providers of outdoor recreational equipment.
    Our building and camp grounds offer naming opportunities for major institutional or individual sponsors.
    General association with the City Tots name and logo offers marketing and public relations value to corporations within the local community.

2. What actual or potential costs/risks are associated with becoming affiliated with current and prospective corporate sponsors?

    Affiliation with disreputable companies or individuals could damage City Tots's reputation.

Exclusive partnerships with providers of equipment, materials or other resources for City Tots programs could preclude access to better quality products and services from competitor companies.

3. What value can/do corporate sponsors offer, in terms of both material benefits and mission impacts?

   Corporate sponsors could potentially provide City Tots with cash income, discounts on products and access to marketing expertise and assistance. Corporate sponsors could lend assistance through pro bono consulting and participation on committees and the governing board.

4. What exchanges of value takes place or can be envisioned between prospective corporate sponsors and the SPO?

   Monetary contributions in exchange for listing of sponsors on our website, publications and facilities.
   Board and committee participation in exchange for public acknowledgment.
   Discounted purchase or donation of company products in exchange for permission to cite City Tots as a satisfied consumer.
   Product endorsements in exchange for cash payments or product donations.

5. What pricing strategy governs or should govern current and prospective partnerships?

   In general, corporate sponsorships are sought to enhance revenue or subsidize costs. Pricing policies should be designed to maximize net economic value to City Tots rather than potential contributions to mission.

Overall, *City Tots* recognizes that it can offer a variety of options with real market value to corporate sponsors, and that corporate sponsorships are not intrinsic to its mission. As such, terms of sponsorship, including payment levels (prices) should be designed to maximize net income and avoid damages such as reputation loss.

BUILDING ENDOWMENT

As noted in Chapters 8 and 10, several factors play into the decision to build or increase endowment. Worksheet A.8 helps an SPO explore these considerations with a series of diagnostic questions.

WORKSHEET A.8 ENDOWMENT

Diagnostic Questions:

1.   Does your SPO already have an emergency reserve fund?

     City Tots maintains an emergency reserve fund equivalent to one month of operating expenses. Priority should be given to increasing (tripling) this reserve before undertaking to build an endowment unless a potential funder is exclusively interested in endowment.

2.   What fixed costs does your SPO face which require steady streams of income support regardless of the level of services you deliver? What are those costs?

     City Tots maintains a building, camp grounds, and a core salaried staff that must be paid for regardless of use.

3.   Is your mission perpetual or is there an end date for completion?

     City Tots mission is ongoing with no sunset date, presuming that urban children will always need pre-school and summer care in our community.

4.   How do your services impact future generations? What is the balance of benefits your SPO produces, between current and future beneficiaries?

     City Tots pre-school and summer camp programs produce benefits well into the future. Current participants experience improved lives as teenagers and adults while future clientele receive benefits over the longer term. Families and children also receive current benefits associated with enjoying school and camp sessions, receiving quality custodial care, and deriving satisfaction from recreational and educational activities. The balance of benefits is weighted heavily toward the future, arguing for endowment as a long-term source of finance to help ensure services indefinitely.

5.   How would your organization raise funds for endowments? Retained earnings? Charitable gifts? Other?

     Retaining earnings (profits) would be difficult given current costs and fiscal pressures. Endowments would depend on gifts by major donors. Possible donors include successful alumni of City Tots who value the long-term benefits of our programs.

6.   What restrictions would likely be placed on endowments from these sources?

Donors may wish to restrict endowments to scholarships for children from needy families, to maintain the redistributive benefits of the program. Scholarships would help fund operational expenses from year to year so long as appropriate scholarship recipients can be identified. Some donors may wish to restrict their gifts to maintaining particular parts of the campground or building new facilities therein. Funding endowments through retained earnings, although difficult, would face no such restrictions.

7. What incentives can be offered to funders of an endowment fund?

Donors could be offered naming rights to scholarships, and to the campground or parts thereof. Donors could also be involved in selecting scholarship recipients. Donors could also be honored by plaques or having their names listed in City Tots publications and on its website.

8. What are the opportunity costs of devoting funds to endowment versus current expenses?

Retained earnings could be used flexibly to increase reserve funds or to enhance the quality of current programs. The same would be true of gifts, if donors could be convinced to offer unrestricted donations instead of endowment funding.

Overall, *City Tots* does not seem well positioned to raise endowment funds. Its priority should be to increase its reserve funds to protect against unanticipated risks. The case for endowment lies in the facts that the SPO does face fixed costs that could be partially offset by a stream of fixed income from an endowment, and it does maintain a perpetual mission that requires the generation of benefits for future generations. However, the potential sources for endowment funding are tenuous and the opportunity costs of locking up funds for the future are high.

TACTICS FOR OVERCOMING FREE RIDING

Worksheet A.9 offers a series of diagnostic questions to flesh out what tactics are available to enhance giving and volunteering to support the provision of redistributive, group and public benefits. As discussed in Chapter 6, all forms of giving are subject to free rider effects wherein potential donors who value the benefits of an SPO hold back on fully supporting them, either for behavioral reasons (inertia, procrastination) or because they are content to have fellow beneficiaries carry the burden. This worksheet uses Mancur Olson's (1965) categories of "selective incentives" and "social pressure" to tease out strategies for overcoming free-riding. Again, *City Tots* is used to illustrate use of the worksheet.

WORKSHEET A.9 TACTICS TO ENHANCE GIVING AND VOLUNTEERING

	Material Incentives	**Social Pressure**	**Remarks**
Small and annual donations	*Gifts such as tee shirts and coffee mugs with City Tots logos; public recognition/ market visibility for local merchants and suppliers of educational and recreational products*	*Members of a parents' association solicit participating families, emphasizing "give what you can"*	*Establishment of a parents' association helps mobilize gift solicitation and creates social pressure to give*
Major gifts	*Naming rights for scholarships and funding of day camp facilities*	*Internal solicitation of members of the governing board*	*Capital campaign incentivizes large donors to make initial gifts and other donors to help reach the target*
Volunteering	*Recognition for service awards; training opportunities for students*	*Solicitation of/by peers in the parents' association; allow low income parents to give time instead of money*	*Volunteers as a likely pool of financial donors, and vice versa*

Overall, *City Tots* is limited in the material incentives it can offer donors, but stronger in the social pressure it can mobilize by organizing its constituency of families, through a parents' association and its governing board. These mechanisms allow access to the principal beneficiary groups for purposes of financial giving as well as volunteering.

REFERENCES

Mancur Olson, 1965. *The Logic of Collective Action*, Cambridge, MA: Harvard University Press.
Dennis R. Young and Richard Steinberg, 1995. *Economics for Nonprofit Managers*, New York: The Foundation Center.

Index